In Tandem

Pedaling through Midlife
on a Bicycle Built for Two

Jay Livingston
with
Szifra Birke

Published by Bates and Hall

Cover Photo by Kevin Harkins Photography
Printed Book Cover Design by Kostis Pavlou
Audio Book Recorded at Wellspring Sound Studio
Engineered by Ka Wa Joshua Lu

For additional content visit: TandemRiding.com

Library of Congress Cataloging-in-publication Data
Livingston, Jay and Birke, Szifra

In Tandem:Pedaling Through Midlife on a Bicycle Built for Two

Summary: A memoir about two very different adults starting over after multiple divorces and a death. The challenges of coordinating the authors' new tandem bike mirror the challenges of coordinating their two independent lives.

ISBN 979-8-9865622-0-9
[1. Sports. 2. Interpersonal Relations.]

2022913277

Dedications

To the introverts and extroverts (and "flextraverts") who find each other and create resilient and unbeatable teams in all endeavors of life. And to Kara who recognized that we might be such a team.

Gus, our late Airedale Terrier, also needs to be recognized for his hours spent patiently waiting in the car while Jay wrote at a coffee shop. And for his nose for editorial intuition, which improved the final product by chewing any of our sticky notes within reach. He's gone but still loved and appreciated.

Table of Contents

Chapter 1: View Back 1

Chapter 2: First Ride..6

Chapter 3: Someone to Ride With...11

Chapter 4: The Captain 22

Chapter 5: The Stoker...28

Chapter 6: An Unexpected Lean..37

Chapter 7: Bicycles Built for Four...42

Chapter 8: Synchronized Pedals 48

Chapter 9: Fitness to Ride...54

Chapter 10: Balance in Motion 61

Chapter 11: A Bike That Fits 68

Chapter 12: Shifting Gears..75

Chapter 13: Uncoupling..79

Chapter 14: Should We Buy a Tandem?...87

Chapter 15: The Grand Junction 92

Chapter 16: A Joint Venture... 105

Chapter 17: Out of the Cocoon... 114

Chapter 18: Speed Bumps.. 121

Chapter 19: The Stoker Isn't Always Right 129

Chapter 20: Cockpit Talk... 139

Chapter 21: Make It Clear.. 151

Chapter 22: Riding in the Drops 154

Chapter 23: Effort, Power and Discomfort................................... 161

Chapter 24: Training for Endurance 177

Chapter 25: Hills and Miles 184

Chapter 26: Death Is a Part of Life.. 194

Chapter 27: Screaming Yellow 199

Chapter 28: Involuntary Flinches 209

Chapter 29: Where We're Headed? 213

Chapter 30: He Still Hangs Around... 217

Acknowledgments.. 220

Who is Jay?.. 223

Who is Szifra? 224

Chapter 1: View Back

As the semi-rural blacktop road rose toward the next intersection, we pushed hard to keep our bike's momentum going. The climb was only a medium pitch, but the effort to maintain our cadence was fanning the embers of heat in my legs, which progressively increased from a warm glow to a significant burn. Every ride has some objective and this one's was to stay close to the younger couples in the group we were riding with. Of course, we were enjoying the intermittent wood lots, the rustling in the bushes along the road that spoke of foraging squirrels and other furry neighbors, and the little plots of vibrant flowers that decorated some of the front yards. But our priority was to hang with our young friends so that we could coast in their slipstream, draft behind them, and rest our legs on the way down the other side.

Ahead, a half-bike swung smartly out of a side street and pulled in front of our group. A half-bike in our jargon is one with two wheels and one rider. Our group was all on tandems, the official name for the more whimsical tag, a-bicycle-built-for-two.

Like all enthusiastic cyclists, our young leaders put a bit more oomph into their pedals. The single bike was like a rabbit to a dog, something to chase, something to best. It's hard for a tandem to climb as fast as a single bike ridden by a fit, experienced cyclist. But tandems have a secret weapon ready to deploy on the downside of the climbs. We descend like runaway log trucks. Each tandem has twice the pedal power of a single bike, less rolling resistance, and with the second rider tucked behind the first, half the wind resistance. The single rabbit was scampering ahead uphill but would become virtual roadkill on the way down.

And sure enough, after we crested the hill, our group flowed by the other bike like a line of downhill skiers on a black diamond run. But the guy on the single knew the drill and ducked onto the back of our paceline. Now

1

he had five tandems blocking him from the wind. Aerodynamic resistance accounts for something like 80% of what cyclists have to work against to build or maintain speed.

Tandem bikes benefit from an aerodynamic plus but can suffer from a relationship vulnerability. Tandem biking is a team sport, and the majority of tandem teams are couples in a primary relationship. The communication and cooperation tandems require will challenge any sloppy habits couples have. Our relationship began in midlife. And our time on the tandem helped solidify us as a couple. The challenges the bike presented became a metaphor for the work it took for two independent people to pedal their way into a functional team.

Neither my wife nor I had ever ridden a tandem bike until her 49th birthday, the year we met. Eleven years after that first spin, eight years into our marriage, when we had ridden only that one time, my wife Szifra—the Polish Sz is pronounced like an Sh, "Shifra"—suggested we get a tandem.

After some research we bought one, a bit rashly perhaps, and had been riding it for two years when one noonday, on a ride near our summer cottage in the Lakes Region of New Hampshire, her voice proclaimed loudly, "We should write a book about how riding a tandem is like a relationship." I couldn't see her expression because she was sitting on the seat behind me. Her proclamation was loud because she knew it was hard for me to hear her over the noise of my breathing and the wind in my ears. It was midweek, and we were riding through a rural area, a mix of old farms, meadows, forests and new houses. At that hour there were no cars in the driveways of the big homes, which suggested they probably belonged to professionals who commuted somewhere—perhaps the thirty minutes to the capitol Concord or the hour to Manchester.

After another dozen revolutions of our pedals—cadence in bike talk—she excitedly added, "All the coordination, the communication, the negotiations, and the need for cooperation! The tandem is a great relationship metaphor!" Those who know Szifra know that she rarely has an idea she isn't enthusiastic about. She approaches much of life with unbridled enthusiasm. But this metaphor fairly begged to be expanded on, and for the rest of the ride we threw ideas back and forth.

Ideas are one of Szifra's stock in trade. She generates ideas to help kickstart anyone within hearing who's muddled with inertia or confusion, or any young person who looks in need of an advocate. She's a therapist turned executive coach who can always create new ideas when her clients are lost in a wasteland of old habits, ineffective thinking, or despair. She shares her ideas with everyone she meets—the people ahead of her in a grocery line or the young woman ringing up her purchase in a department store. Many of them she also runs past me.

I'm a business consultant and executive coach who evaluates ideas. I see challenges where Szifra sees promise. I see problems in corners she doesn't bother to look in. I generate my own ideas or receive hers and turn them this way and that looking for loose ends that need to be addressed. Szifra climbs on board many ideas and surfs a wave of enthusiasm, not really caring that she may be headed for a head-first flip into the sand. Getting a ride within the curl of enthusiasm is motivation enough for her.

And that enthusiasm often does lead to excellent outcomes. She's appeared as an expert in magazines, books, and on national television. She bumps into and ends up friends with celebrities, interesting characters and lovely people. The tandem as metaphor both spiked her enthusiasm and passed my more skeptical "credibility" evaluation.

Any look back on our history—our journey from two single strangers to a tandem team—would seem to beg that both our voices be equally represented in the tale. But Szifra doesn't enjoy writing. She enjoys relating and talking. Writing is one of the few places her enthusiasm gives way to evaluation. She calls herself an editor not a creator, although, in her thirties, she did co-write a book, *Together We Heal,* with her collaborator Kathy Mayer. Since we met, her editing energies have been donated to my authoring endeavors. She reads, edits, and suggests my articles and books into more readable and interesting form. So, her proposition that *we* write a tandem book didn't mean she wanted to draft any part of it. Her input is all over the contents of this story, but the structure, focus and stories are all shared from my perspective.

Relationships don't come with objective video replay, so my subjective memory of our history was the starting point and then Szifra prodded my recall with her memories and encouraged clarifications to reflect her experiences more accurately. Bicycles also don't come with rearview mirrors installed. You have to either look over your shoulder or choose from a selection of small mirrors that mount on the end of the handlebars, attach to your glasses, or stick to your helmet. My bike-shop friend wonders why I even bother to use a mirror, "You can hear cars coming. What good does it do to see them about to hit you?" Of course, hybrids and electric cars have changed that calculation.

After riding thousands of miles on the tandem and on my single bike, I've found the most useful mirrors to be the small, round ones that mount on the side of a helmet. By turning or tilting my head, I can get a panorama of circular glimpses of the receding road or cars approaching. The glimpses are sufficient to keep us safe unless Szifra momentarily blocks my view by leaning out to look around my left side. Then her orange helmet and yellow jersey block a significant chunk of my view behind and I have to wait for her to shift a bit to reveal what's back there. "Back" is cycling parlance for things behind. Alternatively, I can ask her to report what's in my blind spot. Our routine is for her to take responsibility for announcing things back—"Car back," "Truck back," "Bike Back." With her monitoring our back, I can concentrate on things unfolding "Up" ahead—"Car up," "Jogger up," "Gravel up." On and off the tandem, my view back is enhanced by Szifra's input. And more and more she has come to appreciate my ability to keep an eye on what's up.

Besides their limited viewpoint, any rearview mirror, and particularly the tiny, cheap helmet ones, will cause distortions—objects and incidents may not be exactly as they're reflected. In the relationship, each of us also saw things slightly differently. When emotions were running high, our views were often seriously distorted.

In communication terminology, how a person chooses to edit a story and emphasize a point is often called their punctuation. At crucial junctures, Szifra and I often initially punctuated our impression of events very differently. Time and affection have tended to synchronize our memories. These accounts are my recollections of how we built our tandem team and our relationship. The punctuations and distortions are mine. But I've also included what Szifra reported was in my blind spot.

When Szifra suggested I include a story about a failing of mine, I could easily explain why it didn't fit as well as a story about her misstep would. But as the manuscript moved along, having Szifra a part of the writing process offered endless value as she clarified my understanding of her experiences, of what she thought and felt riding behind my back and getting in my face. My punctuation changed and my appreciation of her deepened. In the end, this view back is a much better representation of what *we* went through.

I sit on the front saddle of our tandem and block Szifra's view up. It may seem like I'm in charge. But holding the handlebars is a far cry from being in command. On our tandem, and in our relationship, we both attempt to take and accept responsibility. Szifra has told me again and again that she's pleased I manage many of the road hazards, and she has expressed her delight that I put the work into the initial writing about our tandem and relationship experiences. I'm delighted with her crucial and invaluable ideas and editing

Chapter 2: First Ride

Similar to a bike ride, a relationship is full of fast sections interspersed with hills and spills. Szifra and I met when we were both recovering from relationships that had hit gravel and spun out. Mine from a misalignment of personalities. Hers from the sudden death of her husband. Our bid to couple, and eventually to marry, was her third and my fourth attempt.

The day we met, neither of us had ever ridden a tandem bike. Our first ride, three months later, was my birthday present to her. The day we met, He had been dead for over a year and a half.

Our early relationship was full of negotiations as we attempted to coordinate our cultures, family and personal. Szifra had previously celebrated forty-eight birthdays before our first together. She had a tradition of trying new experiences to mark her day. One birthday she'd gone to a small, exclusive village north of Boston where horse farms proliferated. She and a friend attended a polo match. Another time she'd taken an intracity bus into Boston and eaten at a new fusion restaurant. There had also been movies, concerts, and plays.

Each birthday was a celebration of adventure, a sampling of some indulgence or subculture, a thing to check off her curious-about list. When her forty-ninth birthday came around, she didn't have an idea ripe enough to tempt her. In the past, when clarity refused to appear, she asked someone else to choose from her list or to surprise her. Surprises weren't the key attribute she looked for. Sometimes just having someone else make a choice from her options was the gift.

During the weeks before that first shared birthday, Szifra told me about her ritual and mused about possibilities for her upcoming day. Renting a tandem was one of several things she mentioned. The idea had no particular genesis she could remember. Somewhere she'd seen a tandem and thought, "That would be fun!" In the end, she couldn't choose a birthday activity from her list and asked me to arrange something. I asked, "Do you want to be surprised?"

"Sure! Or no. It doesn't matter. Sure!"

Tandems have been around almost as long as single bikes. They were manufactured starting in 1898 and have been a fixture of the pedaling scene ever since. But tandem dealers are few and far between. I found only one, which sold and rented the big bikes, within thirty miles. That spring neither Szifra nor I knew there was an active, quirky subculture of riders of the over six-foot-long machines. Years later we met teams from nearly every nearby Massachusetts Middlesex County village and town.

During our early days, my modest income and mortgage payments demanded I live within a careful budget. The bike shop I found rented tandems for $100 per day—my normal birthday present for someone I'd only been with a few months topped out at $25. But the chemistry of Szifra enticed me to splurge. At the beginning of our improbable relationship, we kept stumbling over many things that had the potential to cool our heat. His lingering presence was certainly one. I didn't think about it consciously, but the bike-rental fee was a small investment in keeping the hungry-for-each-other fires burning bright.

The morning of her birthday threatened rain. I drove fifteen miles the opposite direction from her house, which was twenty-five miles from mine, to pick up the arranged rental bike. The dealer was located in an older brick building on a street of small shops. Inside was a menagerie of bicycles-built-for-two. A row of fast-looking road tandems stood on either side of the narrow showroom—sexy curved handlebars announced they were road bikes. I stood alone in the shop, breathing in the smells of new rubber and grease. A black frame—the crux of a bike, without wheels or handlebars—dangled from a tripod work stand. New parts, chrome and colorful, hung on the walls behind the parked bikes whose bright blue, deep red, muted orange, and stark white paint jobs sparkled in the bare fluorescent lights.

As I waited, I touched handlebars covered in wraps of grippy tape, squeezed narrow tires, and inspected how the drive components differed between single bikes I was familiar with and tandems. I wandered the shop for about five minutes, and still, no salesperson appeared. The bikes and I waited silently. I looked around to see if I'd missed an indication of how I was supposed to announce I was there. As I considered my next step, a tall, overweight man in street clothes with a tandem at his side, shouldered open the front door. He pushed the front of the bike through the partially opened door, saw me and waited for an offer of assistance to get the bike the rest of the way in without dinging the paint or banging one of the delicately laced wheels. I stepped forward and held the door. He acknowledged my assistance with a "Thanks!", rolled the tandem in, and carefully maneuvered it so that it leaned against a wooden display case. His comfort moving around the space and the newness of the tandem suggested he belonged. When the bike was safely parked, he turned to me and asked, "How can I help you?"

I didn't leave with an elegant machine like he came in with or one out of the row of my waiting companions. My rental was closer to what experienced bicyclists call a "Beach Cruiser"—a heavier framed, flat handle-barred, flat-pedaled, cushioned-seated machine, which was stored in the shop's basement. My salesperson opened a trap door and clumped down a set of old wooden stairs to retrieve it. The bike was a birthday-celebratory orange.

The salesman's instructions were straightforward. He called me "the captain." This had nothing to do with my experience as a semi-professional sailor and racer with hundreds of hours on the water and a license as a commercial Coast Guard Captain. I didn't tell him I was currently only a casual bike rider, although I had once lived in Santa Barbara, California, and had ridden regularly with a group that attacked the serious hills that crowd the city up against the Pacific Ocean.

My instructor called the person who rode on the back seat "the stoker"—a term I associated with the shoveler of coal into a steam engine. The salesman's main admonition was to "Tell your stoker what you're going to do before you do it." He pointed out that when I pedaled, my stoker's pedals were going to turn. When I stopped pedaling, her pedals would stop. When I turned, the bike would be hard to turn unless she leaned a bit. Any other secrets to tandeming would wait for some other day.

I left a hefty deposit check, and the two of us maneuvered the orange bike out the door and across the street to my minivan. We lifted and rolled the tandem into the van, but the rear wheel stuck out and prevented the hatch from closing. I held the rear tire while he opened the side door and detached the front wheel. We then gently finessed the bike in the last eight inches and laid it down so it perched on its handlebars and pedals with its longest greasy chain up, away from the carpet.

Forty minutes later, as the bike and I arrived at Szifra's house, the grey skies turned to drizzle. I greeted her with a birthday wish and hug and invited her out to see what I had in the car. She seemed genuinely surprised and pleased. We decided to stall to see if the day might clear up a bit more and went inside to wait.

I only had the bike for the day, the rain was light, and birthday adventures are adventures, so after thirty minutes Szifra decided we should ride. She helped me extract the bike from the van and held it while I remounted the front wheel. I had her get on and off the back saddle while I held the bike up and measured and adjusted her seat. I explained the communication strategy as it was explained to me. She was enthusiastic. I felt some trepidation. I was responsible for her safety and fun on the bike. But it was her birthday, and there was no retreat, so I kept moving forward.

I swung my leg over the top tube and braced the bike between my thighs. "I'm ready. You can get on," I told her. She fumbled around a bit as she got into position, standing over her top tube.

"Should I get on the seat?"

"Yeah. I'm holding the bike. You can get on." She mounted, and the bike rocked unsteadily from side to side. What a birthday present it would be if I dumped her off the bike before we ever moved. "Ready?" I asked.

"Ready!" she responded, and we pushed off for our first short jaunt. It was one of the last times either of us would ride without a helmet.

Her house had a large oval drive, which we shakily circumnavigated once. Then, to avoid the busy street in front of the house, we slowly headed across her large back lawn toward a fenced walkthrough between her property and the neighbor's. The narrow path, more of a chute between wooden-fence pickets, would deposit us onto a much safer side street. But from our angle of approach, the turn around her end of the fence was tight and constricted by those menacing-looking pickets. Between my tense grip on the handlebars and our dangerously slow speed, we wobbled severely as we gingerly steered around the first post and into the thirty-foot picketed corridor.

We made it safely to the street, and my tension eased as we pedaled casually around her neighborhood on wide empty pavement. One decision took us up a dead-end street that ended abruptly at brush and trees. It was clear we couldn't just roll into a U-turn. We got off, straddled the bike, lifted it off the ground an inch or so, and shuffle-stepped it around to face the opposite way. The process was pretty smooth. But Szifra isn't the most spatially aware or attentive person, and during one of the steps she didn't move her leg out of the way fast enough and the chainring near her pedal bumped into her leg, tattooing her bare calf with the first of many toothy, black-grease, gear marks that she would collect over the years.

The drizzle increased to light rain as we coordinated our remount and agreed it was time to head back to her house. The walkthrough to her yard was a straighter shot from the street end and we finished the ride confident and pleased. The half hour had been full of grin-moments. Although I couldn't see her when we were on the bike, the delight in her voice matched the grin I could feel on my face.

As we wiped road grime off our bare legs with moist paper towels and dried our damp hair, we talked about how easy it had been to coordinate our pedaling and balance. Neither of us imagined that tandem riding would someday become a central pastime in our relationship, that an activity so unfamiliar to either of us would be one anchor of our coupling.

Chapter 3: Someone to Ride With

Szifra and I originally connected through dogs, not bikes. She didn't have a dog and never had. I had always shared my life with dogs. When we met, a major part of my income for the past fourteen years had come from solving the behavioral issues of dogs living in a people world. My specialty was domesticating dogs who were more aggressive than their owners wanted them to be. I developed a technique of soft voice mixed with clear, simple obedience requirements that was quite successful, and I got an abundance of referrals from veterinarians and other trainers. Although to put my success in perspective, it was fairly straightforward to be a top dog in a specialty that most other trainers avoided. I also worked with wildly-friendly dogs and sad, fearful cases—any dog that needed help living sociably in a human-centric world.

Besides the lessons-by-appointment, on any given day I might have up to twelve furry students, from tiny Yorkshire Terriers to Great Pyrenees living in my older, two-story house, which was tucked behind a large hedge on a corner in a quiet, working-class suburb of Boston. All of us, the dogs and I, lived a meticulously controlled life, so the neighbors weren't disturbed and wouldn't complain. I only took one or two dogs out at a time for bathroom breaks. And the dogs were trained not to bark. Complaints were also minimized by my volunteer snow blowing of twelve of my neighbors' driveways and walks during major winter storms.

I liked working with dogs, and their owner's patronage kept my sailboat and house afloat. The dog work was augmented with consulting and executive coaching. One aspect of my consulting work was assisting dog-related businesses. And it was a dog-sitting business that provided the one degree of separation between Szifra and me.

For a couple of years I'd helped a growing doggy-daycare business establish professional practices and processes. Part of my work was training young employees to manage both the dogs and the other employees. One particularly talented young woman, Kara, was a standout. She was compassionate, pushy, full of energy and respectful of the wide variety of clients the business attracted, dog and human. The business owner singled Kara out for extra responsibility and asked me to coach her. She and I met weekly to think through the complexities of dog-on-dog interactions and the tendency of some employees to try to bite their supervisors—metaphorically speaking, of course.

For several years my personal life had also been laid transparent before Kara. I wasn't purposely divulging anything personal, but if she had read an exposé about me in a trashy magazine, she wouldn't have learned anything she didn't already know by keeping her eyes and ears open. The leaks from private to professional occurred because, when I needed to be away overnight, she stayed in my house to cover the needs of my live-in dogs. And many of the clients who came to her playgroups were referred to me for remedial behavioral work, or I had referred them to her for playgroup.

When my wife of fourteen years and I separated, Kara had a front-row seat. Totally coincidentally, when I started dating again, I discovered my new woman friend was a client of the sitting business. When she suddenly left me after a year, her dog blabbed it to the pack. A few months later, a new relationship, once again coincidently, involved an occasional client of theirs.

The continuing drama in my life was at least partially due to my predictable attraction to women with complex inner lives—and I suppose it's only fair to also assume that those women were also attracted to men with challenging complexity. My relationship just before I met Szifra eventually succumbed to the scars of too many tangles. I stepped out from the closing curtain on that drama, once again in front of Kara.

Despite my run of quick openings and closings, and my obvious shortcomings as a leading man, one day after a consulting session Kara walked me out to the business's big front porch, paused a beat and asked, "I have a friend that I think you might like. I'm not sure this is professional to ask you, but would you like to have her call you?"

I hesitated as I wrestled with a mix of scrambled feelings. Though I wasn't really interested in meeting anyone right then, it felt good to be asked. And Kara was so sincere I wanted to give her a positive response. I figured I could always find a way to slide out of the obligation if I wanted to. My response came out rather formally, "Thanks for thinking highly enough of me and trusting me enough that you'd refer a friend. I'd be pleased to have her call and talk."

Kara said her friend's name was "Shif…" something. I couldn't have repeated what she said on a bet. She asked, "Should I give her your work or home number?" It didn't seem very inviting to send a social call to my work number, and besides, I wasn't sure what the woman who answered my phone, and who'd also been there through all of my recent relationships, would have to say about such a caller.

My work phone was forwarded to my associate's house. She answered all calls, explained my services, made appointments and called clients to remind them about their appointments. She and I met in person once a week, mostly because I knew it was hard for her, a social person, to work alone. I liked her and her work and wanted to mitigate some of her isolation.

My associate didn't hesitate to comment to me about my relationship status. Not that she was any paragon of relationship stability or virtue herself. Nothing had ever happened between the two of us, but I could guess from the heat that simmered around her during our weekly business meetings at my house that the stories of her friends' sexual exploits were likely a barely camouflaged attempt to catalyze something between us.

Anyway, it seemed best to have this Sh…, whatever, person call my home number—no cell phones in those days. I shared the phone arrangements that would work best for me and then asked, "Would you please pronounce her name slowly so I can get it."

Kara said "Shifra" very distinctly. I wondered if I would remember it. Kara began to look a bit uncomfortable and started to counter possible judgments she seemed to imagine I might have. She pitched Szifra's strong points. "She's good-looking. She's about your age. She's a therapist. She's fun." All of which ended up being true, but only the fun part was on my list of required attributes.

My past experiences and my personal therapy had gotten me ready to launch a new phase of my relationship career. It was time to grow past "Jay the rescuer" and to fire "Jay the teacher." I was slowly coming to better understand my inability to sustain relationships. I realized only partnership-style relationships would truly work for me. I had to get off my control high-horse and my placating knees and find a woman who was also interested in crafting such a partnership.

Relationships require a lot of tolerance and major adjustments to merge individual visions into a shared enterprise. Fun seemed like a decent foundation for such an adventure. So, if Kara used fun as one of the first few adjectives to describe this Shif... (whatever), I was intrigued. I wasn't terribly hopeful or particularly drawn toward the work of beginning a new couple adventure right then. But I was interested in seeing what fun looked like in its incarnation in this person—however you said her name. And I didn't have to do anything except wait for her call.

Coincidentally, that same day I made arrangements to pick up my new German Shepherd puppy from the breeder. In ten days he would be seven weeks old. A great age to get him. He'd be my new partner, my new family. He'd fill the void left when my previous shepherd and my Airedale had died. I now had just an elderly miniature poodle, the last of the three dogs I'd shared with my ex-wife of fourteen years. My ex was actually my third attempt at marriage. I hadn't shown much skill at choosing compatible mates, but I was persistent.

I was alone. And it was perhaps the first stretch in my adult life when I felt comfortable looking forward to time without an intimate partner. The possibilities felt ripe and sweet. I was mostly free of major responsibilities. For a few months I'd been thinking about a new project, training my new puppy as a search-and-rescue dog. Search and rescue had a level of complexity that appealed to me. Besides training a dog to use its nose in a consistent and dependable way and to communicate with body language that it smelled what we were looking for, there were search configurations to learn, scent patterns to study, first-aid to brush up on and physical fitness to hone. If my new puppy had the nose and work ethic for it, the project would occupy a lot of time and play to many of my strengths.

A few days later I got a call, "Hello. This is Kara's friend Shifra"—that odd name again. On the surface, the first phone call was to arrange what we both assumed was to be more like a business meeting to explore any synergies a joint venture might offer. But the tone quickly became an odd mix of formal and very friendly—she laughed easily and often. Our conversation style was colored by a possibility neither of us would've admitted to, the potential that our personal and physical boundaries might at some point be opened to this stranger. There was no hint of flirtation from either of us, rather we both seemed to unconsciously know that the promise or hint of future intimacy was eavesdropping on us.

She didn't give any sign she was urgent to make this work, and I doubt I did. We both acknowledged, out loud, a large dollop of skepticism. It was easy to be transparent with this outgoing stranger who was comfortable inviting herself to check me out. We chuckled together about our shared doubts and declared we wanted nothing more than a quick cup of coffee someplace midway between our homes. "That may be all that happens," she announced in a friendly tone. I agreed, "Low expectations seem best." She gave a full-throated laugh, a punctuated but not forced burst of mirth. She did sound fun.

Where to meet? I suggested somewhere in Lexington Center, which was slightly more in her direction. She agreed and threw out the Starbucks coffee shop as an option. I agreed, and we set 11:30 on the following Thursday. The conversation felt pleasant, like a drink of clean water—no subtle, complex flavor, no faint aftertaste. After a minute of savoring the possibilities, I put the call aside and got on with my day. On the Thursday, at the time I had noted, I showed up at Starbucks. I found a place to stand by the front door, a small opening among the scrum of noontime customers. Szifra still hadn't appeared after fifteen minutes.

My last serious relationship—a couple of tries past my last marriage—had ended a few months earlier. It started with a reverse of this situation. On our first date, the woman had sat in her apartment waiting for me. I'd put the arranged time in my schedule book, but the time I noted was a half-hour later than what she thought we'd agreed on. I climbed the open, wooden stairs up the side of an older house to the landing at her second-floor apartment. I knocked, she answered the door and immediately delivered an angry ultimatum, "If you're not serious, don't waste my time."

Surprised, I stood on the stoop and stammered, "What's wrong?"

She spit additional accusations at me, "You're late and you don't care! If this is the way you treat people, forget it!" I made a successful attempt to repair the misunderstanding. But it took me almost two years to understand the dope slap she'd given me. By the time I realized I should have apologized for whatever misunderstanding had occurred and declared that I wasn't ready to build a relationship on emotional quicksand, I was too deep into it. The best strategy would have been to apologize and leave for a pleasant dish of ice cream by myself.

Now I was the one waiting, but I wasn't angry. I was just standing in a coffee shop, leaning against a counter, with no agenda and no blame. I wasn't overly concerned about whether I was being stood up. She may have had something urgent come up, or maybe she'd simply gotten the time wrong. If this didn't work, she was the one who would have to explain it to Kara. I had little invested and even felt what might have been a slight sense of relief. I certainly wasn't desperate to make things work. A warm appreciation for my late-developing patience, and perhaps maturity, settled over me.

A chilly March breeze from the hallway that ended at the backdoor of the shop swept through the crowd. And then, among the ordinary-looking people standing in the hallway, an energetic woman with a self-described "streak of white hair"—a white section running through her dark, shoulder-length hair—worked her way forward, looked around, saw me near the front door and smiled a distinctive smile. Without a word of apology or even hint of remorse, Szifra walked up and said "Hi, I'm Shifra. Can we get out of here? I hate Starbucks!"

I still wasn't positive I could repeat her name, but I was agreeable to her suggestion. "That's fine. But wasn't this your idea?" I asked with a slight chuckle.

"I don't like that they are taking over all the small coffee shops. Let's go see what else there is." And I followed her out the front door into the cold air of a New England March 13th. Years later as we fondly replayed this meeting for new friends, we discovered that she had noted a different time than I had. Sadly, upon checking back, my appointment calendar betrayed me. But my whole story of casual interest might fall apart if I acknowledge I was early. So, I'm sticking with the story my memory has stitched together from glimpses in a tiny review mirror—always a risky thing to do.

Even though looks quickly end up not being very important, it's of course hard not to notice physical traits. She had the aforementioned hair and a diastema, a term for the gap between her front teeth—a word Szifra used and explained within the first fifteen minutes of meeting her. Her body was well-proportioned—don't each of us have proportions we think of as pleasing. And she had quick, lively eyes—I'm an eye man, attracted to bright, dynamic eyes.

Szifra stood on the curb waiting for the traffic to sufficiently ease. I waited beside her, not scooting through a break in cars I'd normally have taken advantage of. I waited while another gap passed. If I stepped into traffic first, I'd be crowding her function. She was the one leading us to a suitable place to talk.

Thinking back on that walk, the tandem bike metaphor captures my role. On a tandem, the captain shifts gears, applies the brakes and steers. The stoker pedals and trusts life and limb to the captain's decisions. If Szifra wanted to be captain and steer us out of Starbucks, I was along for the ride. She walked and talked us over to a bagel shop. She braked at the curb, accelerated between cars and shifted into a slower cadence as we approached the crowded bagel shop. After less than three minutes standing in a long line, she signaled a U-turn and walked us back across the street to an empty, second-floor lunch and dinner restaurant.

The stoker on most tandems has to start and stop pedaling when the captain does. The pace or cadence of the pedaling is also set by the captain. Szifra was moving and if I was going for this ride, I needed to stay in sync with her cadence. I was personally comfortable in Starbucks and didn't mind lines when I had someone interesting to talk with. But following Szifra's lead was easy and natural. Her hopping about and exploring weren't my usual style, but I was happy to be her stoker.

Lunch forecast the possibilities of mostly sunny skies ahead—quite different than the prediction of storm clouds, which I'd ignored on my last first date. Szifra and I talked effortlessly. I asked her to repeat her name and I got a lesson on its spelling—a Polish adaptation of an Egyptian name, held dear by Jewish populations. We naturally fell into a level of emotional intimacy that escapes many people in these kinds of casual circumstances. She had two young adult sons, liked being a therapist and contra dancing. Our mutual acquaintance, Kara, was a young friend of hers who had been a babysitter for Szifra's boys during Szifra's post-graduate days at Purdue University. Szifra had lived in West Lafayette, Indiana, for seventeen years.

We'd both been married, although the numbers and details were set aside for these first-coffee circumstances. I shared that I'd been married more than once. She said she was a widow of some twenty months.

I had no idea at the time that a dead spouse is a whole different creature than a divorced one. Dead doesn't necessarily happen after the sparks and joy are gone. Dead isn't the result of a weakening lust or boredom. Death doesn't give the survivor the luxury of throwing blame around quite as casually as divorce does. And strangely enough, dead doesn't end things as conclusively as divorce or being left can. The memories of the dead person retain the glow of the best of the pre-death relationship. And if some memories aren't altogether wonderful, death tends to encourage the survivor to airbrush the blemishes off them. After all, the survivor is now solely responsible for keeping the relationship's memories alive.

Our coffee date was a bit more complicated than I'd imagined it might be. I hadn't known about Him or expected him to join us. Although, as we sat while coffee morphed into lunch, our easy comfort moved him to a seat at a nearby table.

We began laughing at the silliest things. Szifra is a big talker. She pushed the conversation ahead at a dizzying pace, taking corners or making U-turns at unexpected places. As she talked, her foot continually bounced and made small circles under the table. She kept her fingers busy pulling tiny bites of crust off her roll—leaving the soft interior sitting on her plate like the detritus of a squirrel. Once, she made an enthusiastic point and accidentally spit droplets of soup at me through her diastema—that Marlene-Dietrich gap in her teeth. I recommend this as a technique to quickly get past a lot of the nonsense posturing that is the coin of so many first meetings. Wiping soup drops off my face and shirt as we laughed about her antics certainly kept things delightfully real and fun. Her willingness to laugh at herself was alluring.

The fact we were both amused at her foibles was a good harbinger of our willingness to accept imperfections. If two people can laugh at spit soup, they can laugh at padded bicycle shorts on the sixty-plus-year-old body of a partner—padded bicycle shorts make the wearer look like they have a diaper on under their spandex. And there is also comfort in knowing that your partner's experiences with relationships that end unexpectedly suggests they will also have resilience in the face of unexpected falls.

Our casual coffee turned into a lunch of soup and bread and lasted two hours. Months later, when we talked about our initial internal assessments of the possibility of a relationship being born, we'd both found it comforting and easy to identify the things we had in common—our political leanings, training in psychology, a desire to laugh, and the catalytic pheromones that wafted back and forth across the table. We also both sensed strong hints that the list of differences was long. Whether it was that day or some other time in the first few weeks, we acknowledged to each other that, if we had met a few years previously, we simply wouldn't have tolerated those differences. Szifra boldly declared, "You'd have driven me crazy!" I retorted, "You'd have driven *me* crazy!" But we also acknowledged that our age and relationship experiences had toughened our resiliency and tempered our expectations. And our life circumstances rounded the urgency to agree on everything.

Not addressed that first day was whether we would've had the same crackle of energy if He were still alive. An insulating barrier protects well-working relationships from outside temptations. When there's a strong habit of connection and physicality, less stray energy leaks outward. Fulfilled desire doesn't have enough oomph to search for someone else's dry kindling to ignite. I don't think she would have paid me much attention if He and she had still been interwoven in their established habits. Neither of us thought of relationships as "once in a lifetime" happenings. We both had enough experience to know that the opportunity which was opening before us wasn't a treasure chest, but a simple hope chest that would only contain value if we both wanted it to.

The afternoon finally demanded we each move on to our individual obligations. We split the lunch bill, walked together to the parking lot, and were amused to discover our cars parked right next to each other. That we both drove grey Chrysler minivans—hers light, mine dark—compounded the delight. We were a bit high on those pheromones. Szifra offered me the first of one of her frequent hyperbolic statements, "It's unbelievable!"

We leaned on our cars facing each other and considered what next? She was expecting her late husband's teenage daughter to come from Utah the next day for a ten-day visit. With that announcement, He stepped forward, leaned against her car, and settled into his established place beside her—a quiet reminder that He was the one who got to ride home with her. She didn't want to disturb her stepdaughter. We wouldn't see each other again for ten days. And I had to get home to my new puppy—I'd picked him up the day before. Our time was at an end. We stood there leaning on our minivans and let our obligations pull us away from each other, like removing a Band-Aid. Each of us opted for the slow pull technique.

"I'm in trouble with you," she suddenly declared brightly into the quiet moment. "All I wanted was someone to contra dance with. And now I think I'm in trouble."

I understood. I said, "This reminds me of a New Yorker cartoon I saw recently. There's a couple standing at the woman's apartment door and she's saying, 'I had a nice time, Steve. Would you like to come in, settle down and start a family?'" Szifra grinned. I smiled. And we went back to our lives.

Chapter 4: The Captain

When I started captaining the tandem, I was surprised at how different it felt than a single bike. A single gives quick feedback. If I lean my weight a tad, the bike heads in a new direction. On the tandem, it's hard to separate the effect of my actions from Szifra's. Often what seems to be the bike's response to the road, or an unconscious shift of my weight, is precipitated by Szifra. I'm often surprised when I don't do anything and the bike suddenly seems to head on its own for the shoulder or centerline.

For a captain, this interconnectedness makes riding the tandem a complex activity. The stoker is best served if the captain gains mastery of the basics on a single bike, then graduates to a tandem and the teamwork it demands. Not unlike how much easier relationships are if you've already learned to like yourself and to live your own life and dreams. Both tandems and relationships require you to keep your internal balance while coordinating with someone else.

On our second date, we took a walk in the woods of a local community-owned farm. As we shared the first bits of data about our lives, Szifra asked that I not tell her about my past relationships, even if she asked. We climbed a small hill leading to a pasture of spring grass. We chose a large granite boulder to sit on. The rock was still cold from the previous night, but it was dry. Not fifteen minutes had gone by since her request to stay uninformed, but she suddenly asked how many times I'd been married.

Was this a test of some kind? I checked, "Do you really want to know?" She thought a second and said she did. I felt trapped between honesty and her prior request. I'm not good at games so I opted for honesty. "I don't do well with paradoxes and dilemmas. If you ask, I think I'm going to have to answer. I've been married three times. Once when I was eighteen, another time for six months. The last time for fourteen years."

She listened with a therapist's blank facial expression and adjusted her rule a bit. "Well, maybe you could just answer my specific question, but not tell me how many other women there've been or too many details. I'm not ready for that, until I ask."

We got off the cool granite and moved on. As we walked beside a field of last year's corn stalks, I felt a small misgiving. Her restrictions weren't ideal for me. I voiced my reservations out loud: "That's okay for now. But in the long run, I am who I am because of the experiences I've had. Those relationships and what I learned from them are a crucial part of my experience and what you've said you like about me. I don't need to tell physical details, but emotional ones will be important."

I wasn't sure she understood yet. We stopped at the juncture of two paths. I continued, "I can't imagine who *you'd* be if you hadn't been in other relationships. You want me to accept you for who you are. I want you to accept me too. It might feel uncomfortable to imagine you with other men, but you've been with them, that's reality. I'm okay with letting details come out when you're ready, but eventually I don't want to feel like I need to keep secrets. For now, I'm fine waiting until you're ready to know more."

Szifra and I both found process stuff interesting—the strange and rather formal psychological talk about the subtlety of influences and insight is the plus and minus of two people with therapeutic training trying to understand each other.

My past habit in relationships had been to lean so far into the turn my life was taking, that if the other person leaned away from me, I'd fall on my face. This time I felt more balanced. Maybe I was growing up, or perhaps just finally learning. My internal voice was saying: *If she doesn't ever want to know all about you, she isn't the right person.* This was considerably different than my traditional: *I'll do whatever makes her happy, until I can't take it anymore.*

By the time we returned to the parking lot and my car, she wanted to know more about my last ex-wife. My third marriage lasted thirteen years. We'd separated for a year and had been divorced for two more. My third ex and I were friends with tension. She held many of my memories, a bit like a sister. In fact, she shared my sister's birth year—two years older than I am—and shared my sister's first and middle names. Both she and my sister were the oldest children in their families. All this sisterly comparison had a bit of a cooling effect on the brush of jealousy that Szifra admitted she felt. Still, she wasn't comfortable with a recent ex whose attention still occasionally wandered my direction.

At times I've been a challenging partner for women in my life. I offer a lot of transparency and need a reciprocal amount back. If I don't get it, I worry about how solid the connection is. My third ex didn't have much experience fashioning committed relationships. She had been raised to function with less openness and didn't understand my hunger for connection. I found the emotional distance frustrating. And if I'm not on top of my game, my frustration gets expressed as irritation.

We also had very different backgrounds. She was raised Jewish, as Szifra had been. Two other women I'd seriously dated were also Jewish. These women had introduced me to the nuances of everyday prejudices and oppression that Jews have experienced, even in American culture.

My background is an odd mix of influences. My father was a liberal Congregational minister. I experienced some privileges due to my gender, race, the religion of my family, and my exposure to the culture of the upper class—priests and ministers of marginal financial means often serve wealthy parishioners.

The privileges were modified by other aspects of my life. We were poor. My parents were socially marginalized because of their activism in civil, economic, and gender rights from as early as I remember. I was sensitive, anxious, had views different than much of the common culture, and I'd been bullied. As is the case with so many people, it took a nuanced social-political viewpoint to appreciate all the possible ramifications of privilege and discrimination in my background. But it was clear my background had been different than many of the women I dated or married.

I separated from my religion at twenty, when I rejected what I saw as the improbable theologies of all religions. My dad couldn't understand the need for such rejection because his belief system was so flexible it could easily be practiced with almost any variations one wanted. My dad was worried that if I had no religion, no appreciation for the feeling of belonging to a group and no connection to an imagined Supreme Being, it wouldn't endear me to many people. "You won't have a community." He felt my women partners' Judaism was a plus. His stereotype was that they were part of a tight community, and he respected that.

My third ex couldn't get past my Christian upbringing. She was suspect that I could ever be a reliable partner against both real and perceived anti-Semitism. After we were married, she revealed that she didn't want to risk having children with me for fear they would be infected with my latent Christian influences. In many ways that would probably be true, but it was a bizarre notion for my Christian-rejecting head to assimilate. She married me because she liked who I was but rejected what had made me that way.

After our divorce, I'd fallen again for a secular Jewish woman, one with a complex background of parental abuse. We dated for over a year and got engaged, but she abruptly abandoned the relationship. One day she left a phone message that I was not to ever contact her, and we never spoke again. I knew my need for intense connections played a large part in the failures of my relationships, but I also knew different backgrounds and mental vulnerabilities were a factor.

The woman I dated before I met Szifra—the one who warned me to be serious or get lost—was raised in the same Protestant denomination I was, and we shared many cultural values. It was easy to discount her mother's mental illness and the dysfunctional family dynamics she had to negotiate as a girl. My family also had issues.

My father was an abused child, anxious, a bit compulsive, and not interested in adjusting his ideas or actions, even in the face of evidence that his way wasn't working. All this got in his way of dealing with the complexities of his growing children and their feelings. His style of trying to control the messiness of social life around him fueled my search for ways to keep a flexible, open mind.

On a bike, you tend to head toward what you look at and of course will eventually get hit by something coming from whatever direction you ignore. My previous woman friend and I had some glaring differences, but I ignored them and focused on the similarities we shared. I got hit by a degree of interpersonal anger and aggression that entangled and confounded me. I calculated for the therapist I was seeing—not my first and not my last therapist—that my woman friend and I had a major argument every day, except when we were separated or the first few days of each reconciliation. My woman friend constantly called into question my ability to care, commit, or relate. I lived within a storm of emotions, which swirled around me and often escalated for reasons I couldn't fathom and only ebbed with emotional and physical distance.

I allowed the corrosive words and contempt into my body until I had serious back pains, constantly twitching eyes and exhaustion. I understood that no one can argue alone, that I was a part of the catalytic reaction. But friends, family and therapists saw things that made them question why I stayed.

To me it seemed simple. I was responsible for my personality and the way I approached the relationship. If I could pull myself out of my own reactivity and calmly refuse to engage with her anger and blame, things would be different. Eventually I achieved some measure of that, but the onslaught continued.

After one last straw of an interaction, I realized it was time. And with profound regrets for the loss of what was good, and my inability to change while swimming in dangerous water, I stopped seeing her.

At that point I needed a break from a lifetime of immersion in the effort to make relationships work. I didn't feel the old, desperate pull to be coupled at all costs—a feeling that was a significant factor in every relationship I'd gotten into since leaving my parents' home. I was ready for some single life. Szifra's friend disrupted that.

Meeting Szifra upended my quest for single time but delivered some other things I wanted. She was decidedly less volatile but still passionate, knew the compromises it took to couple but wasn't willing to lean too far into someone else's life, had two wonderful sons, had lively eyes and other cute parts, and could laugh. The downsides? We had to negotiate cultural issues again. I stimulated memories of her notoriously difficult dad, she reminded me of aspects I didn't like in my father, she had never considered any of her life partners her best friend, and of course she came with Him in tow.

Chapter 5: The Stoker

Szifra may sit on the stoker's seat of the tandem, but she isn't just a passenger any more than she is just my wife off the bike. She has significant responsibility to power us away from stops, leans to help steer or balance, and holds a bit in reserve to boost our efforts on hills.

It's discouraging how many men we pass try to have fun at her expense. A man standing at a crosswalk amuses himself by shouting at me, "She isn't pedaling!" A rider on a single bike pulls past us and when he is shoulder to shoulder with me delightedly shares his original quip, "She isn't pedaling!" At a traffic light, we pull up beside a car and the driver lowers his passenger window and asks me with a conspiratorial grin, "How do you know she's pedaling?" Sometimes we catch an original shout from a yard as we roll past, "She's not pedaling!" And on and on the repetitive and patronizing comments come at us. Women don't throw them, and men lob them even when I'm not pedaling and Szifra is.

Szifra seems nonplused by all this. She grins and waves at the perp. I try to give a quick retort before we are too far away for the smug witticism generator to hear. I throw back a weak, "Actually I'm the one faking it!" or a puzzled, "Funny, it feels like she is!" or a usually misunderstood compliment, "She's my turbocharger!"

Certain situations do arouse Szifra's competitive attitude. If a pickup truck is behind us as we pull away from a stop or hit a hill, she declares, "I'm up!" and stands to pedal and drive home that she is doing her full share and more. I stay seated and sometimes even stop pedaling to underline her crucial role. We both enjoy rebelling against presumptions.

One of the gutsiest things Szifra and other stokers do is to get back on the bike after a fall or close call. On one rural hill we pulled onto the driveway apron of a house where a woman was working in the front flower garden. I misjudged how soft the dirt was. We dramatically slowed and the front tire pulled hard to the left. Our bike shoes clip to the pedals with fasteners that lock with a push of the foot and release with a twist of your heel. The twist to unclip can cause a delay in getting a foot free and planted on the ground. This time neither of us got a foot down fast enough. The bike careened to the side and we fell sideways into the dirt and small stones.

The first reaction to a fall is to do a quick body scan for the location of any major pain. I had none, and as I disconnected from my pedals and we squirmed out from under the bike, I asked Szifra, "Are you all right?"

She brushed off and twisted to examine her legs. "I'll have a bruise on my thigh," she reported. I picked the bike up onto its feet and rolled it back onto the pavement. She came over to her position and asked, "Ready?"

"Ready," I returned. She climbed back on and in doing so, forgave my misstep.

When you trust your life and limb to another person, and they fail to protect you, remounting is an act of courage. I've also failed to get my foot solidly onto the pavement when we stopped, and we've gone down. I've tried to make too sharp a slow U-turn, and the bike hit dirt and slid out from under us. Each time Szifra brushed herself off and got back on.

I'm lucky. In her family, falling off and getting back up were the norm. Disappointments, divorce and death were all in Szifra's background. Getting on with life was her and her family's tradition, and in their character.

Szifra's father was rabidly protective of his kids. This wasn't theoretical protectiveness. This was war-hardened experience, paid for with the blood of his entire family. To know her story you have to know his and her mother's.

Szifra was her parents' fourth child. Her two oldest brothers died as infants in Siberia, where her Jewish parents fled from Poland during the Second World War. Her older, living brother was born while her parents were post-war refugees in France. Her younger sister and brother were born in the U.S., as was Szifra.

Europe during the war was a horrendous place for Jews, and her parents' native Poland was at the top of the list of places to get away from. As the German army marched into Poland, Szifra's father volunteered to help his friend's eighteen-year-old daughter go search the countryside for her older brother who had left to avoid conscription or worse. The situation deteriorated so quickly that the older man and the friend's daughter had an impossible decision to make—return to their homes and families, which would mean walking back into the trap of the German army and Polish sympathizers or flee across the border into the Soviet Union.

Rules, propriety, customs and religion all demanded that to flee together they had to be married. And so, her teenage mother formed and maintained a loveless union with her older companion, which she upheld until his and then her death. If luck is a relative thing, they were lucky. But escaping the merciless ovens that consumed all their family and friends and losing two children because war made medical help impossible was a terrible kind of luck.

Szifra's life was colored by the lifelong damage the losses wrought on her parents' psyches, and therefore their abilities to parent. This was explained to me, while she patiently introduced me to the personal, intergenerational trauma that surviving genocide imparts—trauma gets passed down through at least one or two generations beyond the immediate survivors. "Szifra," with its Polish spelling, was also her grandmother's name. With that gift came an unspoken responsibility to protect her parents and to never forget that every member of the extended family perished at the hands of the Nazis. Grandma Szifra and her young son were gassed and cremated at Auschwitz.

Of the many manifestations of the damage that her father survived, perhaps the most notable was his bizarre and renowned propensity to express explosive irritation. His invectives were profane and profoundly disrespectful of anything that mattered to the other person. His broadsides were built on ugly verbal images that mocked a person's religion, sexuality, or anything else that struck his fancy. He was verbally abusive to customers in the clothing store he and his wife owned, to friends, to anyone who disagreed with his opinions, and to his wife and family—never physical, but verbally merciless. In one of life's bizarre twists, he was also generous to the downtrodden, laughed with abandon, and was fiercely protective of his children's health and welfare—other than their psychological health. Research shows that verbal abuse from a parent, perhaps even more than physical abuse, can create a life-long flinch reaction. And Szifra flinches in the face of any hint of irritation.

Szifra's mother was almost universally adored. But the scars of losing her entire birth family to hate hardened her heart. When she felt wronged, she would abruptly shun an erstwhile friend for a small perceived slight. And this disowning was visited upon Szifra for equally minor missteps. Despite her mother's occasional emotional abandonment and the continuing threat of its possibility, Szifra learned to delight in connections with her sister, her friends and customers of her parents' clothing store. She is a talker of some repute, and an extravert from her youngest moments.

Jewish heritage and Jewish religion are two very distinct considerations for many people. Jewishness was the bones of the family culture, but her father had contempt for all religions including Judaism. I never met her father, but after Szifra's mother was placed in a nursing home, Szifra and I bought her parent's house from Szifra's siblings. Everyone I'm introduced to in town has a story to tell about her father's outrageous public behavior. As Szifra describes him: "He was an equal opportunity bigot." And to that he would probably respond, "Fuck you Shif!"

We are different in more than the specific religions of our backgrounds. My father acted respectful and encouraged people to be religious. Her father was scornful and mocked people who declared they were religious. Ironically Szifra ended up non-religious and I ended up anti-religious.

Szifra married the first time when she was twenty-three. She met her first husband in grad school at Purdue. I like to think of him as the father of her boys. That label gives a certain distance to their relationship that I find easier to be comfortable with. They started dating and just a few months later Szifra encouraged him to consider marrying her. His resistance to her proposal was that he was eighteen years older than her. Szifra's mother was thirteen years younger than her husband, so that argument held little sway with Szifra.

The boy's father came from a wealthy family that emigrated from Germany many generations before. Szifra's parents flat out rejected him on those historical, ethnic grounds. His having been divorced didn't help either. Szifra persisted, they married, and her parents virtually disowned her.

A first grandson was born. To bridge the ludicrous gap her parents maintained, the grandson was brought from Indiana to Massachusetts to visit. His ever-patient Germanic father walked into the parents' clothing store, handed him to his grandmother, then walked out and left them alone. When he walked back in an hour later, the extended family was accepted— to some degree. A second son was born two years later.

The boys' birth father was initially a devoted dad. But he was introverted and didn't share a lot of feelings. Szifra was left alone in many significant emotional ways. But he was involved, kind, loving, and a good husband, at least until he began an affair with the older boy's kindergarten teacher. By the time I met her, Szifra could say, "I pushed him into being more social than he wanted. I didn't understand how hard it was for him to deal with my energy. There were signs something was wrong, and I ignored them."

But I prefer thinking it was all his fault. Research shows that the best relationships occur when at least one member of a couple is a bit delusional about *his* partner's good points. I find it comfortable to play this role in our relationship. Anyway, putting my tendency to see Szifra as perfect and the boys' birth father's failings aside, a messy divorce followed. The little boys' lives were shattered. The other woman went out of her way to compound the hurt. Friends rallied. Eventually a few other men wandered through Szifra's life.

On one trip home to visit her parents in Massachusetts, Szifra's mother invited a "good customer" from the store to dinner. Szifra was in no mood to meet or to placate the man who, since her parents liked him, and he got along with her dad, had to be wrong for her. But her mother was also persistent, and it became easier to acquiesce than to fight. And as her sister announced when she saw him, "He has a beard!" It ended up that He was also a nice guy.

Under the pressure of an impending return to Indiana, the casual dinner led to a hasty follow-up date, then another. By the time Szifra and the boys headed home, she had a significant involvement with this new man. Over the next two years He visited Indiana, met her friends and was invited fully into her life.

Of course, no relationship is seamless. Some of his viewpoints were dramatically different than Szifra's. He was raised in Utah where gun ownership was a given. She was anti-gun. He was socially progressive, but not as fiscally liberal as she was. His background was Mormon, but he had evolved an anti-religious headset. He was a senior executive in a worldwide computer company. His parenting style, which expected effort and growth, was an important positive addition to the boys' development. And He was a bit compulsive. Well, quite a bit.

His many business suits each hung with its own belt installed so they were ready to wear without decisions or fuss. He had numerous shirts and sportcoats so that He didn't have to coordinate laundry or dry cleaning very often. He used the master bedroom shower as a place to throw dirty clothes. Only after months of not using that shower and finally suggesting that they get it working did Szifra find out it worked fine and only needed to have the dirty clothes taken out.

Trips to the lumber store carried with them the real risk He would return with a dump-truck load of scraps in anticipation of the multitude of projects that could now be done at minimal expense and without additional trips to the store. The inventory of a handyman's store was bought as a possible future occupation and the source of thousands of parts to fix all sorts of obsolete items—if ever needed.

A trip down their basement stairs was a treacherous undertaking due to stacks of potentially useful clutter that temporarily ended up on each tread, waiting to be assigned a permanent home. The piles regularly crept up the last stair, sneaked under the basement door and took up residence on the kitchen floor. He only forced them to retreat back down the stairs under persistent pressure from Szifra.

And then there were the truly collectable items. His 1760s house, which Szifra and the boys moved into, had numerous pieces of antique furniture, tools, signs and other paraphernalia. But the core of his collecting was the brass, model-train engines.

Each HO-scale model engine was a precision cast and finished work of art. The potential varieties that were available to purchase were almost limitless. The real-world prototypes for these models were the endless, different engines pulling, or that had pulled, passengers and freight for dozens of US companies past and present. The selections included every change in a railroad's ownership, which created new paint jobs and therefore, new models. The collection was limited only by His prescription that he would forgo all the steam engines and collect just the diesel variations.

Eventually the corporate world became too political for him and stopped valuing his integrity and commitment. He quit and turned his hobby into a model-train business. But there are few transitions more fraught than that of compelled-collector to dealer. Do you add inventory to your collection so there are additional items to sell? Do you sell items from your collection? And how complete must your inventory be? These decisions pushed hard against his compulsion to have completeness and bled his bottom line toward insolvency.

When Szifra and I met, twenty months after His death, her basement and his business space were still amazingly cluttered. Amazing because, after his death, Szifra's brother had helped sell thousands of dollars of tools from the basement and the business continued to be actively run by an administrator and part-time employee who were selling off inventory. When Szifra decided to move from the antique house, I offered to organize another tool sale. I spent days in the basement sorting trash and junk from items that had some value or might be given away rather than thrown away.

After every sorting session, I carried boxes out to the curb of her busy road, and by the next day they had been claimed by new collectors. Szifra confided in me one day, "I feel like we're feeding other people's addictions. I feel for the spouses. They probably cringe when they see the boxes and know their partner will stop and get something."

In one corner of the basement was a mound of trash, dirt and tools. It looked like someone had swept everything into a pile of debris after an earthquake. The rubbish mound was close to two feet high and five feet in diameter. In it, I found dozens of sockets, ratchets, extensions and screwdrivers, plus hammers, antique chisels, rulers, planes and wrenches. Also littered among the dirt and trash were various small parts, each with a smidgeon of value. There were hundreds of new bolts, nuts and screws in small packages or individually scattered among the debris like silver nuggets. I would pick and throw, pick and set aside. After weeks of discovering things in strange places, I became sensitized to spotting tools out of their natural milieu. Their distinctive shine, shape or size was the tipoff. They had come to rest in the oddest places: ratchets in the garden, wrenches in the grass, screwdrivers in the woodpile.

Besides the large mound and many smaller heaps of tools, parts and trash, the basement was full of neatly hung and stacked power hand tools, large industrial-grade lathes, bench presses, saws and other power tools. Between organized arrangements and random discoveries, there were enough pieces for ten complete socket sets in four different sizes from huge to tiny, and numerous metric and English wrench sets. I eventually put dozens of boxes of marginal stuff out on the curb, created tool kits for each boy, kept a few items for Szifra and me, and then had a second sale that brought in thousands of dollars.

Szifra and her late husband had a good relationship, with only a few areas of strain—like the clutter. He was even-tempered and kind. He stepped into the boys' lives in a significant and positive way. She appreciated his perspective on the boys and expected she and he would grow old together. She and the boys had been set aside by her previous husband, and she was intolerant of people who didn't respect commitments to their spouse. Death wasn't as obvious an end to that commitment as it would seem at first. Her love didn't stop in an instant. When I met her, their relationship was still resolving into its new status.

Szifra told me that the facilitator of her Young Widow and Widowers Group kept reminding the grieving participants that "The person has died, but the relationship hasn't."

Having coffee with me was just one tentative step toward exploring her new single status and how it might coexist with activities that are generally reserved for a significant other. Were feelings of affection or sexual interest compatible with respect for the feelings of commitment and love that she and her late husband had nurtured for each other?

Eventually she began to share a few of their more private struggles. They'd discussed whether they would each contribute to the gun or anti-gun, group of their choice. Should they stop giving because their gifts were canceled out by the other person's? Were the boys expected to do chores that challenged their weaknesses or ones that played to their strengths? Szifra wondered if she would be able to pressure him into decluttering the house when the boys left for college. To insist felt like it risked creating tension and pushing him away, which Szifra told me she always wanted to avoid. The same questions came up around his faltering business. He owed money to suppliers. Should she push harder to encourage him to sell more of his collection to generate income?

Their style of relating was loving and friendly, but not the "best friends" style my parents had while I grew up and that I wanted for us.

Chapter 6: An Unexpected Lean

As we began to pedal our relationship forward, Szifra carried a secret she needed to share with me, but she wasn't sure whether she should just lean into it and tell me or stick to the straight road we were on a while longer. It's threatening to try to negotiate a quick turn in a new relationship. It takes practice to change direction and maintain your balance and traction.

Tandems aren't great at hard turns either. They're not sports-car quick like single bikes. They take team coordination, time and a bit more room to turn. There are some especially sharp turns that tandems can't make unless the team is well-practiced. Bikes steer more by leaning than by turning the handlebars. On a narrow road when we want to make a U-turn, I ask Szifra to "Lean" in order to influence the bike into a tighter turn.

A fast, tight curve on a narrow road can also be challenging. If I see a hard turn coming at us when we're zipping along, I call "Pedal up," a reminder to her to raise her pedal on the inside of the turn so we don't drag it on the road. If we need to dramatically lean into a curve—for instance to tighten the radius of a turn when a car appears too close to the centerline or has shouldered its way into our lane—our inside pedals, which will be at the apex of the circle, and hence closer to the road, might accidently scrape. If a pedal hits and jams into the pavement, the pedal and its crank arm will lift the tires off the pavement and catapult us into an out-of-control flight to nowhere. A pedal strike is almost guaranteed to cause a bad fall.

Besides getting the lean and pedal position right, I have to pick a course through the turn that minimizes the chances our tires will hit sand, gravel, or road debris, and consequently lose traction and cause the bike to slide out from underneath us. Bike tires are narrow strips of rubber whose grip on the pavement can be broken by small obstacles that would be inconsequential to a wider, car tire.

To maximize our potential traction in a corner, it helps to have our weight pressing straight down on the tire rather than threatening to roll the bike onto its side. With the bike leaned considerably over to one side, if we place our outside pedals down, keep our bodies upright, and our weight pressed onto that outside pedal, our weight will be directly above the places on the tires that are grabbing the road. We can add even more direct downward force by putting some weight on the outside handlebar. Done correctly, we swoop around a corner, solidly tracking on the pavement. Done incorrectly, the bike will skid out from under us, and we will accumulate what cyclists call road rash—skin abraded by using it to slide on pavement or gravel. Szifra is still anxious about hard turns on the bike—from the stoker's position it can be hard to tell if we're leaning into a turn or falling over, going fast, or going down.

At the inception of our relationship, it also wasn't clear to her how much traction the relationship would have if she tried a hard turn into absolute candor. We'd only had one meeting and a number of phone calls. She knew there was some potential gravel in our path that I wasn't aware of. She feared we might not safely negotiate what she was about to throw at us—more precisely, she was worried I might not be able to handle it. She worried that what she had to share threatened to abrade our nascent relationship.

Her bind was how much she should tell me about the end of her last marriage, about His death. She'd already taken the first step by letting me know she was a widow, that she had a husband who died. During our lunch she made it clear that their relationship had been good. She'd also let me know it had been a little over a year and a half since his death and that she felt ready to move beyond her initial stages of mourning, to see what it felt like to be in the dating world again, to go contra dancing—always a joke because I had no affection for contra dancing.

Coffee with me was a tentative foray, a dipping of her toe into general social activities. Her declaration that she was "in trouble" with me was an acknowledgment that her plan was threatening to come unraveled before it even got going. She felt a big pull toward me. Feelings, which had been walled off by loss, were threatening to break out and fracture her oath of loyalty to her marriage.

At the time, I didn't understand the relationship she was leaving behind. I just tried to wait patiently for information about its current tenure and His demise. Because she hadn't mentioned the cause of his death, it was clear to me that there was something she was deliberately not talking about. I wondered if she was compartmentalizing her past to keep the present upbeat. Did she need a respite from whatever process she had been through the past twenty months? Or was there something more troubling? I was a stranger still, on the outside looking in. I waited for her to bring it up.

From the inside, she was trying to figure it out. She still hadn't found a way to talk to new friends about her late husband and his death that didn't feel like she was threatening her listener with a profound surprise. Both professionally and personally, Szifra cringes when faced with uncomfortable surprises, and she didn't want to inflict that on anyone else.

His stepdaughter's visit precluded us from quickly having another in-person date. But Szifra was open to emails—texts weren't yet common—so we continued our initial conversation, minus the helpful voice inflections. Each of us was deliberate about not seeming too intense. We both knew that relationships start with hormonal heat that can easily blind, then dissipate. There were lots of reasons to take everything slowly. But we also wanted to keep the intensity of that first meeting alive. After a few days and a couple of emails, she emailed me that it would be ok to call after 9 o'clock in the evening, after her stepdaughter went to bed.

The conversation about her late husband's death happened during one of those calls and was a pivotal moment in our relationship, but neither of us remembers what led up to the crux of the conversation. Perhaps I asked something about Him. She's a person who feels acute pressure to get information out on the table when it might matter to the other person. She says that to do any less feels like she's not being honest.

Her mother either nurtured or created this feeling by telling her that when Szifra lied, her mother could see "little green men" in her eyes. Faced with the inevitability that any secret or "withhold" would be obvious, she usually chooses to deal with the facts and find a way to repair any potential damage. The circumstances of her late husband's death were details that she just had to share to clear the air.

Perhaps she simply plunged in with a "Do you want to hear about my late husband?" Whether truth for truth's sake or deliberate attempt to circumvent any surprise, she eventually said, "I have something I need to tell you about my husband's death. You may want to prepare yourself. It isn't easy."

I heard her serious tone but had no concerns that the information might rock me emotionally. I'd been around a number of people whose spouses had died from tough diseases. "I'd like to know. Are you okay talking about it?"

"Well…" She stammered, then it went quiet as she apparently got her courage up. "He committed suicide," she breathed into the quiet.

There was less air at my end of the call; a deadly quiet settled over us. I remember feeling like we had walked out onto thin ice. I'd need to step carefully. It wouldn't take much to quickly get into trouble.

"Oh, I'm sorry! That must have been tough." I wanted my words to be profoundly helpful; instead they sounded stupid.

She rescued me, "It was."

I needed to be sure she knew she was welcome to tell me more, "Is there more you want to say?"

"I don't need to." Then the therapist in her came forward, "Do you need to talk about how you're doing?"

"This isn't about me. I'll let you know if I need something."

She was again trying to protect me from what had slammed into her world with no warning, "Well the next part is even harder to hear."

"Go ahead."

"He shot himself."

I paused. That wasn't a possibility I'd considered. My first thought was what a challenge that must have been for her and her two boys, who I hadn't yet met. "Wow! I'm so sorry that happened. I can't imagine how hard that must have been." Again, I felt I was stumbling like an idiot.

Again, she didn't leave me to flounder, "I know this stuff is hard to hear."

I thought, *hard, yes. But necessary if we are going to create something together.* Did I dare say that out loud? I dared, "Whoever you end up with is going to need to accept that a third person will be part of the relationship. If we're going to see each other, he'll be a part of our relationship, so it helps for me to know about him and what you experienced."

My instinctive response was apparently the right one. She cried. For years she pointed back to that declaration and my encouragement as the moment she knew she had a chance of creating a lasting relationship with me. But of course, nothing is that simple. Eventually there would be a struggle between loving the person she heard on that phone call—perhaps my best self—and living with the frustrated, irritable me, which reminded her of her father and often overwhelmed her sense of security.

Chapter 7: Bicycles Built for Four

Szifra coasted into my life with two teenage boys. If couple relationships are tandems, she and her boys were pedaling a triple—a bicycle built for three. At tandem events you might see a triple and infrequently even a few bikes with four-positions—quads. Most quads seem to be family bikes. They have two intermediate seats above pedal systems modified for young children with short legs. The real power comes from the two adult riders, but enthusiastic young people can add a meaningful boost at crucial times.

Szifra and her boys had metaphorically ridden relationship quads twice. But each previous captain had hit a bump, let go of the handlebars, and the bike had crashed. Szifra and the boys survived each of the crashes with only serious internal wounds. After both crashes, the three of them climbed back on, Szifra taking the captain's seat, and continued their ride pulling an empty saddle. Each time they managed to maintain their balance and to eventually detach the empty saddle. When I entered Szifra's life, the three of them didn't need or want a new captain. The boys were ready to ride single bikes.

When her stepdaughter left for Utah, Szifra invited me to come to her house for a second date. Her large, white, antique Colonial was perched on a small rise above a busy, yellow-lined road. The paved driveway rose sharply up to the level of the house and ended in a large oval drive shaded by a couple of huge mature oak trees that stood in the patchy grass of the median. The reasonably kept but rambling structure had a low addition added to connect the older part of the house to an attached two-story, two-car garage.

I arrived and slowly circumnavigated the oval. I was impressed by the size of the lot, which had pockets of tangled brush creeping out of its far corners. Beside the house was a two-thirds size, asphalt basketball court with regulation-height hoops. Szifra's grey van and an older dark-blue Nissan sedan were pulled onto the verge of the median across from the entrance into the addition. I pulled in beside the Nissan and took a deep breath.

Szifra had said that her older son, in his second year at a college two hours away, was home. I felt like I was entering the citadel of a family that had come through a brutal siege. The drawbridge was let down for me, but everything was standing ready to return to hunkered-down mode. I was an intruder in His territory, their keep. This wasn't just a coffee date. This time my stomach was tight. This time I had something to gain, to prove, to lose.

Szifra greeted me at the door to the addition with her marque smile. She invited me in, and we took an immediate left through another door into a large modern kitchen. Her older son stood in the middle of the room and greeted me with a warm, "Hello," an easy smile, and he walked over for a handshake. Szifra stands a petite 5'4". At the time she had dark hair with that white streak, and brown eyes. Her older son was a surprising contrast, a lean, muscular 6'4" with blond hair and blue eyes. At 5'10", I had to look up to meet his gaze.

Szifra walked us out of the kitchen, through a small formal dining room into an antique-filled living room that felt lived in—and not at all stuffy. One entire wall was dominated by a large open fireplace. Once we left the kitchen and moved into the original house, the ceiling came down almost to the doorframes.

Szifra's son followed us, and when I turned to look at him, the ceiling floated just above his head. But in the Alice-in-Wonderland world of the shrunken room we were in, he carried himself with the easy fluidity of an athlete. It struck me that he was a serious Queen's Knight, standing ready to protect his monarch.

Szifra sat on a mustard-yellow antique couch, her son lowered himself into an overstuffed chair near the couch and I sat across from them in a wooden straight-back chair. Her son turned his head deliberately, looked at Szifra, then me, waited a beat and with impeccable timing declared, "Isn't this interesting. I'm sitting here chaperoning my mother and her date." So, this was what I was getting into. Szifra had been entertaining at our coffee date, and she had clearly infected her son with her amusement at quirky circumstances.

She appreciated that humor was a primary attribute of an interesting relationship. Her appetite for laughter matched mine. With previous partners, my tendency to point out absurdity had gotten me in trouble and invited stinging criticism. My third ex-wife had told me I didn't have a sense of humor—a reflection that I assume was colored by her discomfort with other more difficult aspects of my relationship quiver. On the other hand, perhaps that criticism doesn't do her justice. From the number of groans and eye rolls I've experienced over the years, I realize my humor is an acquired taste, maybe something like turnips.

During the first week, when Szifra and I were initially holding our place with phone calls, my wordplay seemed to drift over her head or perhaps it lay dead at her feet—it's hard to read nuances over the phone. After one particularly witty bit of wordplay, which just sat there in the dead air until I began to worry that Szifra had taken it the wrong way, I came up with an emoticon equivalent of a wry smile. I hit a button on my push-button wall phone two times and told Szifra the "beep-beep" meant I was making a joke. "It was probably a lame joke. You don't have to laugh. But you should at least know I meant it as a joke."

From then on, when it became clear to me that a joke of mine had gone astray, I would "beep-beep" a couple of times. That became our signal that Szifra should cycle back and look for a joke or at least put down her defensive weapons and ask what I meant. For years we found this technique helpful. Even face to face, I would say, "beep-beep." Or she would ask, "Beep-beep?"

During that first get-to-know-you conversation with her older son, I threw out one of my oblique word plays and Szifra immediately "beep-beeped" to rescue her son from confusion. He looked blankly at her odd expression, and she went into a long explanation of our short history of "beep-beep." Once he understood, she recycled the expression again and again. I doubt he cared or needed it as often as her parental instincts thought he did.

Szifra leaps to the rescue of anyone who she thinks is lost, a strength for a therapist, but it opens her to gentle ridicule from her sons, "Mom! I get it." Playing with her impulse to clarify has become an intergenerational ritual. When she tried to explain to our oldest granddaughter that I was kidding, Granddaughter looked at Grandma with the incredulous eye roll only a ten-year-old could pull off. Our granddaughter clearly gets my humor. Even as a small girl she knew I was kidding long before she understood exactly how I was kidding. Now she occasionally catches Grandma in the game and plays her like a fish on a line. Szifra told her over the phone that there was a squirrel on our back fence. Our granddaughter innocently asked, "What do you mean Grandma? What's a squirrel?" When Szifra started to describe a "little furry creature with a bushy tail" she got a beep-beep.

Szifra's older son lost his beloved birth father to divorce and his stepfather to suicide. By the time I showed up, his attention was focused outside the family, and there was elasticity to the space he had for his mother's relationships. He was ready to allow me to float around his and her life, albeit on a probationary status.

His younger brother was just at the end of his senior year in high school. I didn't meet him for a few days, and when I did, I misjudged the degree of care I would need to use. He had taken his beloved stepdad's death hard—this was the dad he knew and loved. I was a bit too presumptuous in the way I stepped into conversations. My humor also left him wondering if I was being disrespectful. We got off to a rocky start when I flippantly responded to something he said. His back went up. I realized my stumble and stepped back. He shunned me for a couple of months as he regrouped. Szifra stepped in to lay down politeness rules the way any mother might, "He can have his feelings, but he can't treat you rudely. He has to be civil toward you!"

I knew my relationship with him had to be that of two single riders, which at best meant I might hope we could occasionally ride side by side.

"Let him be." I suggested to her. "It'll take time for us to figure this out. He needs to be in charge right now." We needed to find our way to each other through channels he decided to open, when he decided to open them. There was no room for pushiness or any attitude from me except considerate-adult curiosity. I had to take absolute responsibility for my feelings and give all the patience he needed. His stepdad had shocked and hurt him. Therefore, I had a lot to prove if he was going to discover I was trustworthy, respected his abilities and trusted him to captain our relationship for a while.

The two boys certainly had no need for another go-around with an untried captain. They were ready to ride on their own, but they were also reluctant to stop pedaling in support of their mother. Szifra was clear it was a bad idea for them to take any adult-style responsibilities for her. And that's where a spot in their family initially opened for me. If I partnered with Szifra—watched the road, maintained the relationship and stood ready as an adult to assist the boys when they requested—they might set out on their own with less feeling that they had a duty to pull their widowed mother along her life path.

A few years into our relationship, her younger son cleared up his and my missteps by calling me at the hospital I was working at and asking to talk. I invited him to stop by, and he drove over. The weather was warm, so we went out to the grounds and sat on a picnic table. In a fashion I only wish I could have pulled off at his age, he laid the groundwork for our rapprochement by declaring, "I don't need a father." A self-evident fact in my mind. He went on to admit, "I often can't tell if you're being disrespectful or joking. I don't get your humor."

I told him I appreciated him for being so straightforward and for caring enough to clear things up between us. "I respect the hell out of you for all you've managed and for who you are. I'm sorry my stupid humor is so unclear. It isn't just you who struggles with it. Please ask if you feel disrespected. And again, thanks for taking the risk to talk this out."

His courage blew the tangles out of our relationship and set us squarely on the path to a fun, supportive bond. During the whole process, Szifra had stepped back and let me steer. She trusted my good intentions and her son's resiliency. She let us figure it out. That's the same kind of trust that it takes for her to ride as a stoker.

Chapter 8: Synchronized Pedals

Szifra and I are used to spinning through life at very different speeds. She loves social engagements and new activities. Unusual people, quirky restaurants and new acquaintances charge her batteries. I like to untangle the details of interactions and glide through periods of quiet introspection. A known restaurant allows me to focus on my dining companion. A new restaurant allows her to make a new friend of the waiter. From the beginning, we worked to fashion a life that left each of us room to do our thing while still moving our relationship forward. It and we thrive in spite of, probably because of, these differences.

We both felt the best style of relationship for us would gently coordinate our lives into partial oneness. It would give us flexibility to pursue our own interests, but encouragement to synchronize goals and some activities. Too tight a bond would restrict instead of supporting, constrain instead of generating growth. But with flexibility comes the threat of fragmented or wobbly interest.

Tandem designers need to address this same dichotomy—synchronize or independent coasting. Most tandems chain their riders into harmony. Pedals are linked together with a bike chain or a toothed, rubber belt—like a car fan belt. Riders have to coordinate starting, stopping and cadence. When either person pedals, or stops pedaling, the other person has to follow suit, or there will be a clash of intentions—leg muscles will be jarred, and the bike can slow when quick acceleration is required.

A tandem that's synced might start moving something like this: With the captain straddling the bike, the stoker steps over their top tube—the one that runs between their saddle and handlebars. They ask, "Okay?" If the captain's shins are clear, they respond with an "Okay!" The stoker uses their foot to spin the pedals backward until one is at the bottom of its arc, clips their shoe in, and using the pedal, boosts up onto the saddle. While perched, the stoker clips the other foot into its pedal, repositions the pedals at three and nine o'clock, and says, "Ready." The captain clips in one foot and says, "Go!" The stoker gives an initial push on the pedal, the captain boosts their self up onto the saddle and uses the motion to give their pedal an initial spin. They might then give a second push on the opposite pedal to give the bike some extra momentum before they both pause while the captain clicks their second shoe onto its pedal cleat. If the stoker pedals while the captain is clipping in, the captain can get a shin smashed by a spinning pedal, which is being turned by the stoker's pedals.

Once underway, teamwork remains important, or there may be jerky pushes and pulls to the leg of the slower responder. To coast, the captain alerts the stoker with a "Glide," and both stop pedaling. If one rider wants to stand and readjust their behind, both have to stop pedaling. If the captain needs to slow down and the stoker doesn't stop pedaling, the stop might be delayed with accidental consequences.

At tandem rallies, where you might see more than a hundred tandems start a ride at the same time, all but a few have synced pedals. As the mass of teams flows past, bystanders will see two hundred pairs of legs most rotating in a symmetrical rhythm. A synchronized dance where two feet push downward to the five o'clock position before smoothly completing the down motion and sliding backward past six and seven o'clock, then lifting up to the eleven o'clock spot before pushing over the top and starting down again. This happens again and again, sixty to a hundred times per minute.

When we got a tandem, ours was one of those few that didn't sync. We visually clashed with the comforting synchronization of other teams. Our spinning legs visually jumped out. Some people say our feet appear to flail to catch up with each other. Each of us is making those same smooth circles, but like small children on adjoining swings, our feet and pedals roll the circle disturbingly out of sync with each other. We each pedal the circle at the same speed, but our feet are usually sited at a different position on the circle's arc—only occasionally in sync.

Our asynchronous feet aren't as uncoordinated as they appear to onlookers. We're each driving the bike forward. We don't look like most tandems, but neither do all tandem racing teams. Some racers lock their pedals a few degrees off from exact uniformity. The idea is to generate more consistent power during the entire arc of the circle—one rider may be at an inefficient place while another is still able to maximize their input.

If we want, we can deliberately sync. Szifra will watch my legs, briefly pause, then start her pedal stroke in sync with mine— stokers who are visually impaired can do this by placing a hand on the captain's hip and feeling where to start their stroke. I can also initiate an approximate sync. Without turning my head, I can feel Szifra's surge on the downstroke of her pedal circle and join in at the right moment.

Our appreciation for an un-synced tandem is similar to our desire for a successful relationship formula that prizes independence with a good size dollop of togetherness. We watch most teams' starts, locked by their chain or belt into unbreakable cooperation, and enjoy our detachment.

Our team is like freeware. We can each add power when we feel we can contribute; we can build on the effort of each other. Or we can coordinate pedal stroke by pedal stroke. During our starts, Szifra gets us going. But her pedal strokes don't move my pedals, which remain quiet, patiently waiting for me to clip in. If I fumble my clip attempt, Szifra alone can continue to drive us across the intersection or up the incline.

Similarly, when either of us wants to stand on our pedals and get the blood flowing back into our butt capillaries, our independent coasting allows that while the other person continues pedaling. Or I can spin backwards while Szifra rests or spins forward. Coordination enhances our effort, but the independence enhances our relationship.

Not everything is open for independent action. Some aspects have to be harmonized, by agreement or declaration. Because most captains have control over when to shift gears, they have default control over the cadence tempo. Cadence is a significant factor in any bicyclist's comfort and ability to produce efficient power. I've learned to spin at a higher RPM than I used to, and that challenges Szifra, who likes the feeling of a slower, harder cadence.

Even on our un-synced tandem, the cadence has to be synced—both of us must spin at an equal RPM or the slower person is not adding to the power and is spinning uselessly. Even at the same cadence, one of us usually generates more power due to more pedal pressure—pressure plus cadence creates watts of power generated.

A high cadence means it takes less muscle strength to produce more power. A faster spin rate is one way to "save your legs" on long hills and long endurance rides, but the savings come at an aerobic cost. Low cadence—called crunching—puts less aerobic pressure on a rider but requires more pressure on the pedals. Crunching saves aerobic effort but can exhaust legs sooner and puts more pressure on knees.

Relationships require the same sorts of decisions about how much coordination versus independence, about hurrying through difficulties versus slow, methodical problem solving, about whether to start together or have one person pull the team forward until the other person is able to put some effort into it.

We knew from the first that we'd have to work to build a team, that getting synced around lifestyle issues and pacing was going to be a challenge. It was clear to both of us that we'd stumbled upon a fickle window of opportunity that just happened to open when we were both available. If we'd met a few years earlier, it's unlikely we would have been interested in negotiating ways to merge our lives. In the least negative case, we would have probably been invisible to each other behind the active lives of her young children. Or one or the other of us would have been involved in a committed relationship. Even without those impediments, my hunger for tight connection, the fact that my anxiety often manifests as irritation, and my much more moderate fiscal ambitions than hers wouldn't have been attractive or perhaps even tolerable to her. I was just lucky that the window opened, and she hadn't yet met someone who was more accomplished, more extroverted, and/or more emotionally laissez-faire than I was.

We don't always agree about when we need to process a tangle in our relationship, whether to crunch our way up an emotional hill or to ride down the road and ignore the issue. But as a team, we need to agree on a joint tactic about when to spin and when to crunch.

There's a similar situation when we're faced with working our way up an emotional hill together. It was easy for one of us to feel we were doing all the work while the other "soft pedals"—soft pedaling means taking some pressure off the pedals while still turning them, i.e., not working hard.

On a bike, occasionally the chain might slip off the gears and just hang limply. The pedals turn uselessly, and momentum quickly dissipates. The first time we seriously slipped our relationship chain was over a perceived difference about veracity. The tangle was about Szifra's hand size. I made the mistake of not paying attention to the fact that she has unusually large hands for a small woman, or a medium woman, or many big women.

We were walking hand-in-hand on a dirt path along the Charles River. The wide, brownish-green water flowed languidly past us toward Boston and the sea, as we walked quietly upstream enjoying the warm spring weather. We'd spent enough time together in the previous few days that we were satiated with each other's company and ripe for small differences to bother our sense of independence. Szifra casually commented, "I have really big hands for a woman."

I glanced down at them. They looked normal. And I responded: "They don't look big." What I didn't say was that I was so taken with her that I really hadn't paid much attention to small details other than those sparkling eyes.

She then declared her feet were also large for a woman of her modest stature and got irritated when I didn't quickly agree. Apparently not noticing her hands and feet, or quickly confirming her impression of them, made my veracity suspect. My family would have called that being polite. Her family tended to comment bluntly about odd characteristics of other people and their biological processes. We sure weren't spinning at the same speed on this one.

Szifra's accusation and upset left me incredulous. I defended my ignorance of the limits of normal hand size as reasonable. I wouldn't have commented even if I had noticed, but I hadn't noticed. I told her she shouldn't evaluate veracity when I hadn't noticed. She didn't back down. She was determined I wasn't being straightforward with her. She said I was bullshitting her. I looked carefully at her hands and had her hold them up against mine. They were about the same size, maybe a bit smaller. I said, "Okay, your hands are big. Now what? Are we talking about whether I would have been honest if I had noticed? I have a different sense of what's polite to say. I might not have said anything, but don't hang me because of a possible future felony. Tell me your standard and then see if I can/want to meet it."

There were a few tense weeks as I got synced with the fact that the woman I was dating wanted me to name her appendages as oversized, to "PU" her farts, to talk hard facts, not my soft, lover's impressions. My priority was apparently supposed to be demonstrating there was no BS in our relationship.

I liked focusing on the delight of her hand in mine, not the potential she had disquieting quirks of asymmetry. I was the delusional one, but for her I would regularly try to be amazed at the span of her fingers and the width of her palm.

In the long run it wasn't enough of a tangle to tear us apart. I now comment on the gargantuan size of her hands and feet every chance I get. She laughs, and often says, "Stable in a storm," her comforting rejoinder to a comment made by a thoughtless adult when she was young—"Oh, you don't need skis!"—and we go on with whatever we were doing. That we should come into that early conversation from such different places and turn a tangle into a joint understanding captures the arc of our attempts to bring our two lives into sync. The arc that the tandem eventually enhanced and sped up.

And by the way, I still occasionally steal careful looks at her hands and feet to see if I now would rate them as big. I don't dare tell her that I'm still of the opinion her size 10 ½ feet aren't that big.

Chapter 9: Fitness to Ride

Keeping a tandem team fit can be complicated because the amount of training effort that is new or intense for one rider may be normal or a suboptimal effort for the other. When one rider needs a recovery day or an easy ride to give their body the maximum chance to rebuild from a previous hard effort, the other rider may need more intense stimulation to promote an increase in strength. Most tandems are synced. So, in the face of divergent needs, casual riders may give up trying to ride in ways that are appropriate to their current individual training needs. The stronger or weaker rider's inclination may dominate the team's approach.

Training for increased endurance on a bike—the ability to ride thirty to one hundred miles or more at one sitting—used to mean riding for long miles at a slow pace. The latest technique is to do short, intense efforts called high intensity intervals, shorthanded as intervals. These efforts need to be followed by periods of recovery—a low level of exertion that allows your body to recover: rebuild glycogen stores, new muscle fibers and additional capillaries and cellular mitochondria.

Many cyclists fall into one of two ineffective training patterns. They ride those long slow miles to build an endurance base, or they go hard day after day with little chance for recovery from the previous days' hard effort. No recovery means no chance for adequate repair and the super compensation needed to build additional strength.

It took us a while to figure out how to coordinate our training techniques. The solution, on some rides, has been for us to alternate our effort. Szifra rides along with easy pedaling while I put in my hard intervals, and then she does her intervals while I easy pedal and recover. Our bike's ability to have one person coast, while the other works, makes it easier and comfortable for each of us to effectively meet our needs. On many rides, we both work in a similar effort range: Endurance effort for rides lasting over an hour; Tempo for hard efforts of up to an hour; Steady State for ten to twenty minute extra hard efforts.

In our relationship, I am the one who wants intervals of communication intensity, and I had to learn to take adequate recovery time after we had an especially emotional interval. Szifra was good at going off to take a walk with her friends and recover. She had to learn to schedule intervals of concentrated connection.

I need less external social stimulation and more recovery time to build resilience in my life. My most intense social efforts are often suboptimal for Szifra, and her recovery from social events is spaced too far apart for me. Her schedule of social obligations demands too much effort from me. She spins her way through situations that require me to crunch. I end up exhausted while she's looking forward to the next interaction.

He hadn't needed the social stimulation she craved either, but he was willing to let her be their social coordinator. She'd schedule, he'd show up. He might drift to one side to watch TV or catch a nap, but he rarely complained. My flagging energy and interest for social time were not in sync with what she'd gotten used to.

As we attempted to create a blueprint for how we would merge our two contrasting lifestyles, we started with the default that the other person wasn't required to do what we wanted to do. Before we began to tandem, I rode occasionally, and Szifra didn't. I raced small sailboats two days a week, Szifra didn't. While other people that I sailed or biked with reported that they had to negotiate time away from their family or spouse, Szifra supported my sports activities with little need for negotiation.

Of course, "giving" me the freedom to do my thing meant that I was "giving" her the chance to do her things—yoga, exercise classes, walks with friends, etc. She would put in her electronic calendar the dozen or more possible activities that she could choose from for the week. If a block of time suddenly freed up, she'd often dash out to whatever was available.

It was easy to end up spending time apart. I came to our new relationship with a lake cottage my parents had passed to me. It needed substantial rebuilding. When I had a few free days, I would go up to the lake alone to work on projects like raising the house and digging a basement by hand, gutting the interior, or adding a post-and-beam porch. Even after most of the work was done, I continued to go to the lake to grab quiet time for my writing. After hours spent by myself, which included the hour-and-a-half drive there or back, I would arrive home in an introspective daze. I was gliding—coasting without pedaling—while Szifra, who had spent the time with friends, was spinning along full of reports and ready to instantly engage.

We don't have young children, with their school or sports activities to organize our time around. And we each work for ourselves as executive coaches, so we have more ability to adjust our schedules than most working couples. With so many non-shared activities, remaining synced as a couple took deliberate effort.

Our default assumption for the relationship is that sport or exercise are investments in our long-term health and retirement. We try to always be respectful of the other person's activity schedule. We feel free to arrange activities with the expectation that the other person will support our choices, although not necessarily participate in them. We're each responsible for communicating our needs for time together or time alone. We don't want to make the other person guess what we need. And we try our best to quickly signal the need for time together. Particularly if we perceive any potential risks to the long-term health of the relationship.

One clear sign that we might need to slow down and spend time nurturing the relationship was when either one of us felt taken for granted or disrespected. We're both the product of genetics that make us acutely sensitive to other peoples' emotions, and our childhoods honed our emotional flinch impulses. It doesn't take much to feel we've been slighted. Neither of us has a relaxed response to a perceived offense or an irritable voice. If either of us makes a wrong assumption about the other's intentions, we'll get in our partner's face. Under the demands of time or pressure, each of us is likely to pedal for safety, without syncing our direction or intensity. When one is pushing too hard, the other is likely to backpedal.

Without effort, we'd get drawn into an emotional debate where explaining takes precedence over listening. We both trained as therapists, although I quickly lost my patience for therapy and moved sidewise to executive coaching. It's natural for us to end up in deep conversations, dissecting tangles, speculating about motives, labeling tendencies and traits with professional aplomb. It isn't always productive or illuminating, but it's easy to get there.

We're both aware of the value of careful language to keep us from getting tangled—aware at least until emotions step in and override our reasoning. Then my idea of careful is, of course, different than hers. It's easy to assume she is oblivious to how her words affect me. She's usually looking ahead, which means she misses my emotional cues. I express my negative feelings too passionately, forgetting her family history that accentuates every negative. And sometimes I fail to remember she is being cautious searching to find the right words and tone.

Szifra can slide past a question of mine without any acknowledgment I've asked something, or she can appear to ignore me when I say I feel hurt by an assumption she's made. For my part, I don't get on top of my frustration fast enough and regularly a shard of irritation will cut into the conversation, and she will feel attacked.

My irritable reactions to unacknowledged slights probably comes from interacting with my father. He'd never accept responsibility for any negative emotions he had or missteps he made. In disagreements he'd slide out of accountability by placing the blame on me. If I accused him of anything, he'd come back with, "You're mad." I'd explain that I wasn't angry, just didn't agree with him. He'd repeat, "You're mad." And his accusation would set me off. "See? You're upset!" he'd say. It didn't take much of this for me to feel like I was suffocating, then I'd strike out verbally to create room to breathe.

My reaction to a slight from Szifra or her unfair assumption about my intentions is still to strike out with irritation, to get her to back off and give me room to settle myself. I'm rarely relaxed if Szifra says, "You're being disrespectful, you need to apologize!" Am I disrespectful or is she feeling disrespected?

If I get at all irritated, it's like poking a stick in Szifra's eye. At these times, she used to tell me, "He didn't get upset. He would just say, 'That's not fair.'" She didn't exactly throw him in my face as much as tell me there was a better way to be upset, which He happened to have mastered. I hadn't learned to quiet my wronged, inner little boy fast enough to compete with His more adult control. How could He keep his frustrations in check? Did he not have frustrations, or did holding them in check cause him to go off in the more profound way he had?

Suicide grows within an individual, as a problem-solving or problem-escaping solution. The terminal resolution is formed out of a complex interaction between brain chemicals, self-talk, life circumstances, and some large or small measure of other attributes. Suicide is likely to have a component of depression brought on by brain chemistry, and He did have that. Even his love for his wife, daughter and stepsons couldn't quiet his thoughts about the possibility of escaping from the buzz of problems he told Szifra occupied his head at times.

I struggled to understand how he could've given himself permission to hurt and abandon them as profoundly as he did. Even at my most irritated, I've always found ways to moderate speech or actions that might jump in my head, but which also risked irreparably puncturing Szifra's trust. He had been even better at controlling his words—or perhaps didn't even have the thoughts—but had failed to control that last fatal impulse.

That final day, he told one of the men, who occasionally worked for him at the house, that he was going to sit outside for a while. He got one of his pistols and went to sit in a chair in the median of that oval drive—out there under the shade trees, where any of the family coming home might find him.

Gun safety was his thing, but I doubt he thought about safety that day. His was a purposeful shot to his brain. Szifra remembers him talking about how a shot to the side of your head wasn't as sure a fatal act as a shot into the brain through openings in the skull. Fortunately, one of his employees wondered why he was gone for so long and went looking for him. He was found lying on the ground. Szifra's older son came home from high school sometime after the police and ambulance arrived. From a distance, he saw his stepfather's body. He left to go tell his mother at her therapy office. When they returned, Szifra also saw Him lying on the grass. The memory would come back at her at strange times and circumstances. He'd inserted himself profoundly into her future, even as he abandoned her.

He had failed at ultimate control, but for most of their marriage he had controlled the one aspect of his emotions that I still struggled with. I'd spent my adult life learning ways to bring my disruptive impulses under an increasing level of self-control. I'd studied ideas, gotten a master's degree in psychology, and gone to therapy trying to raise my emotional understanding of myself and my intimate partners to a graduate level. I'd practiced relaxation and meditation techniques, learning to quiet my anxiety and its attendant irritation. It was difficult to have Him held up as an example of emotional control. I felt threatened by who he had been before he wasn't.

The first time Szifra told me that He had been better at emotional self-control than she thought I was, it was way too soon for me to critique him, or at least to do it out loud. I might get away with critiquing his actions and his apparent self-centeredness in the way he ended things, but suggesting He had sat on stuff too long or too tenaciously and that was part of why he imploded might give Szifra the idea that I thought she had some responsibility for his actions, or could have done something to change them.

I understood enough about suicide to know it was his choice, his impulse, the result solely of his body and his brain failing to self-preserve. Szifra might be challenging to negotiate with at times, but she wasn't anywhere near frustrating enough to be the cause of such a drastic misstep. He made his way to his decision through whatever foggy thinking he struggled with. I felt compassion for his pain, and angry at how his weakness left his family to pick up the pieces. But I also felt confusion about how to navigate the comparison between us.

Potential emotional swamps, like comparing myself to Him, pose similar dangers as do tricky obstacles on the road. We humans tend to head for what we look at, and we tend to focus on negatives. To successfully navigate a corner or miss a pothole on a bike, you have to look where you want to go, up the road, past the immediate challenge or hazard. When I'm riding and catch myself staring at a deep crack in the road—professional racers sometimes call these "Death Valley" due to the danger of getting a wheel caught in one—my bike tends to drift inexorably toward the danger.

I knew that if Szifra or I stared at this or any other emotional pit long enough, we'd begin to drift toward discord. When I felt we were being pulled toward a pothole-strewn controversy, I would attempt to look up the road, focus us farther ahead, at what we wanted for a long-term outcome.

Potholes were numerous. Any time I showed irritation it drove Szifra into a silence so distant that I felt abandoned. Often, she didn't pay attention to my plea that I was confused or lost, and just kept driving her point home. My irritated voice camouflaged my frustration and pushed her further into her approach. I would finally need to walk out of the room to quiet myself. We worked to fight our instinct to blame the other for our distress. And we did get better and better at reminding each other to look toward a smoother section ahead. On the bike, "Bump" was my warning to Szifra that the road was getting rough, and she might want to lift her butt off the saddle. Her "Shoulder check" was a reminder to drop my tense shoulders—relaxed shoulders take less energy, are more aerodynamic, and encourage a more fluid bike motion.

Our off-the-bike reminders can feel more like they're loaded with the danger of further provocation than a reminder. It's still easy for us to forget to look up the road at all the positive possibilities. We sometimes neglect to keep our eyes on the reconnection we're trying to head for. We're getting better at telling each other about the pitfalls ahead. I often remember to say, "I'm pissed, but I also love you. Can we take a second and concentrate on that?"

Szifra reminds me, "I'm not going anywhere. I love you. This is just how I feel right now!"

Chapter 10: Balance in Motion

Stress itself is a potential danger both on the bike and in relating. The risks are acute when clipped into pedals. Off the bike, when stress is expressed as accusations or accusations kindle stress, the results can be a festering threat.

If you're anxiously alert, minor obstacles look like bigger dangers—adrenaline accentuates feelings of threat and reactions to threats. Every threat or minor spill increases awareness of the myriad of possible next dangers. And anxious awareness creates physical tension, which begins to upset flow and balance.

If Szifra or I get tense, the tandem is more likely to wobble or be hard to steer. Anxiety causes physical tension, which transforms the two-person dance into a struggle. You lose the smooth, fluid motions that allow faster maneuvering. Tense rigidity in either person can turn a swooping corner into a desperate struggle to keep the bike on the road or in its lane, or to keep the relationship wheeling positively along.

When we're moving along and coordinating effectively on the bike, the revolving wheels and spinning pedals create a gyroscopic effect that helps us balance. But when we're starting from a dead stop, balance comes exclusively from shifting our weight. On a tandem, both riders must intuitively feel any impending imbalance and shift their weight about half of the total needed. With experience, you adjust and unconsciously moderate your reactions, so the sum of both riders' efforts doesn't overcompensate and steer or tip the bike too far the wrong way.

Information about the bike's current state of balance comes tactilely. My points of contact on the bike—my butt, my feet, my hands—give me feedback that tells me what Szifra is doing. Over time I've become better at recognizing her reach for a water bottle on the frame, from a reach for food in the back pocket of her jersey, from her leaning to peek around me. She, in turn, has gotten less nervous when I lean into a corner.

Getting started—before the gyroscopes spin up—challenges a team's balance instincts. The stoker mounts the bike, clips in, and back spins one pedal to a forward position to prepare to apply maximum leverage for a strong starting push. The bike's position and stability are a bit precarious. If the mount and prep aren't done smoothly, the bike threatens to tip away from the captain, who is balancing the bike with one foot on the ground and one clipped into the far pedal. The bike is leaning toward the foot the captain has on the ground. The only thing that prevents the bike from falling is that lean. An inexperienced stoker may think the bike will fall to that side and try to compensate by leaning their weight the other way. If the bike threatens to shift away from the captain's planted foot, it's an urgent danger signal. Nothing is standing in the way of a fall.

There are times Szifra will be mounted and ready to pedal, and suddenly I feel my planted foot become unweighted, as if gravity has lost its grip on me. Szifra may have leaned down and away from me to tighten her Boa shoelace ratchet an additional click—Boa laces are nylon strings that wrap up into a small round mechanism; you can tighten or loosen your laces with one hand. When this happens, Szifra has no idea how close the bike is to falling over. I muscle it back toward me by leaning on the handlebars, but now I'm alert. As she brings herself back up, I'll have to counter that weight shift. My foot on the ground may not be planted at a wide enough angle to offer an absolutely secure foundation against her weight shift. I'll need to finesse the lean I'm holding. Lots of unconscious, practical physics.

At stop signs and lights, Szifra usually keeps both feet clipped in while I do my one-foot balance. Again and again, we unconsciously work together to create balance. I have to be careful not to lean the bike over too far, and she has to trust that some lean is safe, that I've got her.

Our first fall occurred at a stop sign after a few months of riding. We'd spent a pleasant hour on a paved, rural bike path with friends. The path terminated with a small, gradual descent that ended at an intersection near where we'd parked the car. At the crossroad, I realized my view of the road to the left would be partially blocked by an overgrown hedge. We crept up to the intersection, and I let us roll far enough forward to have a clear view of anyone coming down the cross street. There was a car approaching.

I stopped with our front tire just into the intersection and put my foot down. Or rather tried to put my foot down. Since the back tire was still slightly uphill, and the front tire was on the flat of the intersecting road, my foot was positioned over the dip where the path and road joined. The geometry of our position meant my leg was barely long enough for my toes to reach the ground.

It was a desperate feeling to attempt to stand and not have any ground under my foot. We leaned dramatically until my foot finally landed. But the mishap was in motion. The back of the bike, and consequently Szifra, continued leaning and pivoting, tipping toward a fall. Bikes have an articulation joint at the handlebars and fork. In this situation I had a good grip on the handlebars but didn't have the leverage to stop the rest of the tandem from pivoting wildly. The momentum of the tilt and Szifra's weight fought my efforts, and slowly, relentlessly, we twisted down. She hit first and harder. Fortunately, she escaped with very minor bruises. And luckily, she was willing to get back on the bike. Her remount was the definition of courage—putting herself into known danger.

Because my hands are on the handlebars, it would seem like I'm the one steering the bike. But I only partially control our travel direction. The bike is primarily steered by shifting our weight. Remember, when Szifra leans out to look around me or twists her body to get that drink or snack, the bike can easily head for the shoulder or the centerline, and when she sees a car approaching from the rear and assumes that the bike needs to hug the edge of the road, she may unconsciously lean to keep it there and make it difficult for me to avoid roadside debris or a hole in the pavement. All of this means that if the captain—or stoker—assumes that the captain is the sole person controlling the direction of the bike, at some point the team will be painfully surprised.

The bike's gyroscopic self-balancing counters our leans to some degree, but the effect dissipates as the bike slows. A long, steep climb can erode our speed until it's only a few miles per hour. At such a slow speed, any small movement of the handlebars or a weight shift will threaten to swing the bike toward the edge of the pavement or swerve it into the travel lane.

Our early relationship had a similar lack, or presence, of gyroscopic balance. When we were moving confidently forward, small wobbles were quickly corrected. But when we struggled to find our way toward cooperation, when we were moving at a snail's pace, it was easy to fall out of grace with each other.

One early wobble started when Szifra found my less-than-urgent attitude toward earning money disconcerting. By both life experience and family culture, Szifra had become acutely aware of the incoming and outgoing flow of money in her life. By the time she met the boys' father, the heir of a wealthy family, he had left his solid IT job and was working his way through grad school. He lived a frugal, artisan lifestyle, making pottery he sold at craft shows. A small stipend from his trust buttressed his meager earned income. Szifra began her counseling career and added to the family income. When he abandoned her with two young boys and inadequate child support, the money pressures increased. As the family's sole earner, she became an excellent manager of their modest resources. She and the boys stretched meals by dividing and taking home half a restaurant's offering, minimizing new purchases when there were used options, and never buying retail when a discount was possible—her father had continually condemned those buying retail as being "monkeys."

Her late husband was a well-paid corporate executive. After they married, his salary became their major income while she moved between states and rebuilt her counseling practice. Eventually her income provided a solid secondary one. After an associate he had mentored was promoted over him, He resigned rather than engage in hardball office politics. He didn't like playing games. He was a hard worker, but his inability to translate his model train hobby into manageable cash flow shifted responsibility for the family's financial fortunes back onto Szifra's shoulders. The shame he felt ate at him.

When Szifra and I met, I had a reasonable income but not a traditional, professional job. A majority of my time was spent training dogs and coaching dog owners. I'd been in business for twelve years and had an excellent reputation in the world of veterinarians and dog professionals. Many of my clients were well-known regional and national leaders in business, finance, sports and the creative arts.

But my retirement savings were meager according to her standards. In my twenties, I regularly quit jobs to free my summers for backpacking trips. I'd worked in many different industries. A quick list of some might give a feeling for the casualness of my background—semi-truck driver, respiratory therapist, psychiatric aide, master mechanic, addiction counselor, wooden-boat restorer, furniture maker, teacher in an alternative high school, therapist, operations manager for a medical device manufacturer, business consultant, coach, professional boat captain...you get the idea.

I had a master's degree in psychology, owned my own home, had a high-tech sailboat, and a modest but steadily growing IRA. But unlike Him, no one would have mistaken me for an ambitious or financially driven person. I liked my long sailing vacations, my days off and my quiet time. In my twenties, I'd lived a vagabond life on my sailboat for six months. In my terms, I was responsible—I'd never been in debt beyond the value of my assets; my income was dramatically more than either of my parents had ever earned. The fact I had no debt wasn't enough to convince Szifra I was a stable financial bet. I'd never had the financial reserves Szifra envisioned were necessary to secure her boys' futures. And I agreed. In her terms, I wasn't.

It's a challenge to fully appreciate the balance of contributions in a partnership, to clearly see from the other person's viewpoint. For instance, I can only imagine what it would feel like to stare at Szifra's back and pedal—despite how much I might like her and her well-defined deltoids. It's easy to excuse our lack of perspective for our partner's viewpoint. In my case, all I have to do is remind people that she sits behind me. But any lack is probably more from an egocentric focus on my experience and/or a failure of my imagination. I'm also aware of the privileges of my gender. It's more my habit to lead rather than observe and follow. And this attitude isn't mine alone. It still pervades the current cultural and tandem norms.

In a previous relationship I had a taste of being the partner who inhabits the supporting role. I was invited by my partner, who had a Ph.D. in psychology and taught women's studies, to be a househusband. After a year, she liked having meals prepared and the house cleaned but didn't feel I was financially pulling my weight—not one of my job descriptions she articulated ahead of time—and she asked me to leave.

Szifra and I first lived in my house but eventually moved to her hometown where I'm introduced by Szifra, her friends, old customers of her parents' clothing store, and now even by me as "Szifra's husband." The pleasant identifier feels natural and comfortable, although I wonder if I'd be so sanguine about that identifier if people assumed I was supposed to be in the follower role.

Szifra embraces her stoker role—despite the skeptical looks she gets from some women who ride single bikes. It satisfies her to focus on her pedaling effort and to only be responsible for watching right and back. She often tells me she enjoys the freedom to look at the passing scenery and interact with other riders and people along the way. Being responsible for the mechanics of shifting and braking, or for our safety and predicting evolving threats wasn't her thing and would have initially dissuaded her from riding.

**

Szifra was clear that she wanted a full financial partner who agreed with her goals and values and was willing to crunch at times to achieve those objectives. I had no desire to be more financially ambitious than I was. After the disappointments of two relationships where her earnings became the primary income, she wanted a partner who had a stable job. My history didn't come up to her standards.

Our relationship slowed to a wobble as Szifra contemplated whether to tandem her and her boys' lives to a person who didn't share her dedication to train hard for the ride to financial security. She returned again and again to her concerns. Eventually I'd heard enough, and we came to a stop. I suggested we needed to take a break so that she could see if she could find the more compatible partner—financially and emotionally—she bemoaned not having.

The issue of my financial ambition was big for Szifra, but my relationship history also worked against me. Not only had I had three marriages, there were six other monogamous relationships that had lasted eighteen months or more and another five or six somewhat shorter, but also monogamous. Apparently worst of all, I had no regrets about my choices. She didn't hear a hint of remorse when I answered her questions about how the relationships had started or ended. When she bluntly asked whether I had regrets, I told her there were lots of things that I would now do differently, but in each case I'd learned valuable lessons, caused a minimum of damage (I hoped) and grown in my ability to form positive partnerships. I'd even come to appreciate the concerns of the women who'd left me for more promising partners. I felt that all my experiences had prepared me to negotiate, compromise, and savor the positives in a relationship. But, of course, if you see a captain constantly showing up with a new stoker, you have to wonder what's wrong with him. I probably looked like I could easily steer her life into a ditch, and she was appropriately cautious. But I wasn't an entirely strange type. Both her former husbands had been married once before, and Szifra herself had been married twice already.

On the other hand, Szifra thought I was funny. She said she loved that she could talk with me more like a girlfriend than the kind of husband she was used to. However, she wasn't sure pedaling with me would ever get her to the intersection she desired.

Chapter 11: A Bike That Fits

Trying to ride a one-size-fits-all bike or create a relationship without adjusting your expectations is a prescription for pain and abrasions. Relationships and bikes need to be adjusted to fit the participants.

People come in many different physical body styles and varying degrees of flexibility, but it's still easier to fit a bike to two people than it is to fit two people into a couple.

Single bikes come in standard frame sizes. Tandems combine these sizes for captain and stoker. A custom-built single or tandem can have its frame, handlebars, pedal crankarms, stem length, and more tweaked to individual body geometry. For instance, Szifra's cranks are shorter than mine, both to fit her leg length and to reduce the speed her legs are required to move at a given cadence of mine—it takes less speed to get once around a smaller circle than once around a larger one. My arms are a tad long, so my top tube and stem are a hair longer than standard to make my reach more comfortable.

Even after the bike is built, there are many adjustments that make it easier to produce power and reduce the potential for overuse injuries. Ride an event where people start together and you'll see lots of riders who look awkward and uncomfortable. They pedal up the road ahead of you, legs bowed out and going in and out at angles rather than powering up and down like pistons. They may have invested thousands in their bike, but they appear to have neglected to invest in a comprehensive bike fit to fine tune the bike to their body's flexibility and physical idiosyncrasies. For instance, I can ride in a bent-over position that a person with more weight around their belly might find restricts their breathing. Conversely, I can't bend as compactly as a younger, leaner rider.

A do-what-feels-good approach to adjusting a bike is fraught with the potential that it won't help the rider be in their most effective position. Pedal in a bad position and you may feel okay, and your muscles will tend to adapt, but the fit won't be the most effective or safe. After lots of hours on the bike it's common to develop "overuse injuries" from even slightly unnatural positions. If after riding in a slightly off position, you get on a properly fitted bike, you'll likely feel uncomfortable until your muscles adapt. Then the new position will feel comfortable. A good bike fit doesn't guarantee you'll be in the perfect position the first time, but it will tend to get you very close.

Bike fitters use a variety of techniques and tools. These days you can get fit with a tape measure, a bubble level, a laser, or a complex video process. None works better than the capability of the person doing the fit. I was once fit on a new single bike in a comfortable position. When I hired a coach six months later, she rode with me, eyeballed my position, and said that my saddle was two centimeters too low. I made the small adjustment, and it reduced my knee pain and improved my power almost immediately. After a few weeks I continued to gain additional comfort and power.

Each rider on a tandem must, of course, be individually fit for their position. Szifra's handlebars are mounted on the seat post beneath my saddle. She needed them moved higher. The adjustment put them so close to my butt that the motion of my thighs and hips caused me to constantly rub against her thumbs. At eighty-five plus revolutions per minute over a couple of hours of riding, rubbing any object, even the hand of your loved one, more than 5,000 times creates a point of irritation. It's like the old adage about relationships: "What you love is what will drive you crazy." It took many tweaks of Szifra's handlebar angle, height, and fore and aft position to find a compromise that satisfied both of us.

The saddle is perhaps the most crucial point of contact with the bike. Most riders have to break in their saddle, which really means acclimating their butt to the pressure of sitting on two small contact points of flesh and bone. Adaptation to a poor saddle may give way to sores, injuries and serious discomfort. Choosing a saddle and setting the height, fore and aft position and angle of tilt are important fit considerations, but they can be frustratingly subjective.

When you first sit on a new saddle—or put on a new pair of shoes—do you reject it because of a hint of discomfort? Or do you extrapolate how it might wear into a comfortable piece of equipment and keep it?

Szifra rejects saddles, shoes, jerseys, shorts and any other piece of clothing that isn't comfortable right from the start. Her first reaction to a good piece of clothing is a delighted swoon, "This is so soft! Feel how soft this is!"

I tend to assume that, over time, the points of irritation will smooth out to some degree. I have shoes that I rarely wear because they still aren't quite broken in. On the other hand, my optimism keeps me hanging in there, and there are benefits that accrue from my persistence. I also have shoes, which are some of my most comfortable, that took time to break in.

This same issue comes up in relationships. There is substantial evidence that in the most volatile and dangerous relationships, hints of problems were there early on but were discounted by the eventual victim. Until you're deep into the relationship, or the break-in process, it's hard to realistically evaluate the fine line between adapting and putting up with unnecessary suffering.

Our early relationship wasn't soft enough for Szifra. The relationship was basically fun, satisfying in many ways, a challenge for her to grow, as it was for me, but not always comfortable. She began to ask herself whether her discomfort might be a signal she shouldn't ignore. Was my occasional irritation a sign of disrespect for her? If so, was it likely to be something I could crank back in time, or would it escalate? Her natural pull was to look for a softer, more naturally compatible companion.

When we started riding, the access to the closest bike path was through a narrow space between bollards—steel posts designed to block cars from entering. At first, it felt like any little shift of our weight might cause us to swerve into one of these obstacles. Initially we stopped pedaling, held still, aimed, coasted and worried. As we learned to navigate the tight passage, we became more confident we could pedal through it.

Szifra only made it through the emotional barriers to a long-term relationship with me by threading her way past images of the possibility of an easier relationship. After about four months, in another of our conversations where we attempted to sort out a misunderstanding, she shared what she was thinking, "I wonder if there's someone else who would be easier for me." She wanted someone who might be softer, more comfortable, require less break-in time. The irony was that she was asking for my thoughts on the matter.

That conversation turned into a series of conversations about her doubts and wishes. After hearing her concerns and wistful thinking numerous times, I let my better thinking step ahead of my anxiety, "It sounds like you need to choose a route to take. Maybe you should leave and look for someone who's easier. Find a relationship you want. I'm not interested in being a second choice. If you don't find what you want, I'm open to you looping back. I don't think I'd have any hard feelings."

She asked what I would do if she went looking. "I'll probably wait at least a couple of months, maybe longer. I can't imagine I'd actively look for someone for a while. I wasn't really looking when you showed up." She was up against a variation of the age-old risk/reward equation—a bird in the hand might not be worth the possibility of even one in the bush. Was the frame of the relationship sized correctly for her? Did it only need a few fit tweaks? Or was she trying to adapt to a fundamentally wrong size?

She told me she had wondered the same thing when she began to get serious with Him. They had many dissimilarities. Could she find continuing happiness with him? The answer was complex. She did find love and happiness. Her boys did find a good father. But His and her dramatic philosophical and political differences were always there.

The one she kept telling me about was his NRA membership versus her support of anti-handgun organizations. He suggested that they both stop sending money to their organizations because, "We're just canceling each other out and wasting money." He may have missed the importance of each person's independence, of each acting on their differences. She missed the importance of deciding whether she felt safe living with his philosophy.

Her initial doubts had been on target. He had eventually abandoned her. He told her he ran when things were tough, and it had taken a while, but he had. Now she had to decide about how to manage her doubts all over again. She didn't trust her instincts when it came to picking a mate; her poor track record worried her. I might be saying all the right things, but He had been saying them too. He was rabid about gun safety. Every gun was locked. The boys had learned to safely handle firearms. But like I couldn't recognize a poor fit on my bikes, he had failed to recognize when his gun habit had become a poor fit for his emotional state.

It isn't easy to replace either a captain or a stoker. Being part of a tandem team requires a commitment. You have to merge your efforts at cadence and balance. You have to go riding sometimes even when it isn't your first choice. Szifra isn't the strongest stoker I know, but I'd rather spend the day with her than anyone else. But if she didn't feel that spending her day with me was relaxing, it would be best for her to interview other captains or find herself a stoker. The interview process wouldn't be without risks. She risked getting dumped. I risked having to ride alone. But no tandem team or relationship works well on desperation, threat, or settling.

Szifra continued voicing her concerns, and I was finally tired of the ambiguity. I insisted she decide what she wanted to do. Her tolerance for the risks of either path was a decision she alone had to make. I gave her a hug and drove home to my growing puppy. I was sad but had no hard feelings or doubts that I was doing what I needed to for me. I only wanted to be with her if she wanted to be with me.

Later she told me that He had forced a decision moment also. She'd waffled so long on creating a shared household that he'd finally joined a racquetball club and arranged to go to a party where there were several single women. She had what she wanted, complete freedom to go her own way. Within two weeks, she decided to move to Massachusetts to live with him. It was strange, at that moment I found myself feeling closer to him than to her.

I walked into my house, affectionately roughed up my puppy, pulled out my search and rescue study guides, and the phone rang. I had no caller ID on my landline, so I answered, "Hello, this is Jay."

"This is stupid! I want to be with you!"

Now I had my doubts. Was I her desperate second choice? My newly developed sense of independence wasn't fit enough to resist the pull back to her. Or maybe there wasn't enough reason to resist. Should I trust my instincts? I loved her. I enjoyed her. I'd survive another fall if need be. I'd go for it.

Coincidently, at the same time Szifra and I were discussing my ambition and struggling about our future, a wealthy client of my dog business threw a non-linear opportunity my way. I was ripe for a change because as my reflexes slowed down the dog work had become more dangerous. The client recommended me for a full-time senior administrative position at a Harvard-affiliated hospital. She told me she had a friend who was looking for someone to help create operational structure and manage a hospital fundraising department. My celebrity client list, my business consulting skills and my psychological training tipped the balance in my favor. Szifra was pleased: "I feel bratty about the job and salary being so important, but to me they are."

At some point Szifra and I settled into the reality that our relationship, and eventually our bike, required a continual process of tweaking and adapting. Either we accepted that and learned to enjoy it, or we were going to be miserable for a long time. Now when someone says, "I can't ride a road bike because they aren't comfortable," we look at each other knowingly. We'd like to ask about fit and whether they've taken the time to adapt. And Szifra, in her helpful extravert role, often does start asking questions.

At tandem events, there are captains or stokers who comment negatively on their partner's effort, requirements, or flexibility. It's at these moments that we often feel most attuned as a team. We fundamentally fit. We've found that we both enjoy ourselves best when we accept the realities of each other's needs and preferences, focus on pedaling, and delighting in the countryside and our good fortune.

Chapter 12: Shifting Gears

Both relationships and bikes can surge forward in quick sprints, cruise along with determined endurance, or climb challenging obstacles. Each situation requires an ability to change gears—to adjust your pace and effort. When Szifra needs me to slow down and pay attention, I need to be able to shift out of my quick-thinking mode and into a contemplative tempo. When I need to be heard, Szifra has to stop driving forward and glide for a minute.

Similarly, on the bike we want the flexibility to choose how we pedal. What cadence? What effort? We don't always agree, but we want the ability to select a range that works reasonably for both of us, that is efficient, effective, or easy to sustain. Bike gears give us that flexibility.

Chainrings—the "front" cog wheels, which are usually attached to the rider's pedal crank—are used to shift the effort into a broad range that matches the desired exertion or pace. On most tandems, the chainrings are attached to the stoker's crankshaft, which is connected by a chain or belt to the captain's pedals. On our bike, the captain's chain and the stoker's chain meet at an intermediate shaft, which drives the chainrings but also allows us each to coast independently.

Most tandems have two or three front chainrings. The smallest gear makes the pedals easiest to push and is used for hill climbing. But when the road is flat or downhill and the bike picks up speed, that small gear might cause our spin to top one-hundred-and-ten to one-hundred-and-twenty RPMs. That rate is unsustainable for most people without serious practice and conditioning. Many riders will bounce in their saddle and produce very little power at RPMs over ninety-five or so. The largest gear is the one to use on a downhill when the bike rolls to a higher speed. But a large gear gives you so little leverage that it becomes very hard to push when the road starts up again or the wind is in your face.

The broad power and cadence ranges of the chainring gears can be finetuned by shifting the chain onto different gears of the cluster attached to the rear wheel—a few bikes have internal gears in their rear hubs. Because of leverage physics, the large rear gear makes whichever chainring you're in easiest to push. Shifting into the smallest front gear and largest rear gear—sometimes called the "Granny" gear—is the combination you might use to climb the steepest hills. This Grandpa and Grandma use that gear regularly on difficult pitches. The largest chainring in front and the smallest rear gear will allow you to keep up with the pedals when the bike heads downhill with the wind at your back.

Choosing the right gear combinations makes it possible to propel the bike without undue crunching on the pedals, and to keep our spin rate at an optimal team cadence of around eighty to ninety rpm up hills, across flat plateaus, or down winding mountainsides. Shifts between gears on either the front or rear are made by activating a derailleur, a mechanism that pushes the chain off one gear and onto another by means of a lever or button on your handlebars.

Bikes have an eccentricity. They won't shift into a different gear unless you're turning the pedals. You can push the shift lever or button, but the chain won't climb up or down onto the next gear unless the pedals are causing the chain to run while it's being pushed onto or off the gear. Dependable shifting requires some spin and no more than moderate pedal pressure. In the middle of many steep inclines—where the pressure on the pedals is considerable—chains that are moved by a cable may ignore your attempts to shift. Traditionally, you need to plan ahead and change gears before the hill. It's possible to shift on a climb if you push hard, accelerate to gain a bit of momentum, and then back off to relieve hard pressure on the chain just as you shift. Done correctly, a moment of "soft pedaling" allows for a quick shift without losing too much momentum.

Electronic shifting derailleurs can make shifts during climbs almost as flawless as on the flats, albeit often with a sizable clunk if the chain is under pressure. They also take less finger pressure than mechanical ones to actuate the derailleur—great for older joints on long rides. Wired connections also eliminate the long shift cables tandems require, which can sometimes stretch enough to make shifts hesitate.

If I try to shift on a hill, but don't tell Szifra to soft pedal or pause, the chain may refuse to climb into the next gear, it may stay caught in its present gear, or it may abandon the cogwheels altogether and hang limply, mocking our spinning pedals. "Throwing a chain"—having the chain abruptly slip off and the pedals spin without resistance—requires us to stop and take the chain, which is undoubtedly covered with dirty black grease or wax, and feed it back onto the gears. I find that if Szifra lifts the rear wheel and I turn the pedals by hand, I can usually keep my fingers clean by using a short, small twig to lift and feed the chain back onto the top of the chainring.

At the beginning, Szifra and I had lots of off-the-bike situations come at us that required a quick change of emotional gears. Our shifts weren't always smooth, and the resultant gear often didn't quite suit both of us.

We were both slow to reduce the pressure on the other, even when we could see it was disturbing. We often missed shifts that might have led to a positive interaction. And there were times our chain came off, and we struggled to get the relationship moving forward again. The secret seemed to be to catch our breath and reduce the conversational pressure. A moment of soft talking helped us get to solutions more in sync with empathy than just having our individual position prevail.

Szifra was acclimated to His cadence, or he had been to hers. When she helpfully told me that His shifts worked better for her than mine did, I could usually quiet my jealousy by rationalizing the comparison. What most often jumped into my head was that no matter what I did, my faults were likely to be judged more critically since they were current and presented the risk they might come up again. I was a continuing threat of aggravation. He wasn't.

The counterpart to the crisp memory of my missteps and the forewarning that living with me augured more of the same, was that her perception of His missed shifts was tempered by the time that had elapsed since she'd had to deal with them. Death narrows a survivor's view of the past just as our tiny, rearview mirrors restrict our view back. The view back of a deceased partner's cadence, their willingness to work hard and their ability to adapt to the survivor's pace, tend to bleed toward an affirmative assessment. The late partner may not appear totally rose-colored, but their weaknesses certainly tend to be washed into pastel shades.

Viewed in retrospect, Szifra felt His spin rate on relationship hills was a better match for her. The line he took through most turns was recalled as smoother and better executed. The times he ran them into the dirt and dumped their joint venture were hardly worth talking about, except perhaps his failure to get his foot down that last time. Szifra acknowledged and talked about that calamity, although it wasn't until later that she trusted us enough to share some of her deepest guilt and questions with me.

Chapter 13: Uncoupling

Our carbon and titanium tandem is glued together into a one-piece frame. Packed in a long box, we can take it on air and rail transportation or ship it at a reasonable price. Those wanting to travel regularly by air and particularly travel overseas, usually opt for a frame with couplers.

Coupled tandems are designed to be taken apart and reassembled easily into seamlessly working machines. They're built with a series of couplers. The frame tubes are strategically cut so the bike can be separated into sections. Joints—barrel-connector style couplers—which can add $2,500 or more to the cost of a bike, are epoxied, or brazed onto each side of the cut. By turning the barrel connector, you can connect or disconnect the sections. Detachment fittings are also added to the shifter cables or wires and the brake cables or lines.

On a few tandems, the couplings give the owners an option to accommodate a changeable number of riders—resulting in triplets, quads and quints. Parents might add sections and saddles for one or more children and then reduce the bike back to a tandem when the children leave home, or the parents want to ride on their own.

Like coupled tandems, some relationships can be thoughtfully disassembled. Other relationships break apart in a way that destroys future possibilities. On a bike, riders must always be alert for the threat of brute-force decoupling from cars, spills, or disrespectfulness. And similar to a bike, relationships can be decoupled by carelessness, poor quality components like self-centered or selfish individuals, miscommunication, or simple misfortune.

Although I had wanted to stay together with my last woman friend, when it felt necessary to uncouple, I attempted to do it with care for the component parts. The frame may not have survived, but we left as two intact singles. Both of us felt the loss of a partner who could pick up the slack when our strength or resolve faltered, but we both endured.

Szifra's connection with Him had been shattered by brute force that left one half broken beyond repair and the other with significant internal damage.

**

Szifra and I started our relationship with her still coasting on her old tandem and me on a single. As we worked to couple our separate lives, I wanted to be sure we were riding a tandem, not a triple, and quietly worked to uncouple Him from the center of our relationship. I knew he would always be with us, but I didn't want him sitting between us. Not providing a saddle for him didn't seem to discourage him from showing up whenever we hit a section of rough relationship. Szifra would sometimes invite him back with a: "He would just go quiet. He didn't get so irritated. He wasn't bothered by my speediness."

He may not have been particularly bothered by any of her personality traits. He may have appreciated them all. He may have been better at both of those than I was. But his suicide had decoupled them in a terrible way.

As with most survivors of suicide, Szifra was threatened with profound guilt about what might have helped. She had known he struggled with depression. He had told her he occasionally thought about suicide. She regularly checked with him about whether he felt close to acting on those thoughts. Szifra had helped him get a psychiatrist and a therapist. But before it happened, she hadn't heard any recent warnings. Still, she wondered about the small clues she seemed to have missed, wondered if she had walked away from a cry for help, shuddered at the thought she'd left him alone with such overwhelming feelings.

It certainly wasn't my place or intent to add shadows to her memories of Him. It was my job to either adjust to the polygamous relationship I was in or vacate Szifra's still healing life space. I had no reasonable choice but to get comfortable with the positive spin in his still evolving obituary. If I allowed his memory to sucker me into a competition, it would be like dragging a passenger who didn't pedal up a major hill. I would surely bonk before he did. And Szifra would have to carry the weight of additional doubts and feelings. He might have negligently done that to her. I wouldn't/couldn't.

I had a tiny inkling of what Szifra had gone through. It was enough to give me a glimpse of her journey. I had two former girlfriends who died sudden, violent deaths in car accidents—one might have even been purposeful. But, at the time they died, I'd been estranged or separated from each of them. I cared about them, but they belonged to my past. I'd had the time to feel disappointed and angry about being left before they died, and grief started to airbrush their faults. My memories of them tasted a bit sour, and that made them less desirable to dwell on. Even at some distance from the intimacy, their violent deaths tore chunks out of my memories and left tears.

At fifteen, my first serious girlfriend had abruptly jilted me. Three years later, when I lived hundreds of miles away, I received a letter from an old classmate telling me that she had died a terrible death on senior prom night. She and her boyfriend were drunk passengers of a drunk driver. She was pinned under an overturned car. Her death brought her back into my life. Each time I drove through Tonawanda, New York, the town she was buried in, I felt compelled to visit her grave. I felt I was the sole link who cared about her having lived. I felt responsible to be certain she wasn't forgotten. I alone held our treasury of sweet young kisses and furtive explorations of intimacy. It took me years of effort to get her full story, complete with upsets, pasted correctly into my memory scrapbook.

The second death came as my summer camp girlfriend, with her best friend in the passenger seat, pulled her Dodge Charger out into a highway intersection, right in front of a fast-moving semi-truck. Both she and her friend were killed instantly. The truck driver said he saw her look up right at him and still pull out. Did she see him? Were the troubles with her family more than she could bear? Her sweet hugs and hesitant kisses, which grew deeper and more intense as the camp session progressed, are still amazingly ripe on my lips after fifty-five years. That she didn't answer my letters or reach out for help are now diluted disappointments. I also wonder who else keeps her memory alive all these years later.

The obligation to preserve both of their memories is an honor and a burden. Since death doesn't play fair with memories, I often wonder what I'm forgetting. Am I honoring who they were or creating fantasy reflections in my rearview mirror? And, of course, even when I knew them, I never knew who they really were.

Szifra and I met twenty months after His death, which didn't seem adequate time to Szifra for a respectful recovery from her widow's grief. And only the one who buries a person can judge such things. After all, I was still faithful after forty years to the memory of a dead, disloyal fifteen-year-old.

When Szifra and I walked the streets of her town, she was concerned people would think we were having an affair on Him. She was worried it might look like she countenanced infidelity. The relationship between her first husband and that kindergarten teacher had sealed her feelings against that. She told me she felt a bit ashamed as her grief mellowed. "It's too soon. It isn't even two years."

It was important that I listen to her feelings and not speak. But I wondered what alternative she had. Did the history of how women were expected to manage grief give guidance? Should she have thrown herself into his grave or retreated to a secluded life in a nunnery?

The house she lived in was originally His house, the bed their bed, the sheets and pillows theirs. The first time we slept together in their bedroom, we prudishly got ready for bed. I came out of the bathroom, and she was already under the covers. As I lifted the blanket and sheet on his side, I pushed the bounds of propriety by asking, "Is this safe? What if He comes home?" She laughed. I got into the bed and we talked about him until she got bored with the subject, and we moved on to other topics.

After a few months, Szifra's curiosity eventually began to push through her fear of jealousy. One evening over a dinner of broccoli in garlic sauce at a Chinese restaurant near my house, she asked about my last woman friend. I'd left her because I couldn't manage the negativity we generated, but still, mostly positive thoughts sprang to mind. I reached across the table and hooked my index finger into Szifra's, "Boy, this stuff is challenging. Even talking about her feels adulterous. I got this thought that, if this doesn't work out, you'll think I'll talk about *you*. Does the ability to move on suggest I would countenance adultery?"

We both sat quietly chopsticking florets of broccoli, dripping with the dark brown sauce, into our mouths. In the quiet space I was flipping through the pages of my past. My question was interesting to contemplate, but her question had been asked first and required an answer. Not wanting to be disloyal to the woman I'd moved on from, I shared a few good things about her. Not too disturbed, Szifra pushed forward, "What was her body like?"

Now there's a question to strike fear. *It was delightful! It was full of pleasure! I couldn't have asked for more!* If I lied instead, did that confirm Szifra's fears that I wouldn't tell the truth about my feelings about her body? But telling the truth opened the question of comparisons, which had no relevancy to my current experience. Still, the comparison was likely to stand there, quietly waiting to be addressed.

The question caught me still enthralled with Szifra's newness. Even a deliberate change of intimate partners is disorienting. One morning you wake up in a tangle of unfamiliar limbs. Perhaps the legs are longer or thinner than expected, the hair is a different color or stuck up in pillow-mashed spikes rather than draped in a tangle over the pillow, the curled body's direction, compactness and curves have altered. But in my experience, it's the smell that refuses to be ignored, that confirms things have changed. The new smell will eventually recede into familiarity, but for a while it's intoxicating. I was still intoxicated with Szifra.

83

I tried an answer and hoped she'd give me room to adjust it if I found better words to reflect my feelings. "I liked her and the physical relationship we created. Her body was very different than yours but pleasing because she offered to share it with me and seemed pleased to share mine. Everything is so different between you and me that it's hard to remember details about her"—that was a bit of a stretch, but quickly becoming true. "Do you really want to know anything more?"

"No, that's enough." Then her comparison urge spoke up, "Are you disappointed with me?" I was more delighted by the sights of Szifra than I remembered being by the past body. But I was delighted by that body at the time. Her question again stood waiting.

"No. I'm not disappointed. I'm pleased. When I left her, I assumed I'd never find an intimate experience quite that appealing, but in most ways ours is better. I wouldn't go back for anything." Then I zinged her for her previous incredulous judgment of my no regrets/apologies attitude, "I have no regrets." She understood and grinned that distinctive grin.

I realized another comparison question stood there, mine. With some trepidation, I waded in. "Are you disappointed with me?"

And there He was, sitting between us again. She took another turn on the barrel connector and another step in untangling us from him, "I really like what we have." She went on and outlined some other things she really liked about me and us. He faded away from our evening. It was funny to feel pleasure that I'd not lost out when compared to her polished memories of a dead man. But that's what I felt.

A few months later, we began to gently laugh together when He stepped into the conversation. One evening we went to a coffee house where an outrageous singer-songwriter, Stanley Matis, sang a song about not letting "the dead guy drive". We both found the idea delightfully bizarre. We began to refer to the "Dead Guy" in affectionate terms. It both included him and contained him.

When his death date passed the two-year mark, Szifra's strictures around propriety loosened a bit more. We shifted into an easier gear. We talked. We laughed. We groaned. She flinched. Occasionally I'd indelicately reference him, catch myself and apologize. We slowly moved him out of our day-to-day lives and into a scrapbook, where he stayed most of the time— except for unexpected appearances when my voice was more irritating than she thought his would have been. At those moments, Szifra threw open the covers and once again He lay beside her. When that happened, I wondered how many ways she was comparing me to him and not saying anything. Were they together judging me as wanting?

I didn't want to tiptoe around his memory, but I also didn't want to poke sticks in her trauma. The line was fine and occasionally I was tempted to cross it. At least once I let my desire to be funny take me into full-asshole territory.

Szifra decided she was ready for us to live together and with lots of anxiety she put her house up for sale. One Saturday we were clearing His clutter out of her attic, carrying boxes of his memorabilia down the ancient, narrow staircase. Among the piles of his once-memories I found a large box of trophies he'd saved from his target-shooting days. I carried it down to the yard where Szifra was taking a sunshine break, leaning against the backdoor, talking with her sister.

Szifra had always been an opponent of His multiple guns in the house, and his use of one to die had compounded her feelings. One of the first things she did after his death was to have her brother take all the guns to a dealer.

I told her what I had in the box and said I hadn't known he'd competed. I asked, "What do you want to do with these?" She told me she had no need to keep any of them. I headed for the large dumpster we had parked in the oval drive next to where he'd died. Szifra turned back to the conversation with her sister. An absolutely disrespectful thought came to me. There was no way I should ever share it with Szifra, or anyone. But it was clever, and we both loved clever. My impulse control slipped. I turned back to her with the box in my arms, a grimace on my face and said, "I thought of something I really shouldn't say. Tell me to just keep it to myself."

She paused, but her appreciation for wittiness, and her curiosity got the best of her. "Go ahead."

"I mean I really shouldn't say it." I emphasized, begging for pre-forgiveness and someone else's check on my impulse, but my grimace was broadening into a grin at the same time.

"Oh, go ahead."

My restraint collapsed, "I just realized that I got the trophy for his last shot." Szifra half gasped, half laughed. Her sister just stared at me like I'd lost my mind.

With the energy of the impulse discharged, propriety chastened me. "Sorry. I should have kept that to myself."

"It was clever. But it *was* over the top," Szifra said lightly. And she turned to her sister to explain why it was acceptable for me to say it, even if it was too much. To her credit, Szifra allowed me to lean into the bounds of impropriety, while she reserved the right to share her feelings. Every time it went well, the relationship coupling seemed more permanent.

Chapter 14: Should We Buy a Tandem?

Our first tandem ride had been a one-and-done experience. We didn't ride or talk about tandems again for eleven years.

During the intervening decade we moved in together and began six months of easy negotiations about how to live in the same space. We both felt open to not ever getting married. But we also felt that a formal commitment placed positive expectations on our relationship. Marriage felt like it encouraged persistence. An ironic idea, given our past failures.

I was neutral. "I'm fine getting married, but I don't need to."

Szifra was more in the not-interested camp. "I don't want to be wife number four."

I countered. "I would be your third husband."

"Four is totally different than three. Being a fourth wife sounds much worse than three."

"I'd be taking a risk. Your last husband died and I'm not certain you didn't arrange it." She sort of laughed.

By then my inappropriate humor was somewhat less of an issue. She didn't always find it worth a laugh, but often she did. And she could let it roll into the gutter without comment when she didn't. I like to take credit for all the desensitizing work my humor has encouraged over the years, but that's also a self-serving bit of almost humor. I will take some credit for not allowing his death to remain a taboo subject or allowing him to be the subject of continual darkness.

I can't get a good enough read on his style of humor to know whether He'd have appreciated my efforts. But He lost the right to object when he bailed out of all the unanswerable questions life throws at us. I just have to keep threading my way between the emotional bollards blocking the pathway to his life story.

Once Szifra had given herself permission to take a break from "us," and then decided she wanted to stay, she committed to us with superglue. The first question we dealt with was her concern that marriage would take away her rights to His Social Security benefits—his corporate job had given him maximum benefits. One day when Szifra was talking to a friend on the phone, I indirectly found out that issue had been settled by her accountant. Szifra informed her friend, "We're getting married next month."

I waved my hand at her and silently mouthed my question, "When were you going to tell me?"

She broke up laughing and told her friend what had happened, "I never told Jay. He just overheard this." Szifra processes lots of things in the privacy of her thoughts and is often surprised that others haven't kept up. She wanted to be married but negotiating the details would happen on an ad hoc basis, with me if she remembered, by herself if she didn't.

I was fine with the decision, as she knew I'd be. No one would describe Szifra as a romantic. She's a data-driven problem solver—sweet and considerate, but reality-based. She told me that after our first coffee date she had reported how much fun it was to her friend Kara. Szifra had then asked what she should say to me if I kissed her on our next date and she liked it. Kara suggested either saying, "That was nice," or "Do it to me again big boy." Szifra had used the former.

Neither of us wanted a public wedding ceremony, so we decided on a simple wedding at home. We had to find someone to officiate. Szifra was cashing out after a physical therapy appointment, and the young man in front of her told the receptionist he was a newly licensed Justice of the Peace. "It was unbelievable!" Szifra reported to me when she got home. "He was so nice that I invited him to make ours his first wedding. Isn't that amazing?" Life is full of wonder for Szifra, romance excepted.

The day we set for the wedding, Szifra's older son and his girlfriend, now wife, were visiting from New York. We had planned for our ceremony to happen after they left for home. But when they found out what was up, instead of heading home they decided to stay. Since Kara had introduced us, we asked her to be there as our official witness.

Our JP started out sort of formal and then turned to us. The ceremony was based primarily around the vows we created to say to each other. Our notes emphasized the advantages of love the second or fifth time around, and we both mentioned how her family had survived the Holocaust and that ours was a mixed marriage between Jew and non-Jew. Each of us had something to say about growing old together and celebrating life.

I started first. And as I spoke my vows, the phone rang. Four people froze. It rang a second time. Szifra and I broke out laughing. It rang a third time. We waited for the fourth ring and then the answering machine picked up and my outgoing message began to play at a volume too loud to ignore. The other attendees looked to us, while Szifra and I stood there grinning at each other. And then my optometrist's voice came on, letting me know my new glasses were ready. The whole thing seemed to add just the right informal touch for our sensibilities.

After the ceremony we headed for a week in Vermont cross-country skiing. On the way out of town we stopped by for my glasses.

Marriage encouraged us to work a bit harder at building shared traditions and negotiating other aspects of our relationship. Together we raised my German Shepherd, and I finished rebuilding my small, inherited lake cottage. But we didn't have a fitness or sport activity that we were both enthusiastic about doing together.

Szifra worked out and went to yoga classes three times a week. She was her normal social-savant and made friends with class members. I regularly rode my single bike and raced a small sailboat at a local sailing club. Some of the other sailors became friends, and I rode bikes with a couple of them.

I slowly began to increase the time I spent training on my single bike. Szifra occasionally voiced regret she couldn't ride with me. I encouraged her to, but she was hesitant, "I can't keep up with you and I don't want to slow you down."

I kept telling her I was fine riding slowly with her. "It doesn't bother me to putt along. I like being with you. Let's try it."

She knew herself too well. "I'd feel uncomfortable. It wouldn't be fun. I'd feel pressure."

When she was about to turn sixty, eight years into our marriage, she again didn't share her thinking with me, but she quietly began considering a tandem. Since she'd enjoyed riding one the first time, she wondered if maybe it could be our joint activity. On a tandem she'd never be left behind more than a few feet (my joke). We both wanted to be active. A tandem might provide a bit of additional relationship glue, which we didn't need, but I craved.

The majority of tandem teams are couples. Among experienced teams there's a lot of talk about how a tandem will blow out a relationship that's already going flat. But for us, the tandem quickly became a place of solace and repair. The lack of distractions encouraged us to focus on us—not on our shared executive coaching businesses, not our social life, not on family stresses. The team effort and our ability to manage the shared responsibilities of the bike solidified us as a couple.

Once we got a tandem, we quickly realized how it required many of the same things the relationship demanded of us. We found ourselves not just talking tandem jargon but talking as if the tandem was both a part of our relationship and a representation of the challenges of coupling.

We've now ridden for twelve years. We've so thoroughly integrated the bike into our lives and our language that we have trouble remembering that we haven't ridden forever. It feels like it was always the organizing vehicle for warm days, a demanding motivation to ride the indoor trainer during the winter months, an escape from the reactive craziness we could easily fall into, and a way to create a relationship that was manifestly separate from all that went before.

And we both felt like that was part of the chemistry of the bike; neither her late husband nor my exes tended to ride along. And we were generally able to leave both her irascible and my judgmental, deceased fathers behind. There was also something positive about not being face to face when the other person seemed abrupt or critical. When we hit a bump on the bike, it was a bit easier to pedal down the road and leave the emotional jolt behind. Off the bike, we were tempted to face off over who was responsible for fixing the flat.

In the pre-tandem first month of our relationship Szifra told me she wasn't willing to start climbing endless relationship hills again. But she hung in there despite some of the hills we encountered. And after we started riding the tandem, we both had experiences of discomfort leading to increased resilience and satisfaction.

There are many ways the tandem can be a metaphor for a relationship. But between its rarity on the road and its popular theme song— *Daisy Bell* (*A Bicycle Built for Two*)—a tandem bike also stimulates flights of whimsy in people. We still enjoy how it generates surprised smiles and waves from strangers. Toddlers, senior citizens and street-hardened adolescents all succumb to appreciative grins at the sight of our elongated, orange bike.

The words are changed but the feelings are the same:

Szifra, Szifra, give me your answer do.

I'm half crazy, all for the love of you.

I'm not a stylish person.

I won't buy a Tesla.

But you'd look sweet, upon the seat of a bicycle built for two.

Chapter 15: The Grand Junction

The first birthday tandem was an urban-style bike with wide, treaded tires, flat pedals that could be used with sneakers, and handlebars that allowed us to sit upright. The seats were heavily padded. The shift and brake mechanisms were durable and heavy, and the substantial chrome-moly frame might have survived, even if it ran into a car. (Chrome-moly steel is the material the bikes I rode as a kid were made from.) These substantial bikes are like the ones you can rent by the hour at the beach. It takes a hard push to initially get their heavy wheels and beefy tires rolling. I'd hate to try to pedal one up a significant hill.

A moderately-priced road tandem can cost exponentially more than an urban-style bike. Even an entry-level road tandem can cost a couple of thousand dollars and a new, top-quality bike can easily run from ten to twenty thousand dollars. For that kind of money, you get a carbon or titanium frame, alloy or carbon wheels, the most advanced gear and brake systems, drop handlebars, clip-in pedals and solid supportive seats. You can choose rim or disc brakes—cable or hydraulic activated—chain or belt drive, and up to twenty-two or thirty-three gear possibilities. Additional options include manual or electronically activated shifting, USB charger in the front wheel for phones, bike computers, lights, etc., and any number of seat suspension systems.

Not many high-quality, used tandems come up for sale, unlike the plethora of nice single bikes that are often available. Many people buy a single bike but rarely end up riding it. After a few years, underused bikes drift onto eBay, Craigslist, or lean chained to a fence with a "Make Offer" sign stuck to them. Both new and used tandems take some effort to find. There are fewer dealers, with few couples interested in joint riding there are fewer tandems bought, fewer still discarded, and finding one that is sized correctly for two different people is a further impediment.

We began looking for a tandem a year or two after I left the hospital development position I'd worked at for six years. I left for the reason most people change jobs. My supervisor's style of managing. She didn't allow independence and poached all my wealthiest prospective donors. She disagreed with my initiatives and insisted I communicate with people in her pretentious style. I liked creating warm, supportive relationships with donors. She warmed up to donors based on the value of their clothes and cars. Rigid social status and trappings of wealth didn't give me a buzz. In addition, I no longer wanted to commute an hour each way or wear a coordinated suit, shirt and tie every day. I'd had enough. I'd worked for myself before and it was time to do it again.

Szifra supported my leaving, but she heard echoes of Him leaving his corporate job. I would be her third husband to abandon a well-paid job and shift the financial burden to her. But so many pieces of our lives were working really well that she encouraged me to go for it. She said she was up for the challenge of keeping us afloat while I built a coaching business.

My hospital salary had allowed us to add appreciably to my IRA and our 401k retirement savings. I'd also stayed long enough that I vested into a small pension. Szifra and I are both comfortable living below our means. We'd paid off our house and had no debt. Our financial situation looked good. I began the tough transition back into private practice and Szifra crunched through the financial soft spots. She earned most of our income until I slowly began generating more than token returns. Every time I hit a headwind, Szifra hunched over the pedals and doggedly drove us on while cheering my efforts. She was clearly our captain during this ride.

Szifra wasn't just tolerant of what I was going through, she also encouraged me to put more energy into both my biking and writing. She cringed but supported using part of my severance pay to purchase my first carbon-fiber single bike. And she encouraged me to schedule more time to write. I took her up on her offer, rode more, and dramatically increased my writing time. She continued to invest her non-work time in yoga, gym classes and walking with friends.

I started to ride regularly. Slowly building up the bike legs I'd neglected for over thirty years. Later Szifra told me that the idea of riding a tandem had been percolating in the back of her mind, but she didn't want to mention it to me until she was pretty sure it would work for her. The fact her sixtieth birthday was coming at her seemed to add an impetus to her musing—she wondered if a tandem purchase might replace a one-day, birthday adventure.

When she suggested the idea and asked me if I thought it would be fun, I easily agreed it would. The drawbacks she felt about riding on her own would be addressed by a tandem—she wouldn't be left behind or have to work too hard to keep up, and she wouldn't have to pay close attention to the road and cars.

Her idea was that I would captain the bike just like I had the first time. She didn't want the responsibility, didn't trust herself to pay close attention to the road and traffic. The back seat on a tandem would give her time to look around and enjoy the ride. At the time, it wasn't evident to either of us that she was signing on to generate a significant portion of the power we'd need to ride the rolling hills and challenging climbs that predominate in our riding areas.

I was willing to be in charge of all the minutiae that goes with safely maintaining and riding a road machine, but I didn't want to be responsible for Szifra enjoying herself. I would need to keep a check on my inclination to feel responsible. This was a danger I'd felt when taking passengers on my sailboats. I easily fell into feeling answerable for them enjoying themselves, for enough wind to sail but not so much that people felt anxious, for producing clear skies, and avoiding seasickness. I could easily imagine I would start similar silly thinking on a tandem.

We tried to figure out how to be sure Szifra shared equal responsibility in the potential venture. I had a thought. I'd buy her the tandem for her birthday—the amount I was comfortable spending on a present had clearly escalated dramatically over the years. If she was the owner, I'd accept the captain role. Ownership threatened to be a bit more responsibility than she wanted but, without completely thinking it through, she agreed.

We began to strategize how we might experiment with tandeming without overcommitting to a sport we still had minimal information about. There were some obvious next steps to explore. We needed to know what a tandem cost—was it much more than my $2,000 single bike? What options and what features should we care about? Where could we find new tandems for sale? Used ones?

We're privileged to live a life with many freedoms and opportunities, and we have the resources to take advantage of the ones that interest us. We have options that only a relatively small group of people do. My practice was filling in, and hers was robust. We still had no significant debts. Buying a tandem would be a financial hit but wouldn't demand we change other aspects of our lifestyle. What we were barely aware of was how much a tandem would increase the pressure to synchronize our lives.

When we decided to go ahead and buy a new tandem, we made a mistake. We didn't get a traditional synced tandem. That misstep ended up being the best move we could have made.

Szifra and I are both professionals who teach communication skills to our clients—high-functioning individuals and teams. The third person in the misunderstanding, which led to our successful tandem purchase, is also a professional communicator, a strong bike rider and long-time tandem rider.

When Szifra finally made the decision that she indeed wanted a tandem for her sixtieth birthday, she called her younger brother in Oregon—those are his bona fides above. Rich promised to be a good resource for us. He'd been riding bikes since his graduate days at Harvard Law. He collects facts and opinions about things he's interested in. He's full of stories about bikes, bike-shop owners, and routes that his bike group used to ride. Like any avid cyclist, he owns multiple bikes, including a high-end tandem that he and his wife ride.

Szifra asked Rich for his thoughts about tandems and thought she heard him recommend, "Look at the tandems from da Vinci Designs, a small Colorado manufacturer. They make a variation on the conventional tandem." We surfed their website. Da Vinci Designs advertised that their tandems were independent coasting. Although the two sets of pedals weren't locked in sync, they could be if we wanted.

We were impressed that the design synced the essential effort of moving the bike forward but didn't demand rigid conformity of action, the same philosophy we were trying to incorporate into the rest of our lives.

It's not clear what Rich actually advised Szifra to do. She thought she heard him recommend da Vinci Designs. Years later she thanked him for his suggestion, and he asked what the hell she was thanking him for. She discovered he hadn't meant we should buy one. He claimed he never recommended them, only informed her there was such a beast.

Regardless, we found da Vinci Designs. The website advertised an entry level road bike called the "Grand Junction"—chrome-moly frame, triple chain rings, 26-inch tires, approximately $3000. Tandems come in large/small, medium/medium, etc. We were looking for a medium/small. Only a large/small was available in stock. The large was just capable of having its seat height adjusted down to accommodate my medium size. (Perhaps the reason I might not have gotten my foot on the ground the first time we dumped the tandem was the large size of the captain's cockpit— seat, handlebars, top tube, etc. Szifra blamed the large size for our fall, so I'm sticking with her story—at least I like thinking that the bike contributed to the accident.)

Sending $3000 to an unknown company for an untried machine was an act of faith—acts of faith are suspiciously close to acts of stupidity. Our trust was rewarded when our Colorado-designed and Taiwan-produced bike was delivered to a friend's bike shop for assembly. We added clip-in pedals, a stoker's seat post that dampened the jolts, bottle cages and a bell for the stoker to express her concerns about pedestrians and other bikes.

The issues and costs weren't done. The tandem was too long to put in the back of either of our Prius sedans unless the front wheel was removed, and the passenger was willing to rest their chin on the dashboard and take a chance the airbag might lethally punch them in the face. For the first trip home, I transported the bike in our utility trailer. Later we tried a hitch-mounted rack, but tandems hang wider than most cars. In traffic I was constantly on edge. Eventually we settled on removing the rear wheel and holding the chain taut with a "chain keeper."

We received and began riding our new bike about a month after Szifra's sixtieth birthday. Well, not *our* bike. Szifra's birthday present bike. It took a few hundred miles of riding before we were certain we'd made a reasonable choice of bike and hobby. After a ride one Sunday to a funky little brunch place—a ride that took us on a series of shaded country roads—we enthusiastically agreed that we'd found an activity to share.

But delight was tempered by a few difficulties. The problems we had were nothing to do with the tandem's design or manufacture. They had to do with its suspension system. Every bike is fundamentally suspended over the road surface by compressed air—by air captured in tubes within tires. A tire needs to be hard enough to keep the rim from crushing the tube when you hit a sharp-edged pothole or other obstruction in the road. The puncture is often called a "pinch flat" or, because of the usual double hole, a "snake bite". High pressure usually protects the tube. But high pressure causes a harsher and slower ride—a hard tire bounces up and down rather than absorbing the bumps and rolling forward.

The trick to a safe, efficient, comfortable ride is to use the least amount of air pressure that still protects your tube. To achieve this balance, it helps to have wide tires, which require less air pressure to accomplish the same level of tube protection with more rider comfort. Tandem tires carry double the rider weight of a single bike's tires and therefore, in general, tandems use wider tires than single bikes.

It's also necessary to avoid as many potholes and as much road debris as you can. And that isn't as easy on a tandem as a single bike. If a single bike handles like a sports car, tandems steer more like a station wagon, climb hills like a truck, and descend like bowling balls. They're good at maintaining a stable, straight line but less quick at avoidance maneuvers.

Our first year, as I learned to captain, I hit a lot of potholes. One ride, we flatted and repaired the tube only to have it fail to inflate. I put in one of the spare tubes we carried. As I used our little portable pump to inflate it, it initially swelled and then quickly deflated. I took out the tube and carefully looked it over. I couldn't find a leak. We had one more spare tube, but before I attempted to insert that one I desperately tried to solve the issue. Was I not getting the tube completely inside the tire, pinching it between tire and rim? Was there a rough surface inside the wheel or glass sticking through the tire tread? Did the stem hole have a burr on it? When I pursued the latter possibility, I did indeed discover a leak at the base of the stem, but no roughness in the hole in the rim.

Careful reconstruction of the inflation process cleared up our problem. To save a gram of weight on the wheel, the bike assemblers had left small nuts off the valve stems—the nuts hold the stem securely in the rim until the tube is inflated, air pressure then holds it nicely in place. The nuts aren't necessary, unless you're inflating the tire with a little hand pump, in which case each pump stroke rocks the stem back and forth, quickly but effectively injuring the base of the stem. We installed our last tube—this time with its nut. Szifra held the pump body firmly against the wheel while I pumped, and we were good to go.

I have an impulse that, while not anywhere near as strong as Szifra's late husband's collecting, is on the same continuum as a compulsive obsession. I came to cycling with an eye out for extraneous weight. I backpack and have knees that are congenitally prone to pain under stress. On hiking trips, I keep the equipment I pack as light as possible—Szifra would say, fanatically light. I work to eliminate every gram in every item I carry, and I celebrate that those silly grams add up to a few less pounds on my back. I embrace the backpacker's motto: "Watch the ounces and the pounds will watch themselves." Szifra likes to tell people that my backpack is worth $100 a pound because of what it costs to buy high-quality, lightweight gear. Actually, $100 a pound would be a bargain. Getting rid of some grams has cost me almost $100.

Attention to weight also helped me become a winning sailboat racer. When all you have is the wind to propel you, less weight, and the careful distribution of the weight you have, is key to gaining incrementally more speed. When you're dependent on the environment or your own human power, you are well advised to pay attention to the inhibiting effect of excess weight. Although, I'll admit this awareness has never caused me to successfully diet off any of the ten extra pounds I weigh.

Bike weight has minimal effect on flat roads but can dramatically affect acceleration and climbing. When hiking, lifting a heavy shoe multiple times takes more energy than carrying weight on your back. On a bike, weight in the wheels is similar. If you're going to eliminate excess weight on a bike, you might as well first get it out of the wheels. The experts said we didn't need the little nuts on the valve stems, so I wasn't going to carry silly little nuts around on our wheels for no reason. Unlike someone with a true compulsion, when I learned that my lightweight impulse was risky compared to using the little nut, to Szifra's relief I quickly adapted. We now carry an extra nut that we put on when inflating the tire with our portable pump. Between times, it's carried in our seat bag rather than the wheel—so I'm not quite as casual as I could be. And I still weigh more than is ideal—actually still about ten pounds. Sigh!

Compared to single bikes, a tandem's long frame tubes can flex and rob a bit of power when you're really crunching the pedals or standing and climbing. If you have an adequately sized, two-cylinder engine—strong captain and stoker—tandems can climb with all but the better single riders. Our climbing weakness was our under-powered engines, our lack of pedaling strength. We weren't in top physical shape. Szifra worked hard in her aerobic and resistance classes, but it was a dope slap for her to discover that her cycling muscles weren't in the same shape as her dance or core muscles. And I had some cycling muscles, but not the endurance strength to push our steel bike quickly up long hills or on rides that lasted into the third hour. That first year we struggled to smoothly get up small hills and only began to find our climbing legs the second year. It remained hard work, but it was clear additional training would moderate the perceived effort.

And that brought us back to the weight issue. The least expensive place to save weight and the place with the most weight to be jettisoned is almost always from the bodies of the riders. Most non-professional riders are carrying at least ten to fifteen pounds more weight than they should be. Szifra and I were pleased we weren't classified as overweight, but we each were at least ten pounds over our best riding weight. Every small rise in the road reminded me I was carrying jiggling fat around my middle. I thought Szifra looked good in cycling spandex, but she saw excess weight emphasized by her skin-tight clothes. We both began to work on our eating. Of course, the same weight that pained us uphill was grabbed by gravity and added coasting speed downhill.

Szifra wasn't seeing a tandem as a primary way to develop endurance fitness. She had visions of fun, casual rides along bucolic paths with lots of quirky little lunch places. Of course, we would get in better shape by riding. But a training regime that lasted year after year, through every season, and required that some rides be intense, wasn't her image of our new sport. The bike, New England roads, and riders in a tandem club had other ideas.

Szifra and I agreed that she would dictate the scope and general itineraries of our early rides. Her anxiety about comfort and safety drove her to lay down three initial rules for how we were allowed to ride: She said she only wanted to ride on paved bike paths, only in fairly flat areas, and only slowly when going down any hills we might find on a bike path.

Her list was reasonable for our beginning tandem team. But problems arose from the very first ride on our local bike path—a six-mile-long, beautiful ramble along an old railway right-of-way, which starts at an office complex and wanders under mature hardwoods, beside quiet residential neighborhoods, next to small lakes, and over tiny brooks.

It was a clear, warm summer midday. Families and office workers were out walking and enjoying the weather. We came up behind group after group of walkers who weren't aware that they were supposed to share the path with bikes. The norm was for three or four people to walk abreast and when I requested room to pass "on the left" they often turned and fixed me with an irritated look. Even walkers approaching us seemed to assume that they had a right to occupy the entire width of the path. They would look at us coming toward them, keep an unchanging course, and belligerently force me to ride within inches of the edge of the pavement—glaring all the while at our intrusion into their space.

Besides the people on foot, little kids serpentined obliviously on tiny bikes. If they were coming toward us, they would stare and steer where they were looking—right at us. If we were going to pass them, they might drift right into our path just as we got to them. If I said something or Szifra rang her bell, they'd stop in the middle and stare. I could see all this developing and had an option to respond, my hands were on the brakes, but poor Szifra—whose view was half blocked by me—didn't have the experience to know how quickly a bike might stop or how close to the edge we could safely ride. She had no idea if I saw what was coming at us, if we were going to be able to stop in time, or if I was about to run off the path into the grass and rocks.

When we came up behind a group and I gave a quiet "Pass on your left," it wouldn't be sufficiently loud or declarative enough for Szifra, and she would quickly escalate the volume and intensity with a loud "Behind you!" or "Look out! Please." At least that's how I heard it.

During our After-Action Reviews—terminology coined by the Army to designate a time for non-judgmentally finding ways to improve a team's performance or interactions—she would say that I mumbled something too quietly for the walkers to hear. She said, "I know you're trying to be polite and a 'good bike citizen' but people can't hear you." She went on to explain that "If it were me, I'd need a much stronger warning and a clearer idea of what you mean. 'Passing on the left' wouldn't tell me what I was supposed to do. I'd need you to say, 'Move right!' Or something."

The fact I'd never run into pedestrians or kids on my single bike, and I was using the established warning wasn't a detail to be debated in the face of her rising anxiety. When deciding what to do when she's unsure, Szifra falls back on her sense of absolutely belonging almost anywhere and does what she wants. She speaks up assertively and clearly and is ready to apologize if she offends. I, on the other hand, walk gently into most new situations and apologize for my intrusion, even when I rightly belong there.

We didn't have a clear team-voice yet. We had a complex mix of personalities. After a brief airing of the issues, we deferred either to her or to me. She recognized my experience, and I recognized her vulnerable position. Not a bad way to enter negotiations where you both want the other person to feel successful.

The foot and bike traffic on the path rapidly drove Szifra crazy and she changed her bike-path-only rule after a couple of rides. She agreed to an experiment, and I routed us onto a few of my quieter, semi-rural riding options. She liked the scenery and quickly grew comfortable with the light to moderate traffic. But riding on roads also meant riding on steeper hills than the bike path. As is the case with hills, those you go up you mostly need to also come down. Thus, we came up against her other two rules.

Our first "major" climb was on a hill across the lake from our vacation cottage. We rode 30 minutes on a road that runs between cottages on both sides of the road. The route is mostly flat or slightly downhill until you cross the one-lane bridge over a narrow inlet to our half-mile-wide lake. To get back to our side of the lake you either have to turn around or take a cutoff to the right after the bridge. If you go that way, the road turns to dirt for a number of miles. As we crossed the bridge, a man and young boy were fishing off one side. Ahead the paved road rose quickly onto a tree and stonewall-lined hill, which disappeared over a crest, way up by the yard of an old farmhouse. The hill was steeper than we had tackled, and its length was unknown. In those days, I was the one who generally pulled most of our weight. I looked at the hill and was skeptical that I could get the bike, Szifra, and me up what I could see, let alone the strong possibility there was more to the hill that we couldn't see. I turned my head a bit and bent my lips to send my words backward, "I don't think we're ready for this."

Szifra's voice came back full of optimism, "We can make it!" This fit her dad's motto: *Why you no try?* Perhaps followed by, *You Prick!* In a diagnostic sense, she might be described as having fewer strategic planning skills than I do. But in that same diagnostic sense, I would be described as anxious about all sorts of slightly risky things.

I'd ridden many hills on my single bike but doubted my strength and endurance on the tandem would match this hill's demands. Szifra had ridden almost no hills but was gung-ho. How could I say no in the face of her enthusiasm? She had already tolerated many things on the bike that I suggested, but which she hadn't imagined she could do. Didn't I also have to listen to my stoker? Knowing I could always put my foot down if I needed to, I capitulated, "Okay! Let's try it."

We pedaled onto the hill. The road climbed steadily through big mature oaks, monstrous pines and white birches that squatted in every gap. We slowly wobbled past two houses with trikes in the yard and sheds tucked into the edge of the trees. The climb continued beyond the first summit we'd seen. As we approached the second crest I gasped, "My legs are beat, I'm just about done!"

Szifra's competitive juices were flowing. She saw it as us against the hill. "We can do this! Let's go!" I felt a different sensation. For the first time I was being pushed up a hill by my stoker. She pedaled hard. She encouraged. She wasn't going to let the hill win.

I kept pedaling. We continued to wobble, but we kept going. The incline increased a bit more. As we topped each rise, more hill was revealed. We slowly crept by other farmhouses, more stone walls and rope swings in large oak trees. We were pushing our lowest gear. My legs burned, and Szifra's delight increased. She gasped, "Look at us! We're doing this!" Our pace slowed even more as the hill continued, and we started to teeter and weave dangerously close to the gravel shoulder. Szifra finally wondered aloud, "Is there a flat spot where we can stop?" We came over another crest and up ahead the road finally leveled out a bit, and we could see where the hill ended. The pavement also ended, and the road turned to dirt as it continued on through the pines and more white birches. We had our clear endpoint.

So, rules one and two passed into our team's history—we were off the bike path, and we were climbing hills. On the way back down the hill, I rode the brakes hard. Only as the incline flattened out did I let gravity dictate our speed across the one-lane bridge. As we quietly coasted past, the man and boy didn't turn, didn't celebrate our climbing success. Szifra's third rule—go slow downhills—was ripe for rewriting.

A week later, as we climbed on a wide residential street with a series of moderate, longish hills, I asked, "Do you want to try going downhill a little faster?" She agreed she wanted to see what it felt like. At the top of the next hill I allowed gravity to accelerate us. I kept squeezing the brakes to drag the pads on the discs, but we started to build up more speed than we ever had. I watched my speedometer, rode the brakes a bit more and, as we coasted out at the bottom, I announced we had hit 30 mph. She surprised me with a confident, "That wasn't so bad."

There was another hill right in our face, "Do you want to go faster on the next one?"

"Sure."

We climbed the next hill, and this time on the way down, we hit over 35 mph. She surprised me with, "That was comfortable. We could try even faster." I let the bike roll on the next one and saw almost 40 some mph on the steepest part. Szifra quickly volunteered, "That was fun!" I said I needed to go home and change my shorts. We laughed, and she declared, "You can ignore all my rules. I'm fine. I'll tell you if I want you to slow down or if I get uncomfortable." Since I had that same right in my hands, it was a fair request.

Chapter 16: A Joint Venture

When I left my hospital job and bought my first carbon bike, it felt as light as taking off hiking boots and putting on running shoes. The bike had an elegance of function that motivated me, almost pulled me, to get on and ride. The ease of acceleration and efficient components were a pleasure, but I suspect a big part was my expectation that "Now I would ride!" And of course, there was a "should ride" internal admonition, the responsibility to rationalize the cost against miles ridden. A $1,500 bike that is ridden a thousand miles—a distance very few recreational riders put on their bikes during their ownership—costs a dollar and a half per mile. The health benefits definitely sweeten the equation.

By the time we bought our first tandem, my friend who owned a bike shop had helped me trade up to a better single bike. As the price of a bike climbs—my new one cost $6,000—the quality appears in little details. "Marginal gains" is the term used by pro bike teams. Ounces can be saved by replacing metal bearings with ceramic. Round wire spokes are replaced by more aerodynamic carbon or fiber-bladed spokes. Drag is further reduced with aero tweaks to handlebars and headtubes. Aluminum wheels are replaced by deeper carbon aero wheels that are marketed in grams, look like twenty-seven-inch frisbees with most of the center cut out and are tested in wind tunnels for efficient aero ability in multiple wind directions. Tire value is judged by the quality of rubber and how many cords are wrapped into it. Stray carbon fibers and resin are cleaned out of the frame during manufacturing to save weight. There's a saying, "You can't buy speed." But you sure can pay to lower the weight and decrease the drag of wind resistance.

Tandems don't double the ease or speed of a single. You still have two people plus a bike that weighs close to twice that of an equal quality single. The longer, more flexible frame robs a bit of power, there are more moving parts to create friction, and the riders may be less disciplined about holding a bent-over, aero position—at any given time one or the other may be creating more drag than is ideal. Remember aerodynamic resistance gobbles up 85% of the effort a rider puts into the pedals.

Since aerodynamic drag absorbs so much of the pedaling effort, the real efficiency in a tandem comes because the stoker is closely drafting behind the captain, diminishing the aerodynamic drag compared to two singles. The tandem needs 130-150 percent of a single's power to keep up, but the tandem has two people trying to create that power. Szifra and I can consistently produce an average of about 240 watts of power during a moderately-hard, two-hour ride—145 for me and 95 for Szifra. That barely equals the 230 to 250 many young amateur riders can easily do on their singles. Pro cyclists can ride at 350 to 400 watts or more for long periods of time. Going downhill, the gravity of two people and reduced aero drag make a tandem a force of nature.

Bike weight, efficient mechanicals, aero wheels and improved frame compliance make a quality tandem easier to accelerate and climb, which encourages the owners to ride. Small understandings, marginal gains in tolerance and reduced ego-defensive drag, make a big difference in relationships too. Easy communication, lighter emotional baggage, training in emotional fitness and a positive attitude all encourage couples to work at getting better at climbing emotional obstacles. A quality relationship implores, "Make me better!" A lesser quality one asks, "What do you think? Is it worth it?"

We rode and enjoyed our entry-level Grand Junction tandem for almost two years and became convinced that tandeming was our joint sport. I wanted to train and ride more hours than Szifra did, so I switched back and forth between my carbon single bike and our heavier tandem. It wasn't that the tandem was bad, but in comparison, I always felt like I was switching down. My nimble, quick single bike exerted a stronger pull on me, and anything that motivated me to spend time on a bike felt positive. I now know that a lot of my hesitation wasn't the tandem's quality but came from comparing any tandem to a single bike—always a mistake. Still there was a contrast, and I wanted to reduce the differential.

There were two fundamental ways to get better performance— improve the bike or improve training. Improving the bike would be expensive and ultimately less effective, but easier than training even more hours per week. My self-directed training effort for two years had significantly improved my fitness and leg strength, but I knew I had a long way to go. After fifty-five, athletic level fitness comes slowly and has a lower ceiling. It can take three years just to get tendons and bones adapted to hard stresses. Seven years of consistently hard training is the figure thrown around as the time it takes to train to whatever your current optimal physical performance peak might be. It was clear that the level of endurance strength I wanted was still years away. But I'd never get there unless I started training more frequently, longer and harder.

After a lot of decision inertia, that September I decided to hire a virtual bike coach. The coach prescribed a lot more high intensity intervals and more hours on the saddle. I began to learn to welcome discomfort— even suffering—into my training life. Physical training discomfort is the gateway to more stamina, strength and more resilience. That winter of training indoors made a big difference the next spring.

I'm more of a gear geek than Szifra, but since she enjoyed riding, she began to talk about a new tandem, one sized correctly for us. Her pitch was that a better-sized bike, one that really fit us would be safer. I shared my need with her. "If we replace the Grand Junction, and you want us to ride the tandem more, I need it to be lighter with higher quality components. A better tandem will increase my incentive to ride it instead of my single."

Szifra said she also wanted to ride more. But the cost of a new tandem made her hesitate. It brought up memories of His rather indiscriminate buying. Besides the tools, trains and guns, he had owned a glider and two cars, including a Mercedes. He had been significantly in debt and not able to stop spending to climb out. My comfort buying sailboats, expensive backpacking gear and bikes didn't ease her mind. She felt she needed to be the one to put the brakes on our spending. That I could purchase luxury items with a minimum of rumination was, to her, an indication we might be on a slippery slope. That I had no history of spending beyond my budget or compiling debt and had a larger than average retirement savings—although smaller than hers—did little to ease her fear. Anxiety has its own rules, and she worried.

I stood by quietly and listened while Szifra talked her anxiety down and herself into moving forward. The safety factor of a properly sized bike and the increased interest we might feel to both exercise and spend time together were key influencers she used to convince herself. Then we began to plan and investigate together.

Because almost every tandem we heard about had synced pedals, we didn't want to just drift into purchasing another independent-coasting bike. We liked the freedom it offered, but the independent system was fractionally heavier and more complex. We'd also read that synced bikes were more powerful climbers—not necessarily supported by any research. We assumed the majority of tandem riders had some crowd sense and we wanted to know what they saw and felt. We wanted to be certain there wasn't a crucial reason for us to change to a synced bike.

We planned a morning of bike testing and went to the bike shop where I'd rented the original tandem. A tandem specialist set us up with a couple of demo rides on high-end, synced tandems. They were lightweight, beautiful bikes. One was a deep grey and the other a stunning black. As the mechanic installed our pedals on one bike—so we could ride in our choice of shoes—I lifted the other one and felt a rush of pleasure. Szifra claimed I sounded like I was having a satisfying sexual experience. I'm sure I was much more constrained than that. But I did moan with pleasure at the elegance I held.

The salesman held the door as Szifra and I maneuvered the first test bike out of the shop. We bumped it off the curb and walked it across the street to make it easier to start our ride headed away from a couple of busy intersections. We didn't need any instructions from the salesman, but we did have to talk ourselves through the different starting sequence for a synced bike. Understanding and doing use different brain regions. We were clumsy in our timing to get rolling, and I flubbed my initial attempt to get clipped in. It wasn't impossible, but the da Vinci was certainly easier.

We quickly found another drawback to being synced. As we accelerated away from each slow down or stop sign, Szifra reported that my initial pedal strokes forced her pedals forward, jerking her hip and knee uncomfortably. I eased my accelerations, but that left me feeling more vulnerable in traffic. We assumed we could adapt, but this also hadn't been an issue with the da Vinci.

We'd both gotten into the habit of coasting independently, and I hadn't realized I back pedaled as we slowed at intersections. When I did that on this tandem, I jarred Szifra's legs. We also enjoyed the autonomy of standing whenever we felt like easing our butts. It was disconcerting that our freedom to independently do these things was lost on a synced bike. Our relationship on and off the bike was anchored in giving each other as much freedom to act individually as possible. We both wanted to minimize the need for negotiations. We enjoyed tandeming because it brought us together but didn't impose too many rules on us. Sticking with independent coasting gained emotional momentum. Not being synced with the majority of tandem teams felt like a diminishing drawback.

We decided that the next step was to see whether da Vinci Designs built a carbon bike with excellent components. Their website advertised a carbon bike, the Joint Venture, which looked like it would nail our needs, but at more than $12,000, such a purchase was quite a commitment. We wanted the bike itself to sell us or dissuade us. The only dealer within two hundred miles didn't have the model we wanted to test ride. Again, we were faced with having to buy as advertised without a test ride. Gambling $3,000 was one thing, but $12,000 was too much to let ride on the spin of the advertisement wheel.

Money is a wild card in most relationships, but once Szifra and I worked through the initial issue of my ambition, money generally wasn't a tough issue between us. She is both interested in and a recognized expert in the intersection of money and emotions. She had quickly realized that her attitude and worries about money were hers, a product of her experiences, not driven by any demonstrated irresponsibility on my part. She is good about expressing her worries but not holding me responsible for her emotions. I'm both interested in and an educator about the process of decision-making. I understand that most complex decisions are usually more intuitional and emotional than fact-based. Each time Szifra's emotions got stimulated, I knew I needed to back off and let her settle herself. Data wasn't useful or helpful.

Of course, I could also get my anxieties poked. There were times she was trying to talk herself down from her worries. She'd announce, "Money isn't actually the problem. I can spend this without thinking about it." Then, I'd feel a flutter of worry—based on no historical evidence—that she might get into a spending spree and overdo it.

Our individual anxieties would trip us up. But our individual expertise tended to settle us and helped us navigate decisions. The many sensibilities we shared about savings, debt and lifestyle were probably the deciding factors in helping us decide to buy the bike.

The question of whether to purchase a new bike quickly morphed into questions about the reasonableness of the purchase. Those questions sounded like they could be answered by data but were beyond any data's scope of competence. How much more responsive would a carbon tandem be? Was a half-mile-per-hour speed increase worth spending a dollar a mile for the first 10,000 miles? How about a mile per hour faster? What if we could climb more easily? How much was that worth per hill? Was this a decision that needed to be based on data or one that was grounded in data, but that we should allow to be heavily informed by emotions? What color would we get a bike painted? Would the money come from our retirement savings, our long-term health savings, or our "personal" savings? It was possible to justify each of these. We needed a next action to break through the clutter.

As we struggled about how we could arrange a test ride of the model we wanted, we fell on the possibility of visiting a beloved niece who lives in Denver, where da Vinci is located. Szifra suggested, "Why don't we go visit Jac? We could test ride a bike and make a weekend of it." It was an obvious option that sprang us free from the trap of endless possibilities. We made reservations to visit our niece and her fiancé, and called da Vinci to set up a test ride of a Joint Venture.

On the Friday we'd arranged the test, our flight from Manchester, NH departed late. We arrived in Denver desperately close to da Vinci's closing time. We dashed through the rental car process, hopped on the freeway, and navigated with a vengeance to get to the small factory before they closed for the weekend. While I followed the GPS through rush-hour traffic, Szifra called ahead to get a reprieve, which was graciously granted. Each turn onto a new street took us into a different neighborhood, and each neighborhood stimulated new speculation about the company we might be investing in for a second time.

Finally, we turned onto a street of low-rise industrial buildings. The GPS announced, "Your destination is on the left." The door was indeed unlocked, and the owner greeted us warmly. With a minimum of fuss, he decided his personal tandem would fit us for a test ride—as a custom builder they stock few built-up bikes. Seats were adjusted, we donned the helmets and bike shorts we'd brought with us, got directions for finding the entrance to the bike path, which was a couple of blocks away, and we pedaled off.

Looking west from Denver, the Front Range of the Rockies rises like a distant wall across the nearly flat prairie. The city itself sits on the flat. Coming from New England where dedicated, paved bike paths are still infrequent, the nearby bike path was luxurious with wide swooping corners and underpasses at intersections.

We'd had many enjoyable moments on our Grand Junction tandem, but this ride brought the pleasure of tandeming into focus in a way we hadn't felt before. From the first block it was delight and grins again. We felt competent at home, but we didn't feel like the tandem fit around us as well as this one did. We'd sprinted before on our tandem, but we hadn't sprinted with the kind of acceleration we could feel in our bodies, and which made us feel like whooping. Because the terrain was so flat, we had been given specific directions to find the one nearby hill that was steep enough to test the bike's ability to climb. After a few miles of the path, we made the prerequisite turns and found "The Hill".

We turned left across traffic onto a sparsely housed street that went up at a breathtaking angle. It was a good place to evaluate whether this bike's ability to climb was worth $12,000, so we hit it hard.

By this point we generally endured modest climbs pretty well. We could even persist up what we thought of as fairly steep inclines. Occasionally we'd survived some very short, bloody-hard climbs. But we'd never attacked a hill and had it surrender to our spin and power like that one did. The bike *was* different. We didn't feel intimidated by our pedals, which on our bike would be demanding everything we had. We pushed and this bike ascended.

"How you doing back there? I asked Szifra.

"Good! This bike climbs better than I thought it would, way better than ours."

After two blocks we reached the place where the incline began to flatten out. We both felt disappointed that it was over. I swung us into a side street of modest homes with brown lawns, and we made a U-turn that took us from right up against one gravel shoulder to just barely missing the far one. Szifra said something I'd never heard her say before, "I still have legs. I want more. Want to try it again?" I felt the same way. We didn't have time for another climb, but we were hooked. We babbled about possibilities on the ten-minute ride back to the shop. Who cared about dollars per mile per hour gain! Buying our way into this level of performance was settled.

We quickly negotiated with the builder questions of which components, which saddles, and what color, and put a down payment on a custom bike. We ordered shorter cranks for Szifra. Top tube heights, which would not impede emergency dismounts, and reach distances to handlebars were to be tweaked to fit us. Yes, we wanted 700 wheels. Yes, we wanted aerodynamic handlebars. Yes, we wanted five bottle mounts. Yes, we wanted a color-fade paint job. Yes, we wanted both front and rear disc brakes. What fun!

We had to make a real effort not to let tandem talk dominate the weekend visit with our niece. Between interesting restaurants, a Sunday walk in the central city, and good conversation, we flew home feeling like we had gotten our twofer, a great bike and a great visit. As we sat side by side on the plane, leaning against each other and savoring the ride experience, it dawned on me. We'd ridden with such ease, climbed with such joy, without any acclimation to Denver's mile-high altitude. Our new tandem wouldn't just be great, it would supercharge our riding.

Chapter 17: Out of the Cocoon

There's an understanding among experienced tandem riders, a tandem can make or break a couple. The saying goes, "Wherever you're headed, a tandem will get you there faster." When Szifra and I first met other tandem couples, we were surprised at how amiable most were. Apparently the oft repeated saying was based on real experience. Either the bikes attracted couples who are compatible, or the bikes quickly sorted out the compatible couples from the incompatible.

There are tandem rallies held every year in multiple locations around the United States and the world. Twenty to two hundred or more teams show up for a few days of riding routes that range from twenty to a hundred miles. The courses might be hilly or mountainous, and for many teams it's the one time during their riding year that they spend three to four hours at a time in the saddle. At these events, a tense voice is unusual and pulls everyone's attention. The best teams, like the best relationships, are made up of individuals who can quickly adapt and compromise.

Occasionally, on a rest break during our rides, we meet women on single bikes who vehemently explain to Szifra that they'd never ride a tandem. Some sound determined and ready for a fight. Szifra and I make eye contact with each other. We know what's coming. The women go on to explain how they wouldn't trust their husband or partner to be the captain—often with what sounds like good reasons. Or how they like being in control—bicycles were one of the original ways women escaped male dominance. There's a message between the words that sounds something like, "Why would a perfectly capable woman ride second saddle? Riding is an independent activity. It shouldn't be a patriarchal led sport."

We want to reply, "Of course a tandem isn't right for you. It takes two people who are flexible, who want to synchronize, and who are willing to work at communicating." Some of these women report that their spouses are the issue. There still aren't many two-women tandem teams, so the key issue of managing your own or someone else's overly directive personality is easily muddled up with gender issues. And because of traditional social expectations and privilege, men tend to fall too easily into directing women.

Each rider's style of riding and relating can affect the chances of forming a fun, solid team. Captains' styles certainly can create issues, and so can stokers'. Creating a resilient team/relationship can be a complex puzzle with pieces of personal history, emotional management, social pressures, and so much more involved. More often than not, when Szifra and I meet the male partners of the unwilling-to-be-stoker women, we often understand why a tandem doesn't sound like a fun option.

The ability to create a team isn't the only issue. Many strong, competent women who ride single bikes appear to assume women who are tandem stokers are simply compliant followers. And who would encourage them to pursue that role? But come to a tandem event and you'll see a gathering of tough, successful, athletic women riders. Many stokers ride both singles and tandems. Their ability to switch between riding styles and pour it on when the road rises is impressive. In fact, if people could get past the notion that the second seat is a subordinate position, I'd be surprised if they wouldn't look and listen to these women off the bike and assume they're the team captains.

Labels may have a role in misidentifying the status of stokers. Over the years some people have attempted to label the two team members to avoid any sense of hierarchy, without much success. *Captain* is perhaps the most popular term in the US for the front rider, but we also hear *Pilot*. Then there's the underused, *Steersman*, which *speaks* less about hierarchy. Switching that to *Steersperson* creates a lot of work for one's tongue and lips.

Alternative labels for the second rider, the *Stoker,* include *Navigator* and *Rear Admiral,* which I feel carries a pejorative connotation, and perhaps my favorite, the *Turbocharger.*

With our first bike, we were ignorant about the culture of tandems. We usually rode in our own cocoon—by ourselves or occasionally with a friend on a single bike. Within our cocoon, we felt like a team. I like people, but I was more content than Szifra to spend time on our own. Szifra is very social and seeks out new people. She told me that in her relationship with her previous two husbands she was the designated "Social Director."

She was sure there must be other tandems in our area to ride with. I pointed out that the odds of finding people who rode at our pace was slim. She's rarely discouraged by statistics or other people's experiences. Tandems very occasionally came at us on the bike path or on popular riding roads. A few of these teams—who shared Szifra's social inclination—stopped to compare bikes, exchange names of hometowns, or simply delight in finding fellow travelers. As we stood over our bikes and talked, I evaluated whether they were serious riders—serious riders had road bikes, cleated bike shoes, and Lycra kit. Each team—or at least each captain—eyed the other bike to check out the quality, saddles, set up to carry extra gear, tire type, etc. We were well set up, and I discovered my reading had given me as much information about the tandem scene as any riders we met.

Szifra was dogged. She took any opportunity on or off the bike to ask everyone with a whiff of bike interest about tandem groups. Her insistent sharing and questions eventually paid off. A bike coach who I considered hiring told Szifra she knew a couple who belonged to a local group of tandem riders. We were about to emerge from the cocoon we'd been riding and thinking in.

I would have probably held on to the people's contact information, anxious that I might call at a poor time. Szifra has no such worries and called the couple within minutes of getting home. She explained she wanted to know about local tandem groups. They were pleased to answer all her questions and arranged to meet us for brunch one Saturday in their nearby town.

The address of the brunch café was clear, but after several trips down the one-way street with return trips back up the parallel one, there was no obvious number on a building that matched the address. I pulled up in front of a rehabbed brick mill building from the late 1800s, and after a close look we found the name and number on a small sign. Our hosts were standing there, side-by-side, next to the cafe's door. They were in their forties. She was standing with her hand resting on his arm.

We parked, exchanged quick hellos, and they led us into the small café. The man was lean and looked dismayingly fit. His slight build was a bike climber's physique. His quick smile, quiet welcoming demeanor lessened the habitual discomfort I feel in new situations. His wife also looked formidably fit. We felt our age weighing us down even before we discovered, during our first group ride, that they were one of the strongest teams in the local tandem group.

The woman followed the man's lead to a small round table, keeping her arm hooked in his until she was at a chair. He asked her what she wanted, and we left her at the table as the three of us went to the counter to order.

Over rich pastries and good coffee, they gave us a thorough introduction to all things tandem, answered every question, and invited us to join their group for a ride. They explained that "membership" was a matter of saying you were a member. As the explanations mixed with bites of croissants, tastes of banana bread and sips of coffee, the woman offered lots of encouragement to Szifra and worked to allay any concerns Szifra had about her current fitness level.

I looked at Szifra, and we each gave a slight nod. "We'd love to join you," Szifra announced. "Can you email me the information?"

On our way home, Szifra and I both reported that it had taken us a while to realize that the woman stayed close to her husband to get his assistance to find her way to the table. She was the first of many sight-challenged stokers we would eventually meet. And like many of them, she is courageously independent. She is also a powerhouse who can propel their tandem with remarkable pedaling endurance and strength. We felt both welcomed and challenged by them and the tandem subculture.

Almost a month later we joined the club for their first ride of the spring. We showed up at the couple's small suburban house with fifteen other tandem teams. A forty-mile ride was planned, followed by pizzas. Couples showed up in all sorts of cars, vans, and even a panel truck rigged out as a bike workshop. People greeted each other warmly after a long winter break. Hellos accompanied remarks about how the tandems were being transported. "I see you decided on the car-top rack. Be careful of the garage. I smashed a front tire and fork that way a few years ago." "How are you holding the bike in the van? I find it's best to keep it to one side." "Wow! You have brackets for all three tandems in the truck and still have room for tools and your extra wheels."

Our latest, clumsy attempt to easily transport our tandem was to shoehorn it into the rear area of our Prius. Its back tire just snuck inside the hatch, if Szifra slid her seat all the way forward. She's only 5'4," but the arrangement placed her knees against the glove box and wasn't airbag safe. No one commented on *our* system.

That ride was also our first full immersion into tandem-team culture. We were introduced to sophisticated individuals who went one by one into the bathroom and reappeared dressed in gaudy colored Lycra with bold designs. Each person's jersey matched somebody else's. Some pairs were satisfied with only wearing matching jerseys and shorts. Other teams worked the coordination down to helmets, socks, shoes, gloves and sunglasses. One team even coordinated their shoelaces—bright orange. We had emerged from our cocoon into a kaleidoscope of butterflies.

Szifra and I each brought our favorite jersey—for her that meant the most soft, comfortable one; I favored my neon-yellow and black one. We'd each bought a helmet by fit, not color coordination. Szifra rode in bike sandals—again, think comfort—that had mountain-bike-pedal cleats, which most tandem people use. I rode in road-bike shoes.

Bike-shoe cleats are a metal or plastic plate that mechanically connects your shoe and the pedal. Cleats increase the range where you can effectively generate power beyond the traditional down part of your stroke. Cleats allow you to more forcefully push your foot across the top of the pedaling circle and pull it back across the bottom. As you get stronger, you might also start to lift the weight off your foot as it climbs up the back of the stroke, and the cleat helps you add a bit of oomph even there.

Szifra's bike sandals—and most of the other teams' shoes—had mountain bike cleats positioned under the ball of her foot and recessed a bit into the sole of the shoe. They allowed her to walk relatively normally—all good bike shoes have stiff soles to maximize energy production, so walking is a flat-footed, clumping affair rather than a normal, flexy roll forward.

My road cleats are screwed to the sole of the shoe under the ball of my foot. They aren't recessed. They stand proud on the sole. Road cleats force you to take short choppy steps while balancing on plastic latticework protrusions. Climbing or descending stairs or inclines in road cleats is a slippery, potentially treacherous, undertaking. And road cleats can easily grab and hold small rocks you step on, which will then prevent you from clipping into the pedal.

As we stood among the fashion-coordinated teams with our unmatched shoes and outfits, we looked more like a rummage sale display than a team. Again and again, people who couldn't identify our teammate had to ask who our partner was, and we'd have to point and describe each other as "that person over there." Individualism was fine, but among tandem teams a different sensibility prevailed. On our way home we talked about whether we could adjust to the silly idea of wearing matched kit—clothes.

It took almost a year of club riding before we ordered club jerseys. And it was another three years before we ended up with matching helmets—even then, the primary reason was we both wanted the visibility of bright orange. I doubt we'll ever purposely coordinate socks, but it occasionally happens unintentionally, so stay tuned because we wouldn't have believed our team uniforms would come—or is it go—this far. When we ride with non-tandem bikers, we deliberately downplay our coordination to discourage derision from the uninitiated. We're relieved that the "Oh my God, they look like twits all dressed up alike!" comments are aimed at teams who might occasionally ride by, and not at us. When this happens, Szifra and I share a knowing look and slight grin.

At that first group ride, we were introduced to another club tradition. We all gathered under a tree for a group picture. At every tandem event, group pictures are a thing. Wearing your club jersey for the pictures is expected. This club's dark green jerseys had a graphic of a newt on it—the symbol of our New England Wicked Tandem Society (NEWTS).

The actual ride started with a line of blue, red, black, white, and orange tandems meandering through small suburban streets of single-story homes. Shortly we merged onto a road that quickly turned rural. As the traffic eased, the teams accelerated to a pace that left us gasping. We felt like we must be dragging a trailer of rocks as we slipped behind most of the group. Our legs soon burned. Occasionally the other tandems waited for us at a major intersection, but we rode most of the ride by ourselves. Near the end, we bypassed an optional steep hill loop, which most of the teams seemed to think was the main attraction of the ride. Despite our shortened route, we finished significantly after the other teams. Our thirty-five miles was a long one for us. Despite our subpar performance, the other teams encouraged us and welcomed us to return.

Szifra loved hanging around and talking after the ride. She found interesting professionals, delightful raconteurs, and supportive women to chat with, along with the few requisite droning know-it-alls. I chose a large, cheesy, veggie pizza to refuel on and retreated to a shady stoop, where I could eavesdrop without having to invest much of my limited social energy.

I'd been with Szifra for twelve years. I didn't expect her to feel any need to fritter away any of her precious social time with me. She loved me and said she felt loved by me, but there were people to meet and new stories to hear. Whatever connection I desired was always a tad more dependent than she needed. Only if I shut off my need and ignored her did she feel the gap widening and reach out. I was fine with her charging her social batteries, and I get pleasure hits by watching her delightfully drift her way through the peloton of socializers—peloton is the name for a compact group of racers.

Chapter 18: Speed Bumps

From our earliest days together, there was a marked difference between our private and social connection. Early on, Szifra felt she needed to avoid any display of disloyalty to Him by acting casual toward me in public. In Szifra's mind, the twenty months since his death was way too short a time for her to be dating or for us to look like we were riding together—metaphorically. When we went for a walk around the town she lived in—the town they had lived in together—He walked with us. Szifra worried she was announcing her disloyalty by holding my hand, and we certainly didn't show any other kind of public affection. She pointed out people she knew from being with Him and tried to calculate whether they knew he was dead. Restaurants they'd been regulars at were uncomfortable choices until we tested the proprietors' reactions by acting like mere friends out for dinner. My role in public was to hang back, act inconsequential, and not do anything that required an introduction.

At one of their favorite restaurants, Szifra introduced me to the owner, who was almost a friend, as "My friend, Jay." The owner shared a knowing smile with me, and we silently agreed to let Szifra keep her discomfort private. Szifra felt like she was having a secret affair, but my impression was that it was a secret to almost no one. During our semi-undercover forays, we never ran into anyone who acted surprised, and certainly no one who seemed to disapprove. But the possibility of public censure was an organizing factor in all sorts of decisions Szifra made.

I wasn't worried about how the community reacted to our relationship; I was caught on how they and she reacted to me—how I compared to Him. I wasn't exactly threatened, but a former partner and lover is a window into your love's personality and desires. I wondered, what about Him she'd simply had to tolerate for years and how his shortcomings compared to my flaws? What did He do that delighted her and how much did she dwell on that loss? Did her friends like him as much, or more, as they seemed to like me?

As many little pieces of their life were shared or slipped out, who he had been became clearer. And that helped illuminate who he still was in her life. As she had told me, her speedy conversations with their numerous non-transitional slides from topic to topic were more problematic for me than they'd been for him. He'd shared her fast pace and was better at following her circuitous verbal pathways. For instance, the pronouns she uses don't necessarily follow the identifying noun closely enough to give me a clue as to who she's talking about. It's often a previous conversation thread that holds the connection I'm missing, the link I need to understand who she's talking about. She might say, "I walked with Kathy yesterday. We had a good talk. By the way, she's coming to the party."

"Kathy is coming to the party?" I ask, incredulous.

"Kathy? No, Sara!"

"How did we skip to Sara from Kathy?"

"I just wanted you to know Sara is coming to the party."

"How was I supposed to know the "she" was Sara, not Kathy?"

Which would usually earn me a confused look, which I interpreted as: "Just keep up!"

She (That "she" refers to Szifra, not Sara.) tends to start new threads without announcing them. The identifying noun has often been silently pronounced in her head and the out-loud pronoun refers to that silent noun. As my problem-solving brain tired, my frustration and concurrent irritation would appear—He apparently didn't get frustrated or hadn't shown it.

Szifra's wildly funny, uncouth, rude, profane, brilliant, infamous, and verbally abusive father had liked Him. Szifra had no doubt that I would have been a member of the sizable segment of people who her father would have trained his ego-ripping critiques on. Her mother had introduced Him to Szifra as successful and a good fit. By the time I met her, Szifra's mother had started a slow creep into Alzheimer's, and there were many times I wasn't sure she knew who I was, or that I wasn't him. To her I was Szifra's "Boyfriend" even after we were married.

During my first visit for a dinner at Szifra's mother's house, every member of Szifra's family—her father was dead by then—casually ignored me after a series of inconsequential nods of their heads in response to Szifra's introduction. By her family's standards, which I became accustomed to over time, this wasn't discourteous. By default, they assumed everyone would feel comfortable and welcomed. They were more interested in their individual stories and jockeying to express expertise in their current discussion than they were in actively understanding or alleviating the emotional quirks of their sister's new man friend.

Szifra's mother also just nodded, but I wasn't to take that as a negative signal either; she was busy preparing food. A few years into our relationship, I followed a tearful girlfriend of Szifra's older son out of the house during her initial visit. She was trying to escape from what felt to her like derisive indifference. She thought nobody liked her, and perhaps they didn't, but their behavior wasn't the definitive clue.

The cultural differences were challenging. Initially, no one except Szifra's sister asked questions about my life. The family just seemed to expect, and still seems to expect, me to push anything I want to share into whatever monologue is happening. And then to be okay when the conversation is immediately grabbed and taken back by another speaker without any apparent acknowledgment that I've spoken or curiosity about who I am. Szifra explains it as, "If you have something to say, just say it." They like me and are as interested in me as they are in anyone else. I'm not being treated any differently than any other family member. And gratefully, much better than her father would have treated me. But there it was again. Her father had treated Him well.

The differences in family styles showed up on the tandem too—even after we'd navigated the issues many times off the bike. We struggled to find a reliable way to share information with each other and get confirmation that the other person heard us. We started with a sizable gap of assumptions and clarity developed slowly.

My family's tendency to speak quietly—all right, to be fair *very quietly*, not to mention our incessant mumbling—drove Szifra crazy. On the bike she reminds me regularly that if I have something important to say I need to speak up or wait until the cars have passed, otherwise she can't hear me. I can speak up. My stage and presentation voice have been praised, "You were the only one I could hear without a mike." But I'm most comfortable speaking softly. I don't want people on the porches we're passing to hear what I'm saying. I'm full of joy when I can ride through my world like a whispering breeze, leaving few traces that I've passed. I like the quiet "whoosh" of bike tires on pavement, the sounds of air rushing past my face. "Leave behind only footprints" was one of the things that attracted me to backpacking in the Rockies or High Sierras, where a single footprint can take months or years to return to a natural state.

Szifra whirls through her world with a sense of belonging and wants to share her joy with passing strangers. Her attitude is, "How could you not want to share a momentary encounter? And besides, what can happen if they don't want to?" From early in our relationship Szifra shared her "Don't ask permission, beg for forgiveness" philosophy. Her dad was a model for her of a relentless force moving through the world. He commented on everything, insisted on his right to enter anywhere, and even stole when the impulse struck him.

When Szifra was nine or ten, her dad took her to Brandeis University to hear a speech by the then Prime Minister of Israel, David Ben-Gurion. Her dad sat them on the aisle. He wanted Szifra to say hello as Ben-Gurion walked past their seats in the crowded auditorium. Szifra wasn't comfortable with the idea. As the prime minister and his security entourage entered, everyone stood. As they came abreast of Szifra, she froze, and her dad pushed her into Ben-Gurion who caught her and was very nice to her. Her dad's later explanation, "He sits on the toilet and shits just like everyone else. Never be afraid of anybody." My dad would have been thinking about how Ben-Gurion felt, not how I should make my way boldly in the world.

Of course, on the bike, with the wind in her ears and me facing away from her, not all the problems of hearing rested with my cautious family culture. I'm convinced there are times my volume is at a good level, but the receptor is distracted. But when we're flying downhill or along a flat section, I'll admit my normal voice is too soft to be heard above the twenty-mile-per-hour wind blowing past Szifra's helmet straps and across her ear. At that speed we're not moving through our world like a whispering breeze. We eventually addressed this with wireless headsets.

Our first headsets had their own drawbacks. Someone had to remember to charge the batteries, and in the case of our units, to remember to unplug the charger after six hours so the batteries didn't get fried. It was also no snap to get a pair of sunglasses, a headset, and helmet straps all braided over your ear. Each piece went on and came off in a specific order—glasses, helmet, headset. After three hours my ears sometimes had a painful groove, indented by some piece of equipment. If I reached into my jersey pocket for a food bar, I was liable to hit a button on the walkie-talkie that killed my broadcast or one that diminished Szifra's incoming voice to a whisper. I regularly opened a food bar, forgot the little foam-covered microphone hanging in front of my face, and pushed it into my mouth along with the bar—it felt like getting a bite covered with dryer lint. If I moved the mic a bit too far away from my mouth, I effectively turned down my broadcast volume. Too close and Szifra felt like I was yelling at her.

After a couple of years, we stumbled upon an upgrade, a set of wireless mics and earpieces that stick to our helmets. The modern technology is great, but there are still problems. On single bikes, with distance between us, the new ones would be great. On the tandem we're so close we can hear both the originating words and the transmitted words. But the transmitted words are delayed a fraction and each communication is an irritating series of echoed repeats.

I get the worst of it. Because I'm facing forward and talking quietly, Szifra can often barely hear my originating words. She, on the other hand, is aiming her voice right at me and usually speaking loudly enough for me to hear without the transmitter. Over the miles of riding and hearing the incessant echoing, my brain has learned to sort through the overlapping chatter and usually I understand what she's saying.

The transmitters also amplify communication with people off the bike. If either one of us calls out to another tandem team, we unwittingly blast our comments into our partner's ear. The same thing happens when minor urgencies surprise one of us, "Car Right!" or "Go!" We're still working on our communication volume control.

And then there's the slower pace of much of my, and my family's, conversations. Apparently, that's why Szifra and her family change the conversation at unexpected times. To them, a pause means you're done, and they can begin. The potential of using "white space" as a way to emphasize a point or set up the punchline to a story is lost on them—except when they're telling a story. Szifra carries this family habit into our lives. She tends to get so involved in a story I'm sharing with someone that she often bursts through her impulse control and inserts the punchline into my pause long before I've finished the setup. She's so engaging that my listeners are usually entertained by her intrusion, and I have very limited room to object. And no room to be irritated unless I want to be accused of stepping on her right to speak. It's challenging to hit the right tone in my rebuke, and often easier to just enjoy her enthusiasm and let her take over my story. Of course, once she's stepped on my lines she pauses and waits for me to continue with the remaining details that the punchline made superfluous. In the long run, she appears the witty one, and I the clumsy storyteller. But she has no malicious intent, so how can I not love her.

Sometimes on the bike, Szifra will ask me a series of questions in rapid-fire sequence while I'm negotiating a rough patch of road or approaching an intersection. My "Wait!", "Intersection!", or "Not now!" can be a bit abrupt, but she says, "Thanks!" It gives her the right message. "Safety always comes first," she tells me when I apologize for my curt tone. I'm both attracted to Szifra's faster pace, and it frustrates me. But that's Relationship 101—what we like is most likely closely related to what irritates us.

**

Szifra clearly liked me from the beginning. But a bizarre question kept circling in my head when I assessed myself in the context of the new relationship: "If He magically resurrected, who would she choose?" This silliness usually morphed rather quickly into the more reasonable: "Would she ever come to think of our relationship as her primary one?" I often found those old, romantic song lyrics come murmuring through my head: "When the angels ask me to recall the love of them all, then I will tell them I remember you."

In my relationship immediately before Szifra, my woman friend and I spent time bouncing between physical and emotional passion. Both of which boiled and frothed. When I walked away, I assumed I'd just been through a once-in-a-lifetime experience—for good and bad. On my third date with Szifra, she put a Dave Matthew CD in her kitchen radio and danced in place while she sang. Her dancing was free and uninhibited— arms out at shoulder height, hands moving in gentle waves, hips swaying sensually in time to the music. She asked me to dance with her, pressed up against me, and I was reborn into a "boy's dream". We kissed, and the moment gently drifted away.

Later, I told her she was pretty forward for someone who claimed she was too uncomfortable to talk about sex. She looked at me blankly, "I don't know what you're talking about."

"The words you were singing along with on the Dave Matthews' song were pretty graphic."

She still looked blank. "I don't know what the words are. I don't listen to them."

I tried again, "Do you know what, 'Hike up your skirt a little more. And show your world to me. A boy's dream, in a boy's dream' means?" She looked oblivious and then a look of horror blossomed on her face.

"Oh god! I'm such a dope!"

"Not most of the time," I responded. She laughed and apparently begged herself for forgiveness.

She smiled even more broadly and told me about another time her inattention to nuances got her in trouble. "One birthday when the boys were teenagers, I gave one of them a package of boxer shorts. We'd gotten a pool table and I thought it would be cute to give him underwear with pool balls and a cue on them. He looked surprised and asked me if I knew why the balls and cue were on the boxers. I didn't get it even then. He had to explain it to me. What a mother! Giving him sexual underwear!" She had long since forgiven herself for that faux pas too, and just laughed at the memory.

I'm much more strategic and careful and nowhere near as fast to forgive myself. I ask permission a lot. Anything to keep from having to beg for forgiveness. In general, I'm pretty confident and have few long-term regrets. I'm not an uncertain or a doubtful lover and Szifra wasn't shy about sharing her appreciation that we'd discovered each other. But as the pleasure of our physicality ebbed into soothing peace, questions would arise in my mind. Was He sitting on the other end of the couch watching me kiss his wife? Was He leaned against the counter in his kitchen when I came up behind Szifra and held her in a long affectionate embrace? Did He walk on the other side of her as we wandered streets in their town or pathways at the community farm? Was He there at our most intimate moments? Was He evaluating? What did He know about her that I didn't? When we were together was He whispering in her ear, reminding her about their good times? Was any part of our affection her making love to him one more time?

It took many turns of the coupling that held the frame of their relationship together before we disconnected him and converted our sometimes triple into a permanent tandem.

Chapter 19: The Stoker Isn't Always Right

At elite levels of competition, individuals and teams focus on the winning concept of incremental improvement, also called "marginal gains". From the beginning, Szifra and I understood we needed to devote energy to ourselves as a team, both on and off the bike. We realized we wanted to create a space in our lives where fun crowded out potential stress. To do that, we needed to bring the experiences and the consequent wisdom we'd individually accumulated to our team riding. This meant nurturing incremental improvements in our communications and celebrating every success, particularly communication attempts that decreased the tension level for either of us. Overall problem solving and the quality of our interactions advanced with each small clarification. It was similar to the concept of focusing on each pedal stroke to climb a hard hill, to push ourselves to ride past at least one more telephone pole, or keep going for one more minute. But we also discovered we needed to formally run through a quick, post-ride check-in to assess the quality of each of our experiences. During these brief conversations—our after-action reviews—we clarified and underlined how we could improve.

Off the bike our roles are flexible. Szifra isn't the stoker, she's a co-captain. I'm not the captain, I'm a stoker at times and co-captain at other times. And this team attitude has modified our on-the-bike communications, even when an occasional urgent situation demands a command-and-control style decision from me.

Any team activity, e.g., tandem riding or relationship building, brings up questions of leadership, responsibility, methods of critiquing, control, trust, and the most effective style of communication. On the bike, Szifra hands most of the in-the-moment control to me. I make the quick decisions. I initially set the cadence and choose the gear. I choose the moment to start braking and how fast to descend. She has significant input, but the implementation of that input is on a time delay, caused by all the other inputs I am processing. "Let's stop" from her is a suggestion, not an application of the brakes. But we both take responsibility to make it comfortable, safe, and interesting for the other person to be on the bike.

Off the bike, Szifra and I can ride into a quagmire of who's responsible for the latest slight or abruptness. When our communication or coordination process breaks down, whoever is retelling the story of that breakdown—in defense of their position, and occasionally to a "jury" of our peers—that person has license to declare where they feel the narration should start. The storyteller's "punctuation" can reveal an assumption of cause or blame, as this sequence does:

"Your voice was irritated, and it made me want to walk away."

"You were ignoring my question."

"You asked in an irritated way."

"The first time I asked I wasn't irritated."

"You can't hear yourself."

"You didn't hear me the first time I asked."

And on in a spiral of blame, pointing out the reasonableness of *my* reaction to *your* misstep.

Alternatively, stopping the blame that the other was responsible for our words or tone, and recognizing that cause and effect is often a circular occurrence, leads to something more like this:

"I felt irritated at your voice, and I wanted to walk away."

"I didn't hear you answer my question and that felt frustrating."

"When you asked, I thought I heard irritation and didn't feel like answering you."

"The first time I asked I didn't feel irritated."

"Is it possible you can't hear yourself?"

"Is it possible you didn't hear me the first time I asked."

"What do we need to do to get back into good communication?"

Originally, our failures to look for solutions and instead to assign blame could make it sound like we thought the conversation blew up from a single pinch flat when we hit the current pothole. Of course, the puncture was caused because our couple-tread had worn thin from multiple, iterative misunderstandings or slights. The idea of calling a pinch flat by its alternative name, a "snake bite," is also appealing in this context.

Many missteps and failures, both on and off the bike, happen suddenly. When that occurs, we each feel shocked that the other person has switched precipitously into what feels like dismissive, rude, or oblivious behavior. I might respond to an obvious question of hers with what I thought was a lighthearted, "You think?" And she would pounce on me with, "That was disrespectful!"—at least it sure feels to me like a pounce. I might pull into an intersection while a car was in sight, and she stops pedaling because she feels risk. Each of us is surprised and feels the other has ignored our joint safety.

Other small habits build into irritations. She keeps quick, phone conversations going, long after our agenda is accomplished, without checking whether I'm in a spot where I want to continue. It shouldn't feel surprising, but it's easy to blame her for not noticing my needs or putting them on a par with her interests. Similarly, I often neglect to text her back to let her know that I've gotten her text. She is left wondering whether I'm ok. Or how could I disregard her need to close the loop? She's told me this is important to her, but it's not to me. Each of us is surprised that the other person would ignore the norms of our personal social standards, and that can quickly magnify slight differences into hurt feelings. Each misstep can easily feel like a disturbing breach of trust, lazy ignorance, or an assumption of willful disrespect.

We both know these situations are catalyzed into "issues" by our fundamental emotional wiring and our childhood experiences. When I feel Szifra come at me with an attitude, it's hard to see, until the situation has passed, that she may be internally entangled with her judgmental, harsh and disrespectful father. And she misses that my quiet, self-centered father may be sitting on my shoulder and fueling my sense that no one cares what I think or feel. It's similar to how, when we pedal our tandem toward someone, initially they can only see me and assume I'm on a single bike. As we pass them, they can see that Szifra and I are connected by orange tubes and balanced on two tires, not four. Their assumptions lead to surprised delight at an exotic bike. Our assumptions lead to heel-digging-in defensiveness

And since surprises and misrepresentations feel like they originate outside of ourselves, we each look outward for the unexpected cause. Each bike or interpersonal communication failure initially feels like the other person's fault.

A "You made me feel…" when our feelings are our own and not controlled by anyone but the hurt little kids who have lived in us since childhood.

"If only you would…" when we need to be saying, "If only I could quiet my fears."

The "your faults" pile up when "our mistake" is a better route to less stress next time.

It is incredibly easy to overlook our own culpability, our own temporary ignorance, inattentiveness, faulty assumptions, or misinterpretations. Whatever happened, there was almost always an opportunity where we—the victim—missed a chance to correct our own actions or thinking before the more obvious failure occurred. In our minds, and in our retelling of the incidents, each of our versions, the teller's and the listener's, were punctuated with all those "it all started with your action, and my reasonable response." But the actual truth of every story is more like a circle than a straight line. There was a series of unfortunate miscommunications or missteps, and then our personalities and emotional hot buttons played a role in compounding the failure.

Finding a way to correct or prevent a future failure meant we each have to take both 100% individual and 100% joint responsibility. There is no value in partitioning either responsibility. There is value in examining what might have prevented the failure. On or off the bike, we are a system and have shared responsibility. Remembering all this and adjusting our reactions needs to happen while we're still struggling with our traitorous thoughts that the preponderance of blame probably isn't ours. Our climb toward shared responsibility led us toward corrective actions, to look down the road, not at the pothole, to recognize the team functioning well as primary. All options, other than blaming, take practice, like all kinds of personal and team improvements. And all the other options are much more effective in creating a resilient team and relaxed, happy individuals than blaming is.

A few years ago our tandem group took an early spring ride to a little fishing port on the coast of Rhode Island. All twelve bikes pulled into a state park with bathrooms. People gathered waiting for their other team member to come out of the bathroom, waiting in line for the water fountain, or chatting with one another. One of the captains complained to some other men that his stoker—his wife—hadn't trained all winter. One of the other captains admonished him with a faint hint of mockery, "The stoker makes no mistakes." That was the first time I heard that dictum, which I learned is attributed to an expert tandem captain. Now that I'm listening for it, I often hear it at least once per gathering of tandem teams.

That traditional maxim pretended that no miscue, no mistake, and certainly no accident was the stoker's fault. It was the captain's role to assume that every suggestion, every critique the stoker offered, must be treated as if it were correct. Extrapolating further, the captain is accountable for every emotional tangle and every relationship bump, unless the stoker chooses to accept responsibility. And even then, so accepted wisdom goes, it's the captain's responsibility to deny or to at least moderate the stoker's guilt.

It's not surprising that it took the overstated maxim to get some controlling captains to quit critiquing, ignoring, and assigning responsibility for their team's poor performance to the back seat, or defending their own actions. And I suppose it isn't surprising that stokers laugh and welcome this ditty. The philosophy appears to give them additional influence over their captains and their fate on the road. What some teams are missing is the more complex and counterintuitive understanding of 100% *individual* responsibility, and 100% *shared* responsibility. This means no blame, no finger-pointing, no looking to the other person to solve the problem, no sliding out of taking responsibility for failures or for finding a solution. A team needs to find a team solution.

If a team member makes a mistake, the appropriate question is what could each team member have done to help avoid or mitigate it? How might you act differently in the future to sidestep such a problem? If the other person doesn't train and you do, how do you adjust your expectations so that there's no fault finding and more fun? This more complex idea can be daunting to effectively and repeatedly implement on or off a bike.

When I hear someone proclaim the "stoker makes no mistakes" philosophy, I hear an implication that the captain is the benevolent leader and should take a stance of patronizing appeasement toward his stoker. The patronizing tone also makes it sound like the captain would suffer passive-aggressive chills or abandonment if he didn't appease. On our team, any hint of patronizing in describing our responsibilities must be clearly rejected. If I simply acquiesced to an idea or request from Szifra because I thought she needed to be placated, and she got a whiff of that attitude, it would start to dissolve the glue that holds our team together.

Szifra is often right, more often reasonable, and almost always sounds at least formally respectful. I probably match her in the number of times I'm right and reasonable, but not so much in sounding perfectly respectful. I feel respectful, but my tone is probably less consistently respectful with her than it is with others. I relax my tone modulator with her. I treat her with less care at times. It's disturbingly easy to treat her less gently, to take advantage of her as a safe place to express my frustration. Szifra isn't always right when she says I'm being disrespectful, but she's never wrong when she says I *sound* disrespectful to her ear.

"The stoker makes no mistakes" dictum is a valiant attempt to encourage captains to drop their assumptions of blame and take responsibility for the comfort and safety of their stoker—as if the stoker is a passenger. Captains are usually men, often act overly confident, and do carry the heavy responsibility of making numerous quick and fateful decisions. Captains are regularly adrenalized—adrenaline promotes action versus contemplation, anxiety versus calm, anger and aggression versus negotiation. It's not surprising that many captains announce decisions more often than they attempt to reach consensus. We captains often fail to adequately balance the needs of our other team member instead of following the urgent feeling our brain is generating. We need to act now! The feeling is often a false alert, but when our adrenaline has convinced us a predator is waiting in the bush it feels safer and more efficient to move down the road, rather than to stand still and negotiate. And of course, at times it is.

It's a mistake for stokers to embrace "The stoker makes no mistakes" as a Get Out of Jail Free card. The stoker may never be wrong, but they certainly aren't always right—a subtle but important difference. Being found wrong invites blame, while not being right can and should invite corrective action.

Szifra and I learned that when I shouldered all the responsibility it didn't best serve her, me, or our team. She wanted to ride a tandem so she didn't have to keep her eye on the road and make all the decisions a single rider has to make, or to learn to manage the bike controls. I wanted to ride together, so I was happy to initially take on those responsibilities.

But Szifra was not just a pedaling passenger, and any notion she was left a serious weakness in our team's safety and coordination efforts. If either of us saw her as a lesser team member—one who only pedaled without responsibility for our safety, merely a passenger, even a working passenger— her incentive to keep her eyes on the myriad dynamics of every interaction with pedestrians, other bikes and cars was diminished. Having four eyes watching and two people evaluating hazards is always safer than trusting one person to see and manage the risk.

I'm exceedingly lucky in the stoker department. On the bike, Szifra works diligently at assuming her fair share of all poor messaging, miscommunications, and mishaps. "My bad," is easy for her to announce on the bike. Negotiating 100% responsibility protocols off the bike wasn't as smooth.

When either of us is trying to report that some interaction has tripped us up emotionally, we both tend to default to sentence constructions like "When you do that, it makes me feel disrespected." That can easily be misinterpreted as "You did this to me!" We aren't meaning to place full blame on the other person, but the construction can tend to arouse their defenses. It can sound like "*You* make me feel…" Szifra and I know our reactions are rarely or never the other's fault. They're feelings generated by our past experiences, not implanted by the speaker. We do better if we work to share our hurt feelings in ways that don't stimulate each other's default assumptions. We're learning to phrase things in ways that clearly underline that we're taking responsibility for our own feelings while also working not to spike the other person's defenses.

We started asking each other to rephrase reports of perceived injury to something more like, "I feel," "I react," or "I can't manage." Or possibly, "When you do that, I start feeling disrespected." The other piece of construction that helped was to inquire into the other person's intent, "Did you mean that?" or "What were you trying to say?" At other times we simply preface our report on our feelings with, "I'm not blaming you. These are just my feelings."

It's a slow, glitchy process to want to share your pain and then have to slow down and edit for impact. When I hurt, I want to wail in a childish attempt to gain sympathy. Those are often contradictory goals, but the pull is strong, and voicing accusation feels so good in a moment of pain. Szifra had a more philosophical resistance to rephrasing. She didn't want to feel like she was taking responsibility by saying she was sorry or by acting like it was anything but my psychological imperfections or faulty assumptions.

I use "sorry" as an empathetic balm. She used it as a marker of culpability. Neither of us remembers our fathers apologizing for anything they'd done. Each of us tailored the way we eventually reacted to our fathers' stubbornness, to their arrogant protection of their fragile egos. I spread sorry on any hurt, and she saved it for truly marking her missteps. Szifra felt for my hurt but wanted to be certain I didn't think she was responsible for whatever caused the pain. I was sorry she felt she had to be so careful. But on the bike "Sorry" came easily for her. She was quick to feel responsible for her leans, miscommunications and anxious, loud yells in my ear.

Some patterns it was easy to carry onto the bike. Initially it was effortless to have me be singly accountable. I'm stronger and bigger—there was some advantage to having more weight and strength to force a bike to follow my needs, overriding Szifra's. I was also a more experienced rider, the case with most captains. Without much effort, we initially fell into the traditional expectation that Szifra would follow my lead. Even when a strong stoker recruits a new captain, the effort to influence the new teammate to want to ride can mean that the stronger stoker defers more to the captain than is healthy. Gender roles just exacerbate this tendency.

There are tandem teams where the captain is a woman. At events we see women captains with male stokers who are visually or physically compromised, or who prefer the backseat. And occasionally, we run into women who are such strong riders and so interested in biking that they've driven the tandem activity and are the obvious choice for captain, or teams of two women riding together. But as in most situations where women take on a role that men have claimed, women are underrepresented as captains and too often under-respected.

We started in the traditional fashion, with me clearly in charge, but soon found neither of us wanted Szifra to back that far off. The assumption I was in charge was insidious. I'd ask Szifra where she wanted to go before each ride. She'd answer, "I don't care. You decide." I'd have to be careful I didn't just decide and go. I didn't want to always be responsible for deciding. I wanted her to be equally involved in our route, to share the successes and failures on any given day. I'd regularly ignore her disinterest and ask, "Flat or hills? How long? Want to go south to Concord or north to Dunstable?"

She'd say again that she didn't care, but then ask for an easier ride or to go someplace "I haven't been."

As we attempted to break the pattern of captain-in-charge, we talked about our roles, responsibilities and feelings. We also laughed. We knew that even though we had a habit of lots of talk about our process of communication—often called metacommunication—we weren't immune to wearing ourselves out with process talk. One way we broke our pattern of digging deeper and deeper into the minutiae was to laugh about how, if we recommended all this processing as the starting point for tandem teams, it would quickly sour most couples. We had both worked with couples in coaching and therapy and knew that even the thought of minimally processing communications can exhaust many couples.

Our interest in maintaining our communication process was as important to us as keeping the bike functioning smoothly. We carefully maintain our mechanical equipment so the bike is dependable when we're miles from home. We methodically apply lube to each link in our chains, drip by drip—our tandem has three chains: the captain's, the stoker's and the standard drive chain. We'd double-check tire pressure before every ride, confirm our light batteries are charged, and that we have tools and spare tubes aboard. Many teams maintain their equipment, but that care doesn't predict an equal awareness of the need for communication or empathy training, or for relationship maintenance.

Szifra's late husband and I shared the need for orderly preparation of equipment. He understood the downsides of casual neglect. But He and I certainly weren't equally concerned about the need for maintaining the lines of communication within the couple. Or if he was concerned, he wasn't able to implement an effective program.

At the highest level of relationships and sport, superior self-control—the quality of your mental game—is a solid predictor of consistent success. Communication maintenance starts with training your emotional reactions to shift gears in order to meet the needs of the moment. My need for practice is always pulling me forward.

Chapter 20: Cockpit Talk

Sharing roads with mechanical beasts that weigh hundreds of times more than our bike make the communication and safety challenges more urgent. Szifra hadn't ridden a single bike in thirty years, and she wanted to avoid all the issues she imagined a captain would have to pay attention to. We'd been tandeming for two years before she accepted my offer to buy her a single bike. Always the social extrovert, the pull for her was a chance to ride with some women friends.

After she'd ridden a couple of times on quiet streets and a bike path, she told me, "You juggle so many things. I'm stunned at how difficult it is." With that appreciation, I realized it was time for me to retire from my role as the leader and primary safety officer. She was ready to be a more active part of our team, and I was ready to have her use her eyes and ears to help keep us out of trouble. Negotiating how was new territory for both of us: How could we use her to increase our safety? There were times I felt pressure to do too many things at the same time; those situations seemed like a good place to start.

The tandem, with its longer wheel base and a stoker needing warnings about bumps, takes a bit more focus to navigate when the pavement is an obstacle course of rough patches, cracks, potholes, or debris. It's helpful to use the entire lane to slalom through the obstacles. It would be helpful to have an extra set of eyes to assist while I try to keep my eyes on the road surface, look for cars ahead, and continually check for cars coming from behind. I asked Szifra to watch and warn me, "Car Back."

On an early ride under this new regime, we were cruising down a rural road with raised patches, unfilled potholes and big cracks. The road rounded a farm that exuded the pungent smell of cattle. Just past the weathered barn, the road ran along a barbed-wire fence that enclosed a plowed pasture and began a gentle drop toward a river a quarter mile away. "Watch back," I announced into my microphone.

"Ok," she responded.

The road was straight, and the downslope pulled us faster. A hundred yards ahead and to the right was a gate to the pasture. Farm equipment had tracked clumps of mud and manure out of the gate and across our lane. I stared at the mess, trying to find a reasonable line through the plops of impediments.

In my earpiece Szifra announced, "Car Back." I glanced in my mirror and saw an old pickup rounding the farm. I didn't have an option to keep tight to the right, so I immediately moved a few feet toward the middle of our lane to claim all the road we might need to run the gauntlet of tire droppings. Szifra urgently repeated, "Car Back!"

"Got it," I said. My mistake. I should have acknowledged her alert the first time. She couldn't see that I had no choice but to assert our right to the full lane. The pickup had to wait for us to navigate the obstacles.

We also decided it would be safer for me to keep my hands on the bars and have Szifra give the hand signals at turns and intersections. Since I was the one who made the final decision whether it was prudent to proceed, we needed to establish a clear protocol for signals—Szifra isn't that fond of rigid protocols. The first step was simple: I'd call the turn, and she would signal. But just like she needed to know that I heard her say "Car Back," I needed to know she heard me. "Let's use a 'cockpit talk' approach," I suggested. "In airplanes and on large ships, a command is given and the person on the helm repeats it so that both people know it was heard correctly."

I gave her an example, "For instance, if I say 'Right Turn,' you respond, 'Right Turn' and give the hand signal." She hesitantly nodded. Szifra likes to learn by doing, so I didn't pay much attention to her lack of enthusiasm.

The street we turn onto to exit our neighborhood gave us our first chance to try the new approach. I declared, "Left Turn." I saw her bright yellow arm signal to the left in my helmet mirror, but she didn't repeat my directive. Or was it a proposal or announcement? Announcements aren't the same as proposals but are a bit softer than directives—probably, maybe? Transitioning my voice as well as my role was an ongoing process for me.

At the next couple of intersections I announced—or declared—our turn, and I saw her signal. I announced, "Right Turn," she signaled, and I pulled into the parking lot of a local convenience store.

"I need you to let me know you've heard me say we're going to turn so I don't have to look in my mirror to see if you're signaling. It pulls my attention away from the road."

"Yeah. Got it! That's not good," she immediately agreed. But she wasn't ready to just follow my directions. Instead, she figured out a way to stamp her independence on the process by modifying *my* rule. At my next "Right Turn" she came back at me with, "Signaling Right." The slight variation was all hers, and perfect.

At times each of us is the originator of an idea or the skeptical risk-assessor, and occasionally the observer. We may willingly follow, but unless we feel ownership of the project or process, we aren't a team, just rider and passenger.

After we settled into the habit of call-and-respond, I asked Szifra to share responsibility for checking for cars at intersections. This was a major change. At first it seemed obvious that the one who holds the steering and brakes had to be the one to check both ways at intersections. But really, why? Szifra was also risking her skin, bones, and head at every intersection. Shouldn't I trust her to jointly evaluate and call the dangers? She was as concerned as I was that we stay safe. She trusted me to look carefully and make the best judgment. Shouldn't I trust her to do likewise?

"I'm thinking it would be good if at intersections you were the one to check cars to the right. What do you think?"

"I already do that," she told me

"I mean you would be the only one to look and tell me when it's ok for us to go. I'll look left and you look right. I'll take the left because cars in the left lane are the closest point of danger and might require the quickest reaction." I explained.

She was quiet, thinking. "You wouldn't check the right at all?"

"I think if I check, you might not look as carefully. I want you to have full responsibility for the right side. Does that make sense?"

She decided it did and agreed she was ready to own the right.

There was no halfway in this. Either she was responsible for her side, and I had full trust in her judgment, or I didn't trust her and she wouldn't take full responsibility—and would probably hit me with the tire pump when I wasn't looking. I had to be willing to enter an intersection without looking *her* way, just like she was willing to ride across a street trusting my decisions. How could we ask her to have her head fully in the game, if I wasn't willing to risk my health and life on her judgment? If we each looked both directions, who made the final call to go? Me again?

We initiated our new protocol, announcing, "Clear right" or "Clear left." But the first dozen intersections were a challenge. I had to fight my self-preservation instincts. It felt crazy to pull out into a cross street without double-checking both sides. I fought the instinct to turn my head. If I did automatically look, I would quickly look back to the left and wait for her call. When I got clearance, I called the final go. But I was tense, waiting for the impact of an unseen car. I felt like I was closing my eyes and hoping. Probably a small reflection of what she must feel every time she gets on the bike—and she does admit to closing her eyes on some fast downhills.

It took a while for the tension to ease and our new intersection habit to feel fully comfortable. We both knew we had to get the process right. Szifra showed every sign she was at least as vigilant as I was. Once the habit was established we began to relax and started to negotiate small modifications. This is the way we do things in most areas of the relationship. We fully establish a simple habit, then consider modifications—we function on the basis of precise rules, until we gain enough expertise to function with unconscious competency.

One of our first variations to the rule came when obstacles to our right blocked Szifra's view—an overgrown hedge, a wooded lot, a house close to the corner. In those cases, as we approached an intersection, Szifra would let me know as early as possible that she couldn't see traffic on her side. The front of the bike is farther into the intersection so I can often see what she can't, therefore I take responsibility. "I've got the right," I let her know. If all looks clear, I'll announce both "Clear left. Clear right."

There are times I find it easier if I don't try to manage both sides. If the left is easy for her, I announce, "You take the left."

She responds, "I've got the left." And we wait until each of us confirms it's safe on our temporary new side. We also arrange a similar switch at merges where I'd have to turn dramatically to look back over my left shoulder. As we approach those intersections I ask, "Can you take the left back?" Occasionally I give her a heads up that the right isn't quite where it usually is, "Check hard right."

We now use another variation at some challenging corners—at the bottom of hills embedded in forests, proceeding twisty curves, or where I need to keep my eye on rough pavement. I ask her to look ahead, "Please confirm there's no one coming through those trees." I want to take the full lane, but I don't want to meet a car that's drifted across the center line. In those cases, it's too distracting to stare at the partially hidden road looking for a brief glimpse of an approaching car between the trees or way up the road.

The process we used for the first couple of years, and the one I still use on my single bike—me making all the decisions at intersections—comes back at me sometimes when we're waiting for traffic, and Szifra forgets to announce that her side is clear. In the hesitant moment, I find myself making an instinctual check to the right. When I catch myself, I force myself to wait for her "Okay". Responsibility has to be an every-situation habit for both of us. The right side is hers. I have no standing to casually step in or overrule her unless I see a danger she doesn't. When the delay stretches, I sometimes ask, "Is your side clear?" She apologizes, "Sorry! Clear right!" She quietly returns the nudge at intersections when she announces "Clear," and I forget to declare the status of my side before I go, or if I sneak a peek right and then go before she clears us. "Was the left clear?" she gently inquires.

Sometimes "Clear" is a little too permissive and "Not Clear" a little too restrictive. We found we also needed a shorthand way to declare that a car was coming but was sufficiently far away or slow enough that we could easily merge into the lane ahead of it if we got started immediately. We needed a modifier that communicated permission, but with the additional information that the window of safety was closing. We started using "Clear Enough" in those circumstances. If Szifra says, "Clear Enough," and I need to wait longer for my side to clear, I assume I will need an additional confirmation that things are still clear before I go. When I'm ready I ask, "Still clear enough?"

The use of "Clear" cycled Him once more back into our everyday relationship. We considered using "Go" for permission, but felt it was too easy to mistake it for "No." Szifra and He had a similar conversation in a different context, and he had told her that "Clear" was the word to use. So Szifra suggested "Clear," and we began to use it. More than a year later, she told me that every time we declared "Clear" she quietly thought about him. I had no idea. As we use clear so often, Szifra has found the association with him has faded. He still occasionally visits me when she says clear.

One day Szifra and I were near the end of our ride. We stopped at the second to last light before home. This busy intersection is always tricky. There are delayed lights for each direction, and plenty of cars turn or go straight. Cars are always trying to take our lane—crowding alongside us even when we're well into the lane—instead of waiting for us to clear the intersection. When we stop in the middle of the lane to wait for the light and prevent the crowding, they sometimes still pull alongside or honk at us.

In this instance, when the light turned green, Szifra pedaled us through the intersection while I clipped in. This is an intersection where it's safer to accelerate hard for half a block to discourage cars who are pinching our side of the street as they wait to turn left. If we take too much time in the first hundred feet, some drivers behind us will try to pass between us and the left turners. The gap is way too small for our comfort.

At slow speeds, three feet is the minimum distance cars are supposed to leave between them and us. Car-driver impatience is a regular phenomenon. People pass us on blind curves and hills, accelerate past even as cars come at them, yell obscenities when they have to wait for us before turning, pass us in the last half block only to make us wait while they turn. When we ride assertively and boldly, it tempers some drivers' risky behavior.

This time we accelerated out of the crowded intersection with a line of cars right behind us. About a hundred feet down the street on our right, we pass the entrance to an apartment building's parking lot. A car coming toward us turned immediately in front of us without a turn signal or warning. I braked hard, and the older woman driver casually waved her fingers at us like a friendly two-year-old. I shouted, "Be Careful!" She gave us her middle finger and yelled, "Fuck You!" That was our first really close miss on the tandem. But it got Szifra thinking about other ways she could help us stay safe.

One was to alert me when she saw something developing ahead of us. Some people call this backseat driving. Once again, I think of it as four eyes being better than two. I love having her watch, particularly at busy intersections or crowded streets. It's extraordinarily helpful to have her spot cars that might not see us, cut us off, pull out in front of us, or turn into us. So far there are very few times I haven't already seen what she points out but having her scan for risks feels like a huge safety plus.

She's practicing not telling me what to do, i.e., "Stop," "Go," "Turn," but instead telling me what she sees, i.e., "Car right," "We missed our turn," etc. I can misinterpret her voice as a command as quickly as she can misinterpret mine. Having her tell me what she sees helps me think rather than just react, to consider the safest response to the car or how safe it is to make a quick turn.

Cars and trucks are the lethal threats, but dogs can also be significant dangers. My years as a dog behaviorist have given me a sixth sense for where they may be and whether they're likely to be a threat—like all sixth senses, mine is a library of templates created by numerous experiences. I alert Szifra that I think there may be a dog ahead, and she scans for the dog and tries to tell whether it's threatening to chase us. Once alerted, I decide on our response—keep cruising along, stop, or make a run for it?

The list of shared responsibilities has grown over the years as we try to be more efficient in how we prepare for a ride or attempt to find a better way to assign tasks during the ride. We share the goal of being certain I'm not distracted from potential dangers. We also work to be sure we're both comfortable. Responsibilities include:

- Each of us has a blinky light on our end of the bike that we take responsibility for—is it attached, turned on, charged, switched off?
- We each assume responsibility for topping up the tires—one of us does it, but we both check whether it's been done.
- We double-check the tightness of the wheel skewer on our end of the bike—front or back.
- We both assume we need to pay attention to navigation, and then we figure out the easiest way to share those duties. Usually I set the direction on rides I've been on before, and she manages the navigation when we're on an event ride or a new route.
- I shift gears to keep us in a range that has traditionally worked well. But Szifra calls for shift changes when she feels she's spinning up so fast she can't generate her share of the power or feels she's crunching so hard her legs won't last. She also calls shifts when she's standing. If her call causes me problems—strain on my knees, etc.— I let her know I may need to shift again soon. Sometimes we simply agree that the one with the most strength left gets catered to.

There are times all of this planning and agreement doesn't work that well. In our third year of riding, we joined a group of our tandem friends and other teams on a ride organized by the dealership where I'd rented our first tandem. Some first-time teams were test riding tandems. Our group included a few couples who were hesitant to ride on the roads. Even after the first few miles, the group moved at a cautious pace. I wasn't comfortable in the middle of the pack surrounded by inexperienced riders. I knew the area and moved us out front on one section of a busy, narrow, rural road. Szifra and I were focused on a steep little rise coming at us and the cars accelerating to pass during the breaks in the line of cars approaching from ahead.

We missed the planned left turn just before the hill. Szifra urgently announced, "That was our turn!" I slowed to let the cars behind us pass so we could make a U-turn. The shoulder was sandy. I knew if I stopped, it was questionable whether I'd get my foot securely planted in the sand. And it wasn't safe to stop on the pavement. My brain was seized by the problem we faced. I kept slowly pedaling up the hill. Szifra couldn't see all the variables I was considering. She stopped pedaling and repeated, "We missed our turn! We need to stop!"

We were on the hill, I was quickly tiring from pedaling our combined weight and I told her, "Pedal!" She didn't. My brain was full of a matrix of problems. We were wobbling from lack of speed, and I worried that we would wobble off the road. I demanded, "Pedal!"

Szifra didn't like my tone. She felt disrespected and ignored. She still didn't pedal. I couldn't maintain our momentum without her effort. We began to weave dangerously. I demanded again, with authority, "Pedal! Now!"

She heard my tone and thankfully started pedaling again, convinced I was being an asshole. I found a marginal opportunity to stop, where I felt I could safely get my foot down. Once we had dismounted and shifted the bike onto the sandy shoulder, we faced off. Who was right? Who had to listen to whom first? Who had the right to be aggrieved? At that moment all that mattered to either of us was our emotional wound and the righteousness of our complaint. Our off-bike world, with all of our history, our fathers, our hurts, had just intruded on our ride.

My punctuation of the conversation was that Szifra kept getting in my face about why I hadn't just stopped. She didn't appreciate the urgency I felt about our safety. She protested, "You were disrespectful. You can't talk to me like that!" I retorted, "Was I disrespectful or anxious?" She was sure, "Disrespectful. You should have just stopped!"

"I couldn't stop!"

She was holding the bike, so I flipped an "I'll see you on the other side!" at her and walked across the street during a break in the traffic. As I crossed, I felt guilty and childish. Wasn't the captain supposed to take charge of the bike? I'd just walked away in a pique. Szifra waited for the next break and competently wheeled the bike over to where I was.

The process of sorting out feelings, rights and protocols threatened to hamper our attention for the rest of the ride. But when we had loaded the tandem on the bike rack and were finally alone in the car, we both acknowledged that we needed to figure the situation out. We needed to do one of our non-judgmental after-action reviews. And as we sat there, we began, initially in fits and starts, to listen and communicate.

Szifra said she felt left out of my decision-making process. I felt she had ignored our safety needs by not pedaling when I said I needed her to. She wanted explanations at a time my hands and brain were full. I couldn't think what to say, how to do a better job of including her.

Teamwork is complex—full of variables. Part of the problem was our shared responsibility style. We hadn't been clear enough about when a "Command and Control" process was the only safe one. If my brain was threatening to freeze up, what did we want my priority to be? We both agreed in principle that getting us to physical safety was paramount. Once we were physically safe, we could take time to reestablish emotional safety. In theory we could do that on the bike. But given our personality flaws, what should we do until we grew up?

One of us had to start the repair process. If not me, then why should she? I laid down my armament and said, "My tone wasn't that good. I'm sorry I don't have the control I want. It's my responsibility to try. I'm sorry I'm not there yet."

She paused and said, "Your tone was demanding, but it made it clear we had to focus on safety." I waited, but she didn't offer an "I'm sorry."

I went on, "I should have given some indication I heard you. If I'd said, "Not now!" you would have at least known I heard you. If I can't do that next time, maybe I could just cry."

She smiled and said, "You know, that might work." Then she shared what she'd been thinking, "Once I realized you were worried about our safety, I said to myself, 'Safety trumps everything. Tough shit you're feeling hurt! Just pedal! We'll figure it out later.'" I waited again for her "Sorry" but knew it wasn't likely, knew it wasn't her thing. She sounded like she cared about me. She sounded like she recognized she had responsibility that she hadn't managed that well. I could accept that or stubbornly hold out for the specific words I wanted. I capitulated into the offered reconnection.

Given people's natural instinct to defend and explain their actions, we have to continually work at taking full responsibility for our actions, our inactions and our emotional responses to surprises or each other's abruptness. Managing our emotions is a full-time job that can exhaust our affection at times. There are moments I want to give into the feeling of being hopelessly alone in my frustration and alienation.

Szifra likes a sailing metaphor I shared with her early in our relationship. Sailboats come in two fundamental hull shapes, flat bottomed and round bottomed. A flat-bottom boat initially feels very stable—not much tip, even if you shift your weight dramatically to one side. But once it tips past a critical point, a flat-bottom boat loses all its stability and can suddenly flip over and throw you into the water. And once flipped, it's very difficult to turn right-side up again—it's now stable in the upside-down position. On the other hand, a round-bottom boat will initially tip easily— shift your weight a bit toward one side and the boat leans over. But the more it leans the harder it is to make it lean any further. And if it flips, many will almost immediately turn back upright on their own.

I think of Him as flat-bottomed—controlled and hard to tip. But once He hit his critical point, he flipped and couldn't right himself. I am rounder bottomed—tippy, reactive and easily hurt by accusations or slights. But I've been flipped many times in my life and so far I've been able to quickly right myself. Szifra has also been through a lot, and she's also always found a way to pick herself up and get on with life. She agrees she's round bottomed—although she is never as comfortable with that description as she is calling her hands and feet big.

Since our earliest months together, each of us has had a strong inclination to right the relationship when we tipped. If the connection ever broke, we wanted it to be unavoidable, not because we were inattentive or self-destructive. His way isn't our way.

Chapter 21: Make It Clear

Szifra may use mysterious pronouns and share aloud the later tidbits of a conversation she started earlier in her head, but I'm not immune to leaving her wondering what I'm thinking or doing. Again and again, I catch myself making an assumption that she'll know what I mean, even if I haven't filled in all the blanks. At those moments it may not be obvious to me, but I guess I'm assuming she can read my mind.

We both feel unambiguous communication is key to resisting the temptation of assuming the other person is unreasonable or disrespectful. Explicit communication is our best defense against dangers on the bike. It's a challenge to keep things clear even when the day is relaxed, and danger seems a distant risk. We get better and better, but making assumptions still comes back at us in the most mundane circumstances.

On a recent ride I wanted to catch a full view of the road back. I rotated my head slightly left and then right. I centered my mirror's image on an older white car about a block back. I shifted my focus to the road ahead. On the right, about a hundred yards in front of us, there was broken pavement. If I held "our line"—our course around corners and in our lane—until the car got to us, it wouldn't give him time to react when we would need to pull out. He might be beside us and force us to ride into the roughness. Best to move out into the lane now and give the car lots of warning that it would need to alter its line.

I glanced again in my mirror and turned my head a fraction to bring the car back into view. It was still far enough away that there was no need to ask my stoker to signal our move to the left. I began to drift the necessary eighteen inches out to give us plenty of room to clear the cracks and a hole that became apparent as we got closer. Szifra felt the bike move, apparently checked her mirror, and announced, "Car back!"

151

"Thanks," I responded with our agreed confirmation that I'd heard her.

I wanted to be out another foot or so, but the tandem fought me. We were pulled back toward what now looked like it could be a wheel-eating hole among the roughness. I leaned into the handlebars slightly more to move the bike toward the center of the lane. It responded. Szifra again declared, "Car Back!" and unexpectedly we were drawn back toward the dangerous pavement once again. I compensated with an even harder tilt of the bike. We veered left and cleared the cracked pavement and considerable hole.

The white car, an older model compact, was well into the other lane as it passed us. I tweaked us back toward the right side of our lane as I glanced in my mirror. No other cars back. I twisted my head further until I could see the left side of Szifra's bright orange helmet, its black straps, her little-round mirror, and a slice of her rosy cheek in my tiny mirror. I can't see much, but I can always feel when she moves.

After any odd occurrence we try to figure out how to avoid a similar incident next time. There's no blame involved, just curiosity. I checked whether she was fighting my move at the rough patch. "Were you doing something back there? The bike kept heading for the shoulder."

When she reaches for one of the water bottles, the space I've left in our lane for an overtaking car can quickly dissolve. The contortions it takes for her to dig a snack bar out of the deep back pocket of her bike jersey can wiggle us onto and off our line. She's responsible for monitoring who's approaching on our right side. But if she leans, even carefully, to look around me, it leans the bike and can career us toward the shoulder. None of this is a serious issue, unless I'm carefully slaloming between chunks of rock, branches, or potholes.

She answered, "I don't think I was doing anything."

"I was trying to miss a nasty hole, and we started heading for it. I wonder if, when you saw the car back, you unconsciously tried to keep us close to the right side?"

Her answer was slow coming. She seemed to be thinking. "I don't know. I don't think I was, but it's possible."

I attempted to soften any perceived blame, "Tricky stuff. I've got the bars, but you're steering us too."

"I know. Keep reminding me," she said congenially.

I felt her palm rest gently on my back, then a slight circular caress. It's a sweet gesture, her hug-equivalent on the tandem. I couldn't give it back. The best I could do was tell her, "Thanks. That's nice." I checked my mirror and then forward along our line. There was something ahead in the shadow of a tree. Could be a rock or just a deeper patch of shadow. Safest to move out into the lane.

"Coming out a bit," I announced. That's what I should have done last time.

She lifted her left arm, indicated our intention, and responded, "Signaling out." This team stuff is an ever-evolving communications project.

When either of us gets anxious, on or off the bike, we usually forget to share our concern or ask questions. Assuming is easier. We both assume the big things are ok. But we allow assumptions about the little details to trip us up.

When Szifra emotionally drifts slightly away, I begin to feel alone. I forget to ask her if we're ok, or to remind myself I like being alone at times. When I get quiet, trying to avoid running into frustration or changing my line and routing myself into irritation, Szifra leans hard toward trying to please me, rather than asking what's happening. We have to constantly remind ourselves, "This person is my best friend. They're trying to do what's right. I can share my anxiety with them. They love me."

Chapter 22: Riding in the Drops

Our road tandem elicits strong reactions from many non-riders. "I wouldn't be comfortable with handlebars that force me to ride all bent over." "Those little seats would make my butt sore." "Those tires are so skinny. They're scary!"

Drop handlebars—those bars whose ends curl into a "C" shape—allow you to ride in a more aerodynamic, tucked-over position. But you can also use them to ride sitting straight up or with your hands in three or four different positions. This allows you to relieve stress on your hands and your butt. Even some experienced road cyclists echo non-riders, "At first I found the drop handlebars uncomfortable, but now I love them." This was Szifra's reaction after she got used to them.

Counterintuitively road-bike saddles are most supportive when they're narrow and not too soft. They also take adaptation. A harder saddle keeps the pressure on your sit bones, not your sensitive soft tissue. The narrow design keeps your thighs from rubbing on the saddle when you pedal. The best riding technique is not to sit too solidly on the saddle—don't use it like a chair. Sit lightly with more of your weight pushing down on the pedals. The stronger you push the pedals, the less pressure you have on your sit bones.

And the skinny tires? Road tires are narrower (25-32 mm) than mountain bike tires (120-180 mm). But in the past, road tires used to be even narrower (22-23 mm). People thought narrow and hard offered less rolling resistance and less wind resistance. Now we know it's more complicated than that. If tires are too narrow, they need a lot of pressure to protect the tube from getting pinched between the rim and the bottom of the tire when you hit a hole. But high pressure means less compliance and more bounce. Each time the bike moves up and down, it robs power from your forward momentum. It's faster for the tires to be a bit wider and softer so they don't bounce as much on rough pavement. And of course, softer tires mean a more comfortable ride.

In another counterintuitive notion, bike tires without tread slip less on wet and dry pavement than treaded ones. The total area of rubber that contacts the road is greater when there's no tread than with tread. Also, there's no risk of hydroplaning a bike tire in the rain. Its narrow footprint easily pushes water out from under the tire. Tread is helpful in dirt and on sandy corners.

Road bikes aren't like a pair of new slippers, comfortable right out of the store. And the options a road bike offers are of little value unless you ride longer than an hour at a time. A road bike will likely be uncomfortable until you toughen your butt to sit on your two sit bones and condition your muscles to spend time in a bent-over position. It certainly takes some conditioning—practice.

Once you get used to the tucked-over position, you can feel how the design places you in a more efficient pose to cheat wind resistance. Remember, overcoming the drag of moving your body through air requires more effort than any other aspect of bicycling—up to 85% of your power. And again, this is why tandems can be more efficient than two single bikes— the second rider is more hidden from the wind behind the first rider. When I feel a cool breeze, I ask Szifra if she's cool. Her answer is often "No" because she gets hit with less wind than I do. Similarly, on a hot spring day when bugs are hitting me in my face and mouth, she's blissfully unaware we're bursting through intermittent, dense clouds of black flies. (I haven't eaten animal flesh for over 53 years, but I don't consider swallowing random bugs as switching away from a plant-based diet.)

Initially Szifra was certain that if she ever rode a single bike, it would need to have flat, commuter-bike style handlebars so she could sit up tall. And her first single had those. After a season of casual riding, she wanted a bike that was easier to get up hills—lighter, more efficient. She decided to try a road bike. I bought her a carbon one, and she quickly learned to appreciate the flexible positions the drop bars offer.

As I watch my partner getting ready to go for a ride, with her cycling muscles and adventurous spirit, I'm struck by how good a fit we are. But we're no fairy tale. Fairy tales leap to happily-ever-afters. They don't tell us about the need to continue learning and adjusting to each other. Our partnership isn't magical, but in the real world of relationships and tandeming, we're in a great place—learning, adjusting and happy most of the time.

My earliest relationships were built on the assumption that my partners would adapt to my sensibilities, because I irrationally assumed my way of doing things was the most reasonable. I've moved most of the way past that vestige of my dad's attitude. The price my early partners may have paid for my non-compliance is a conjecture for another day. What I know is that they were smart to get off my tandem—the "my" reflects my youthful arrogance. It took numerous missed shifts, thrown chains, and a few blowouts of my heart before I was motivated to adjust with my partner.

A satisfying, intimate partnership demands a willingness of both people to change habits. Many couples jump into serious relationships without paying attention to the amount of practice and number of changes it will likely require. It's clearly best to begin adapting before you make a long-term commitment. At nineteen, I embarked on a design-build experiment with my first marriage. I failed fairly quickly.

By the time Szifra came into my life, I'd experimented my way through the equivalent of a graduate program in relationships. My marks weren't that good. Like many people with advanced degrees, I certainly didn't know it all, but I'd discovered a lot that I needed to learn and how to learn it. To improve further, I needed to constantly do my homework.

I'd learned I couldn't build a satisfying relationship without the tolerance and interest of a committed, mature partner. I'd begun to understand that each person I'd dated or married was remarkably different, and those differences had to be recognized and respected. Areas of strength, flexibility, endurance are constantly developing or waning within each of us. And the interaction of two people is a swirling, complex and chaotic stew of possible delights and misunderstandings.

Szifra once pointed out that those of us who've been in multiple, serious relationships have been forced to face things about ourselves that people who've been in only one relationship may not have had to. We serial relaters have gotten repetitive, often annoyingly repetitive, feedback about our weaknesses from numerous, intimate witnesses. Messages about weaknesses are harder to ignore when the same notification comes from different people, again and again. It's an especially awakening dope slap when you think you've addressed the issue, and you get accused one more time. I found it easy to discount one person's critique. But when two, three, and eventually fifteen or more people accused me of the same things, it was hard to keep casually rebuffing the feedback. I was forced to either bury my head in a hole of my own making or take an in-depth look at myself.

Initially, when my partners said I was critical, I discounted them as too subjective. After a couple of failed relationships, I had to assume there was something about doing things my way that wasn't effective. Eventually that tiny step morphed into awareness that I was overly focused on my partner's behavior, and not giving my own adequate attention. I looked a little closer at my inner world, and I discovered I was a mess.

I clearly had to adjust my ideas about many aspects of life. The basis of my thinking was fundamentally faulty and negatively focused. There really were no rights or wrongs in most of the situations where I thought I saw them. I had to get comfortable living with less surety, less knowing.

I didn't want to go through the discomfort of changing into the new positions required to adapt to my partners. But I was also tired of fighting the winds of conflict as I pushed my upright superiority into it, and I was weary of the resultant road rash when I lost my internal balance.

There were times in my twenties when I faced such confusion about the way forward that I despaired of finding my line through life's twists and turns. I was fired from a dream job in a children's psychiatric hospital for no reason anyone would tell me. I went to one of the complex's high buildings, sat with my legs hanging over the edge, and considered ending the frustration by pushing off.

At another time my live-in fiancé and I woke up one Saturday morning. I asked, "What shall we do today?"

She said, "I'm leaving" and moved out.

I locked myself in the bathroom, held my antique straight razor, and considered cutting myself. It's hard to know why I didn't pull the trigger in either of these cases, as He had, but I didn't. I chose instead to go into training, suffer through discomfort and learn to adapt.

Szifra said that He and she had tangles, discussed their feelings, and looked for solutions. But he never got comfortable in the position his new life circumstances demanded. His initial attempt was always to fight the winds of change with data, not to make Szifra's and his communications more aerodynamic or to bend to the effects of emotional feedback. He told Szifra that he never felt any better after they had crunched their way up a relationship hill. He preferred to buy his way into solutions. He explained it with an analogy. A couple squeezes the toothpaste tube at different points. The mangled tube bothers one of them. The solution was to buy two tubes and let each do what they wanted. His approach was a little like Szifra and my attempts to not overly sync our activities if it takes too much adaptation. But I get my batteries charged when we find the next step in continually improving our relationship. He didn't seem to. And when he needed to adjust the fit of his entrepreneurial business, he was unable to do that.

Szifra and I notice, and wonder, at the differences we have and the way they interact and stimulate reactions, both negative and creative in each of us. In previous relationships, we'd get frustrated or complain, and we carried that approach into this one. But we learned to adapt and discovered how much less stressful it is when we quiet our judgment, pay attention to our feelings, and reflect. Or at least, it's less stressful once we quiet the child in us that's raging at every perceived injustice or slight. Szifra would never call this fun, but she's willing to do the work. And she's developed her relationship muscles enough to keep crunching when necessary.

Our changes are partially the result of all the feedback we've received from our multiple relationships, but they're also because each of us vowed to learn to tuck into a more aerodynamic position—less stiff-backed defensive, more relaxed shoulders, more heads-up aware.

There are clear differences in our styles of adapting and our sensitivities, and these are easy to see on the bike. At this point in my life, I have a wider range of comfort for different equipment and kit. Szifra has a narrow zone of tolerance for discomfort in either. Some bike fitters talk about this difference as macro versus micro sensitivities to adjustments. I can ride hours in almost any padded shorts. Szifra spent years trying and rejecting shorts with various chamois, waist heights, and sizes—bike shorts have a chamois insert to reduce skin irritation. She will cut out her bike jersey's soft cloth tags, where I might forget to remove the cardboard price tag. Szifra went through any number of saddles before she found one that felt comfortable. She's apprehensive when bike fitters suggest she adjust the saddle angle as little as .5%.

Szifra's body is extremely flexible, yet she notices slight changes in handlebar height and position. I'm bound up like a rubber band left out in the sun too long, yet I hardly notice the different geometry and fit on my bikes. It took me years to notice that each of my bikes was adjusted slightly differently. Even now I ride my gravel bike, my road bike, and the tandem with different saddles. Each works well enough that I barely notice the variances. As I go into my winter indoor-training season, I have a yearly check on my bike fit to advise me about adjustments I might need, to respond to my increased fitness and increasing age. Without the fit, I would have no idea what to change.

I'm learning to both spin at higher cadences and to crunch more. I'm okay with the initial discomfort of widening my range and can be unaware I've reached Szifra's red zone until she alerts me. She's begun to work at increasing her cadence, if for no other reason than to make it easier on me to spin. In general, we're smooth about shifting gears and cadence, but without Szifra's alerts I can go into my "shut-up legs" mode and stop thinking about adjusting the gear and cadence to maximize our joint productivity.

We also have different needs for the frequency and duration of rest stops. Szifra likes to get off the bike and sort out her eating, apply more chamois cream—to reduce saddle irritation—and engage in social activities. I'm learning to eat and adjust my position regularly so that I either don't have to stop as often, or I can make shorter stops. At event water-and-food stops, I try to keep my time off the bike brief. If I spend too much time standing around, my legs feel wooden and need to be re-warmed. Szifra's legs almost never seem to tighten up during long stops. This makes off-the-bike breaks a bit of a compromise. She ends up shortchanging her social desires and resumes our rides earlier than she might. I walk around waiting for her, trying to keep my muscles halfway limber.

We pay the price of slower restarts, but each of us gets a bit of what we need. When we remount, I can feel Szifra pushing more than her norm to compensate for my slower start. After a few minutes she'll ease back knowing that my legs are up for it once again. We both agree that all this adjusting is a small price to pay for the fun of being out and about together.

Chapter 23: Effort, Power and Discomfort

Both bikes and relationships are, of course, powered forward by effort. Each requires work that can be uncomfortable at times. And each rewards you with health and satisfaction.

Bikes are powered by pushing pedals in circles. Selecting the right gear modulates how hard a push it takes and how fast we have to spin. Power is the combination of push and spin. Speed is based on how much power we can generate, how steep the road is, and how strong a headwind we're facing. We push hard and fast enough to move along our route at the clip we can sustain, enough to climb the hill we face, or for long enough to complete a ride. How much discomfort we're willing to tolerate, and for how long, are the main considerations underlying the amount of power we generate and where we can ride.

Not every ride requires discomfort, but most hills or long rides demand some. In the parlance of endurance biking, if we want to improve, we must be willing to suffer. We need to push beyond our comfort zone, exhaust our muscles to the point of minor injury, and then take time off the bike to recover. Time allows your muscles to super compensate—build additional strength to handle future intense challenges. During an event, we want to use the fitness we've developed, but not risk serious injury by dramatically overworking our muscles. The trick is to recognize the difference between fatigue-generated suffering and pain that warns us we're really about to hurt ourselves, to understand where pushing builds character and where it risks more serious damage to muscles.

Experienced athletes can judge their perceived effort pretty accurately and can usually safely push themselves to train and ride at a predetermined level of discomfort. But if you're less experienced with intense training sessions, it's easy to over or underrate your effort and over or undertrain. Is the interval of high-intensity work you're doing hard or very difficult—is it a 7 or a 9 on a scale of 10? Are you backed off enough to adequately recover, or are you still riding a bit too hard?

Heart rate was the original upgrade for rating effort from subjective measures like perceived effort. Heart straps, which measure heart rate, are relatively inexpensive. Since each member of a tandem team can wear one, they can get a rough estimate of their individual effort. But the heart rate feedback loop is slow and will underreport during short, high intensity intervals—the kind that is part of effective training to build endurance and power. Heart rate may take minutes to react to a hard effort. With only heart rate feedback, it's not uncommon that for an entire five-minute interval you can't be sure you're working as hard as you want. Or perhaps you're working harder than is good or necessary.

To get the most effect from limited training time, many cyclists now train and ride with power meters. A power meter is a strain gauge that reads pressure a rider produces on the drivetrain. It can sense cadence and uses both cadence and pressure to compute watts of power produced. The power feedback loop is immediate. The data tells you how intense or easy you're riding at the exact moment. By tracking the amount of time you ride at a given percentage of your maximum, you can optimize your training effect.

Power meters can be mounted on crankshafts, pedal shafts, wheel hubs, or chain rings. At $400 to $1000, they're five to ten times more expensive than heart rate straps. Even the least expensive meters work well enough to give you a useful relative reading. To get the same useful training metrics on a tandem, you need power meters for each rider. The question will always be: Is that information helpful enough to any given team that the expense is worth it?

If Szifra and I wanted to be able to keep up with the tandem group, we needed to train smarter. Just like our first group ride, most times we were left in the proverbial cloud of dust. We would pose for the group photo at the start. Then all the teams would mount up and a line of us would snake onto the first road. All the social chatter slowly quieted as teams jockeyed for position in the peloton. Szifra and I always seemed to need twenty minutes or so of slow warmup for our hearts and legs to get up to speed. The other teams apparently didn't need as much. If we tried to keep up with the group, we would immediately be pushing so hard we were sucking in quick breaths and building up an energy deficit that would beleaguer us the whole ride.

As we got more experienced, there were times we could stay with the group for a while. Unless we hit a hill in the first fifteen minutes. An early hill still caused us to pop out the back like a watermelon seed—spit out and discarded by the others. At the first intersection some members of the group might wait, standing over their bikes chatting about the weather. The minute we rolled up, everyone would remount and start again. By the third hill or so I'd warmed up and hit my stride, not fast but steady. Our normal position quickly became "Off the back," by ourselves, perhaps within sight of one or two other teams ahead or behind.

Group rides were also longer than our regular rides and pushed us beyond where we were ready to stop. The group would often ride for a couple of hours and then gather at a convenience store or bakery. We'd roll up just as most people were finishing their snacks. Our legs would be melting, and our butts compressed. We'd feel like we'd finished a good ride, but the endpoint might still be twenty miles away. As the group pulled out for the second half, we'd once again try to stick with them. Our legs and lungs would shortly begin to burn, our heads would chatter to us about discomfort and quitting, and soon we'd once again be riding too far back to see most of the group. Clearly, we needed to train more or differently.

My first foray into serious training was to purchase a heart strap and a simple bike computer. Now when I rode, I could look down at my handlebars to see how my heart was doing. Besides my heart rate, I had other numbers to keep track of—speed, distance, pedal cadence, total elevation climbed, total miles ridden for the year. All the data just made me realize I didn't know what it meant or what I was doing. I began to read training books and their primary suggestion was to ride more. The strong secondary suggestion was to get a power meter.

After two years of training, I felt like I was seeing improvement slower than I should. I bit the bullet. (Bite the bullet is an expression that always causes Szifra to cringe from memories of His death. It comes from biting on a lead bullet while undergoing an amputation or other painful medical procedure before anesthesia—the softer lead might slightly protect the clenched teeth. But for her, it means undergoing a flashback to his last day and gives her no relief from the pain. So out of respect for her trauma, let me start again.) I bit the belt, hired an online coach, and purchased a crankshaft-mounted power meter for my single bike. The power meter immediately changed the way I trained. It showed that previously I had failed to hit my training intervals hard enough to generate the minor muscle breakdown that would stimulate supercompensation, and I hadn't taken it easy enough on recovery rides to fully recover.

I wasn't interested in becoming an expert at determining specifically what my workout should be on a particular day or period of my riding year. It was a relief to outsource that expertise to my coach. I could let her figure out how to arrange my training schedule based on scientific research. I just had to get on the bike and do the workout she prescribed.

Serious training meant riding inside during the New England winters. Riding on a trainer introduced me to the concept of suffering during painful workouts and the need to regulate my aversion to boredom. During the indoor-training season I slowly saw my ability to generate power rise. It was intoxicating. I began to dream about next summer's rides.

The following spring, at the end of our initial outdoor ride, Szifra exclaimed, "It's amazing. I can feel you're stronger. On some of those hills, I could feel you power us up." How could I not love this woman? But a tandem team is a two-cylinder engine. A past-his-prime captain needs the other cylinder firing alongside him.

Szifra values her health and fitness. In high school, she was a cheerleader and basketball player. As an adult, she played competitive racquetball. She was an early adapter to weight machines and yoga classes. And remember, she was the one who encouraged us to try a tandem. Despite her commitment to physical activity, fitness and health, she doesn't like to set formal goals, deliberate or permanent practice schedules, or to track data or incremental gains.

She tells a story about joining a gym in the early 70's. The owner/trainer gave her a chart to keep track of her workouts—weight used, reps, sets, etc. She told him she didn't want to track anything. He explained, "You have to write it down or you won't know what you did last time."

She laid out her ultimatum, "*You* can keep track if *you* want, but if you try to make *me* do it, I'll quit. I'm going to work hard, but I'm going to do as many as I feel like and then move on." He capitulated, and she continued at that gym for ten years. That's the same determination that caused her to push back against my suggestion she use a power meter, and it's also the tenacious attitude she can harness to push us up major hills.

I, on the other hand, am motivated by clear goals, performance numbers, personal bests and practice schedules. I thrive on incremental gains, an attitude that made executive coaching such a good profession for me. I'm good at motivating myself to both start and to persist at practice routines.

Szifra loves classes—she wants to show up and socialize while she sweats. I don't want to adjust my schedule or workout to be a part of a class or riding group. I like to keep my sessions personalized and simple. I hate it when trainers or coaches design workouts for me that put a premium on keeping me entertained. I detest trying to remember the sequences of a complex workout. Give me involved routines, and I'll resist or quit. A coach should change the intervals as often as necessary to maximize effect, but let me manage my mental game, my own boredom.

And boredom is another clear difference between Szifra and me. She seeks out new and different experiences. I'm comfortable repeating an activity to gain familiarity and expertise. When I'm motivated to improve, I can sit with boredom and eventually find or create value. She leaves boredom to its own devices and goes out looking for value somewhere else.

During the first summer after I'd started training with a coach, on one particularly long, steep hill I realized that Szifra was chatting to me

165

about some topic that caught her attention. I gasped for air, "If you can talk, you may not be working hard enough."

I could then feel her increase her effort. After a while she said, "I wasn't working as hard as I thought I was. I can't tell whether I'm pushing as hard as I should."

Once we had topped the hill and stopped to catch our breath, I told her again how helpful my power meter was and suggested we get one for her. She resisted with her normal explanation, "They're too expensive. I'm not going to train that much. I don't want the pressure to meet a number goal."

Not wanting to push against the river, I switched tactics and suggested she try one of my old heart rate straps. "It won't cost anything, and you don't have to report any numbers to me." She half-heartedly agreed to try it.

My heart straps have an elastic chest band with a small sensor unit that makes contact with your skin. They're quite simple. Put it on. Wet the contact strips to make a better connection with your skin. Pair it with a bike computer, and ride. Szifra couldn't get a heartbeat reading with my older strap. I tried it and it worked fine. We put it back on her, zero heart rate. She tried my new one, no reading. She tried gel designed to make a better connection, still inconsistent readings. After lots of fiddling we got it to read, most of the time. Rides became a frustrating series of stops to fool with her heart strap.

On her first ride wearing the strap, we hit a hill. She kept chatting. I broke my agreement and said, "What's your heart rate?"

She was quiet behind me. Then she reported, "It's about what it's been the whole ride. I thought I was working harder until I checked." Suddenly I could feel her pedal. We continued to climb a while longer, and she spoke up again. Only this time she sounded a bit out of breath. "I had no idea. I haven't been pushing myself all day. I had no idea. Seeing my heart rate is really helpful! Can you feel any difference?"

"Absolutely! We've got better speed. I can feel you working."

She quickly became an advocate of heart straps for other stokers. She pitched them as the way to step up their game. When she heard a captain say their stoker wasn't working hard enough, she took it on herself to help by proselytizing to the accused stoker. Despite her advocacy, our agreement was that I wasn't to encourage her to train or ride harder than she wanted to, and the data was not for organizing her training.

Eventually she got a heart strap that wrapped around her arm. It works consistently for her. Still, she resisted getting a power meter for indoor training: "The money; it isn't necessary; I don't want to have to hit certain goals." My power meter worked great on my single, but there wasn't one that fit our tandem. Or rather none that would individualize my power from our joint power. I wanted power data to train. It meant I couldn't ride the tandem on days I needed to do intervals. As I trained more there were fewer opportunities to ride together.

The Garmin company finally came out with a potential solution, power meter pedals. The downside to power pedals was that they required a specific road-shoe cleat. At that point, I had switched to mountain bike cleats on the tandem—considered safer by most tandem riders. I was comfortable with road cleats on my single, so I decided to use them on the tandem too, and I bought myself a pair of Garmin Vector power pedals for the tandem.

During the winter, I used my single bike with the crank-based power meter on my indoor trainer. That meant my tandem power pedals sat unused and were available to Szifra during the indoor season when she also trained on her single bike. I offered them to her. She continued to resist, "I like my bike sandals. Can I ride in my sandals?" I'd forgotten she didn't own a pair of shoes that would take road cleats. Off the bike Szifra will almost always be found wearing Birkenstocks; her "big" feet with narrow heels make regular shoe fit a challenge. My plan to have her ride with power dragged to another stop. Our bike shop friend reminded her she didn't have to walk in the shoes, and he suggested a pair that he found comfortable for his narrow heels. She reluctantly agreed to give them a try with the announcement, "If I don't like them, I can always sell them for most of what

I paid." Much to her surprise, she found they fit and were comfortable, although warmer in the summer than her beloved sandals.

During her second indoor ride with power pedals, I was eating lunch at the kitchen table while she worked out on her indoor trainer in the adjacent living room. I heard her stop pedaling, and when the trainer spun down to silence, she called out, "Thank you, Jay. You were right. They're really helpful. I love them."

I called back, "What about the shoes?"

"They're fine. They're comfortable enough. I would definitely ride with them." Szifra calls herself an "incremental adaptor" to certain changes. She stalls, but when she hits a tipping point, she's all in. I ordered her a pair of her own pedals for the tandem, and we became a power-training team.

Two months later, in deep winter, we flew the tandem to Tucson for three weeks of riding. Szifra never complained about walking in road shoes or the temperature of her confined toes in the warmish Arizona weather. It was satisfying to hear her enthusiasm as she shared her ride-to-ride power readings and her Normalized Power (NP) on tough hill climbs—NP approximately equals power averaged over every thirty seconds during a ride, and then added and averaged for the entire ride, with a few extra factor mixed into the equation.

In the effort to make a relationship work, it's tempting to look for absolute equality between both partners. But each person's strengths come into play at different times, and the balance of effort shifts with "pulls" from one person to the other—the out-front person faces most of the wind's resistance, "pulling" those drafting behind, giving them an easier ride. In a solid relationship, one person sees their partner flagging emotionally, puts their head down, and burns through a "match" of exertion. A match equals an extra push of effort, which if repeatedly spent without recovery will exhaust a person's reserves; even a fit rider has only a limited number of "matches" to burn. The partner who is floundering in emotions needs to draft their stronger partner, needs to recover their equilibrium, their ability to relate without merely reacting. To balance a relationship, these self-sacrificing exertions need to be reciprocal, coming in waves of patience, tolerance and willpower. The stronger partner invests their emotional and physical resources. Their exertion may be begrudging and self-righteous, or affectionate and sympathetic, but the investment is made until the other partner can collect themselves and get back in the game.

There's no power meter that can measure relationship effort. And like a tandem, it's hard to isolate one person's input from the team's total. It's easy for me to perceive my investment of energy as more than hers. Because I'm privy to all my feelings and internal tradeoffs, my exertion feels more persistent, disciplined, and I imagine I feel more discomfort than she appears to. Not surprisingly, due to her inability to see my internal efforts, Szifra also feels that she's working harder than me. She can also easily fail to recognize my work as equal to hers. We both know our feelings of not being unconditionally appreciated are suspect, but the feelings leave us expecting changes, apologies, and more reciprocal effort from our partner.

Most of our emotional snags, both on and off the bike, are about messages we mistakenly thought we heard the other person sending. Our knees jerked in reaction to assumed slights. Particularly at the beginning, tension always threatened to tangle us in extended clarifications and explanations. Quickly we'd feel a building sense of threat and frustration. There were a lot of ground rules we needed to establish. We hadn't yet found ways to de-escalate tension and re-establish our loving connection.

We both knew from experience that quality coupling takes patience and work. We'd both been through similar touchy, post-honeymoon periods in other relationships. I like to claim it takes at least a dozen relationships to sort things out, but I seem to be a bit slow. I've passed the dozen mark, and it still isn't easy. I kid my ninety-nine-year-old mother that her 65-year-long marriage, which lasted until my father's death at 92, lacked the variety of experiences needed to teach her how to create a healthy couple.

Szifra had also been through the exertion of multiple couplings. Her relationship with Him took work, negotiating differences, and getting the corners of his and her concerns rounded a bit. After their first dates, she returned to Indiana. They frequently traveled to see each other. Indiana and

169

Massachusetts are far enough apart to minimize irritating differences. Eventually he brought up the subject of joining households, and with the prospect of closer living came doubts for Szifra. Doubts fostered negotiations and the need for compromise. She was well aware that her friends had not warmed to him, to his confrontational conversations, his conservative fiscal views, or to his guns. Still, she liked who she saw.

When they began to figure out how she and the boys might relocate to Massachusetts and live with him, she and He had to negotiate the things he would need to change in his house. It was clear to Szifra that he would have to move some of his furniture out to accommodate some of hers and the boys'. His resistance to giving up physical possessions—similar to collections for him—was high. Although she persisted and brought it up numerous times, he struggled.

After we met, when Szifra decided to sell her—His—house and move in with me, she assumed we'd have the same negotiation. She was reluctant. She didn't want to go through that again. She wondered whether it might be easier to start fresh in a new house, so we looked together for one. After days of frustrating open houses, she began to reconsider my house. She obliquely suggested, "Your house is much smaller. I don't see how we can fit all my stuff in."

"That's not a problem," I said. "I'll empty my house, and you can move your stuff in."

She looked at me like I'd lost my mind. She stood there trying to figure out whether to take care of me by resisting, to negotiate, or to just accept the offer while it floated there. My attitude gave her so much room to maneuver that she chose to switch and became my advocate. "But you need to have your things too. It isn't fair to just have my things."

I explained, "You need to feel ownership of the house. I've lived here twenty-five years. I have a solid sense I belong here. We'll furnish the house with your stuff and hang your pictures to try to balance things a bit. In fact, why don't you choose new paint colors for the rooms."

Part of the reason Szifra is easy to live with is that she goes out of her way—too far out of her way at times—to be sure my needs are taken care of. That makes it satisfying for me to reciprocate and pull, to take care of her needs. When either of our energy wanes, the other often is ready to ride to the front and pull for a while.

Szifra had to fight to get Him to move a highboy bureau, which he wasn't using, out of their bedroom. I had to fight to get her to move the couch she and the boys liked into our living room. She began to say I was the easiest roommate she'd ever lived with. That may have been true in the sense of household considerations. But emotional negotiations with me still required more investment than she was used to.

At the beginning, we didn't share a sense of how to approach the work of negotiating emotional potholes. Each of us was frustrated that the other person didn't quite get what was important to us. And we felt that if it was important to us, the odds were great that it was the most important thing to deal with. Szifra was clear that she wasn't ready to commit to a long process of sorting out what was happening. Who can blame her! It seems like a new relationship should float over the rough patches on substantial tires and a compliant frame. One wouldn't expect the rigid geometry of habits to show up until our butts were tender from hitting multiple bumps and patches of rough pavement.

Early in our relationship, we were sitting in a coffee shop. It was a nice spring day, but we'd stumbled into a misunderstanding about tone of voice. We were quickly pulled into discussing the complexities of our assumptions and expectations. The content was the crucial focus for Szifra. The context, our style of dealing with disagreements, was mine. I suggested we needed to slow down and try to understand each other. Szifra threw a quick acceleration at me, "We fix this in twenty minutes or I'm out of here!"

I was stunned. I thought we had something solid going. When I'd collected my wits, I responded, "Are you kidding? We need to figure this stuff out. I don't want it to keep coming up. Twenty minutes? Is that a threat, a delusion, or a joke?" To her credit, Szifra didn't throw a real uppercut at me for my incredulous comment.

171

Her experience suggested that, given my impatience, more bumps were coming her way in our relationship, and she wasn't willing to risk saddle sores. The question she kept asking herself was essentially, "How far am I willing to ride with this guy and for how long, given that I don't know how steep a hill he is for me? Is his irritation an early hint that he's disrespectful or might be abusive?"

It was easy to look at Szifra with unsubstantiated optimism about her, and my, willingness to invest in the hard work and practice it would take to modify our significant habits. She assumed I would quickly adapt to her relaxed, avoid-discomfort style. We both assumed the other person would see the value of our way and work to make us comfortable—and we weirdly assumed that if they did things our way, they would see the value. But you can't train for endurance sports or enduring relationships without challenging yourself to the point of discomfort.

I struggled to expose my vulnerabilities to Szifra, and she felt exposed showing hers to me. The challenge we both felt, to manage the pain of perceived emotional wallops, was similar to endurance training—if we wanted to improve, we would need to tolerate discomfort and even suffering. Practice and a willingness to persist through hurt feelings were fundamental.

Szifra's threat to leave in 20 minutes didn't come to fruition. She never looked like she was actually ready to walk away; she pedaled into discomfort and kept pedaling. We struggled for forty-five minutes or more to resolve the tangle enough to take a break. We evaluated and talked about our communication process until we felt back in sync. It was an endurance exercise and the beginning of creating a dependable frame to hang our relationship components on.

Her threat to leave made me redouble my efforts to corral my frustration. And my persistence encouraged her to quiet her desire for immediate peace and look for better solutions. With less adrenaline there was less tension, less defensiveness, and more room for empathy.

Emotional tangles on the bike carry the risk of physical injury—from the road or another object, not from each other. To ride safely, you need to be fully aware of what's happening and have minimal tension. You need to be fluid enough to respond easily and smoothly. There's very little margin for distraction. A busy road, either in a car or on a bike, is one of the most dangerous places any of us regularly spends time.

Szifra and I are different in many ways, but safety on the bike is paramount for both of us. We work hard to decrease the odds of an accident. We try to be as visible as possible—we use front and rear lights for both day and night riding, and we wear shockingly bright clothing. We also work to be sure our maneuvers are predictable to others.

Disagreements on the bike create stress and physical tension. Riding with tension is like riding on a macadam road surface that has been ground down. The cuts create grooves and waves that can throw you. A few years ago, I rode a route I'd ridden before—near our lake home in New Hampshire. For the first time, I went around the sixteen-mile loop in the opposite direction so I could rip down a mile-long decline. In the first hundred feet past the crest of the hill, a squirrel ran across in front of me—squirrel bodies, alive or dead, can create a significant road hazard. I missed the dashing streak of fur by six inches, but I tensed, waiting for another surprise.

And the surprise came. I rolled past thirty-five miles per hour, and a quiver started in the bike. I tightened my grip to exert control over the tremble, and the bike started seriously wobbling. *What was wrong?* I felt desperate. My reading and mental prep kicked in. *Was it my tension? Relax!* I took a breath, and counterintuitively, eased my death grip on the handlebars, and the bike settled down. I wanted to be certain I'd figured it out. I stopped, dismounted, checked the wheel skewers, the tires, and the head bearing that the handlebars pivot on. Everything seemed tight, so I decided to experiment. I remounted, got back up to speed, and tensed up again. The bike rolled on smoothly for a few dozen feet, and then the quiver returned. I took a breath and relaxed my arms. The bike settled.

If we want to get home with all our skin and bones intact, there's no place on the bike for emotional stress. Besides the muscle tension, stress causes a physical narrowing of your field of view—you'll tend to see fewer variables occurring in your peripheral vision and your immediate environment. Emotional stress also lessens our ability to think creatively, which may mean in an emergency we'll consider fewer and/or weaker strategic and tactical options. It's just plain hard to see everything we need to see when our attention is turned toward an emotional threat.

Szifra was quick to appreciate this and found ways to contain her anxiety or irritation until we got off the bike. Her priority was crystal clear, she wanted my full attention on the myriad of things I'd told her I needed to pay attention to—cars, road obstacles, approach and exit lines at corners, intersection threats, pre-positioning our gears for imminent hills, etc. I also work to contain my negative reactions so we remain loose and flexible.

On a long, downhill run, coming off Mt. Lemmon in Arizona, Szifra was anxious about our speed and asked me to talk out loud about every decision I made as I managed the bike. I ran a stream-of-consciousness report on stones, twigs, rough pavement, wind, gear selection, lines into and out of corners, ground squirrels in the roadside grass, assessment of passing cars' likely actions, and my attempts at catching a quick view of her smile in my rearview mirror. I told her about slight noises I evaluated, reminding myself to relax my shoulders, alternately using the front and rear brakes so the pads and discs didn't overheat, keeping my legs slowly turning over so they didn't get stiff after the hard work of climbing. She said the details were valuable reminders and helped her understand my headset. "It's relaxing to know that you're paying close attention to things I probably wouldn't even know about. I'm afraid I zone out sometimes." She appreciates my ability to focus, but she kids me about being almost too good at it. With a smile in her tone, she added, "I guess being able to focus for long periods of time has some benefits." And then adds, "And yes, I am smiling."

After a moment's thought, I added, "I also have to keep talking to myself about how manageable our speed is on long downhill runs. We're safe, but I feel anxious and assume that means there's real danger. I keep telling myself, 'You're just anxious. Relax!'"

She shared, "That's comforting. It's easier for me if I know you're not feeling like taking any risks. Sometimes I close my eyes when we're going fast. I get nervous when you tuck into an aero position. I'm afraid we'll get going too fast. I really appreciate how many things you need to keep track of, and I appreciate that I get to ride the bike with you without having to pay attention to all that."

"You know you can sit up and slow us down? That would fight my aero position."

"Yeah, I do that sometimes. But usually I'm trying to quiet myself. I keep telling myself you must feel it's safe or you'd slow down. It helps to know you're not all that comfortable at high speeds."

Off the bike I also tend to report what's happening. Szifra likes that I pay attention to how I feel and that I can easily share my changing emotions. But she often finds it draining. "I get tired of all your processing. But it's helpful when I find out you're thinking something different than I assumed you were. When I hear an edge in your voice, I react like you're saying I did something wrong. It helps to know that isn't what you're feeling."

He'd also been open about some of his feelings, but when Szifra pushed back, he parked his needs. I persist, willing to upset our short-term equilibrium for potential long-term peace. Szifra wondered what He had been thinking. What he had not persisted in talking about. Had he just backed off, not said things clearly enough or with enough emotional punch to get her attention? Had his neutral tone failed them?

What makes my reports different than his, according to Szifra, is the ongoing, gnarly problem with my tone of voice. If I use a neutral tone, Szifra often minimizes how I'm feeling. If I use a tone commensurate with my feelings, she often maximizes and takes it more personally and intensely than I feel. Hills and emotions present similar challenges.

Research shows the effort it takes to climb a hill is partially a product of the way we perceive the hill as it appears before us. Does it menace us or present an attractive challenge—either prediction will color our physical experience. Szifra and I are challenged to not predict serious problems as we approach steep or long physical or emotional downhills. How we perceive them affects how easy it is to remain relaxed as our speed picks up.

Does Szifra's aversion to conflict, irritation and other negative feelings make our emotional hills feel steeper to her? Does my comfort feeling emotions reduce the emotional challenges for me? I try to make the emotional hills appear easier for Szifra. If I can see one coming, I say to myself, "Pay attention to how hard you're making her work. She's had less experience making this climb than you have. Lighten up!"

Chapter 24: Training for Endurance

Practicing an activity or attitude that stretches your abilities or capacity, and then taking time to recover, creates additional strength that will be available the next time you're challenged. Training on the bike builds endurance, physical strength and efficient technique. Relating is also an endurance undertaking. Practicing ways to quiet emotional upset and regain emotional equilibrium gives you the capacity to quiet yourself and re-engage.

During our early riding, I tried hard to quiet any dissatisfaction I felt about Szifra's physical training schedule and her progress developing her bike prep, nutrition and recovery strategies. I was able to park my concern that she wasn't systematically testing her riding kit, her bike fit, or methodically building the intensity of her on-the-bike efforts. It was crucial that I keep the boundary between my behavior and hers clear. She certainly didn't have to do things my way. She and I were different. And I loved her for that, and because of that. What drove me crazy was also the thing I loved—again, Relationship 101.

I pushed myself in training because I wanted to increase our capacity to ride both longer and more challenging rides. But that was my goal, not Szifra's. She said she wanted the same results, but she didn't want to set any specific intermediate goals. She evaluated her effort after each ride and then projected her ability to complete any future rides by the way she felt. Her strength and endurance were growing, so she was doing something right. And whenever she forgot a prep task, she laughed at herself. That damn laugh of hers always upset my focus on negatives. I couldn't stay irritated when she laughed.

As our time on the bike accumulated, I became better at sensing when her effort was lagging a bit, when it was synced with mine or when she was charging ahead of me. We each try to bring the skills we teach our executive coaching clients onto the bike—to acknowledge small improvements and positive moments, and downplay any negatives or failures. Only when we feel lots of emotional safety do we invite each other to offer critiques.

During rides, I could feel a notable differential when Szifra stopped pedaling. It would suddenly feel like I was pulling us through mud. Clearly she was adding to our power. I kept my negative impressions to myself, but when I felt her power us up, I announced, "I can really feel you pushing." I'm sure Szifra also swallowed most of her negative feedback about me. But she too spoke up when she saw or felt me do something she appreciated.

After a few rides with the tandem group, Szifra shared with me she wanted to arrive at the finish when the main group did. She wanted to be there for the entire after-ride social event. I also had ambitions for the rides—to cause less waiting and arrive less wasted. That would be quite a challenge for us. Some members of the group rode at average speeds between 18 and 21 mph compared to our 13 to 14. Szifra began to explore ways to compensate for our deficit.

My initial impetus to improve my average speed on rides came before my first hundred-mile event on my single bike—called a Century ride. I'd read that riders generally were grouped by those that rode at less than 15 mph, 15-17 mph, or 18 or more. My goal was to be faster than 15. To prepare, I read an old book on "base training"—lots of long, slow miles at the beginning of the season. I trained by riding a lot of miles. As the event approached, I rode a bit more intensely. During the Century, I averaged a disappointing 14.5. I was motivated to train more deliberately for the next one.

I read more articles and books, looking for modern training techniques. Coaches were talking about High Intensity Interval Training or HIIT—short bursts of intense effort that build endurance faster than base training. I incorporated HIIT into my rides. I improved some, saw a bit of a bump in my average speeds. But there was a lot to know about planning workouts, and without specific ride plans it was easy to ride less frequently and too casually. If I was going to reliably gain more fitness, it was time for an individual coach to plan my workouts.

Szifra watched my deliberate practice and incremental goal setting with a combination of appreciation and respect, but my approach didn't fit her style. Her training technique was more to keep all-around active with strength training, flexibility and balance work. She did attempt spin classes, but the saddles didn't work well for her. So, she primarily stayed with yoga, resistance training and aerobic classes.

Having a joint pursuit was new to Szifra. She and He had played racquetball, but usually not together and almost never as a team. He could easily get caught in cycles of poor eating and no regular exercise. He was overweight. With lots of junk food around the house, Szifra had worked hard just to maintain her weight.

During a fuel break on one of our rides, I asked her, "Can you imagine you and Him riding a tandem?"

She visibly flinched. "If He started something, it captured him, and he went all in. He would have bugged me about riding every free moment he had. I'd have wanted to cross train. He'd have just kept riding hard until he injured himself. I don't want to imagine it."

We each feel lucky that we've found a person who shares our concern about health as a priority. Living together has made it easier for each of us to eat healthy and keep our weight down. But I have to set specific weight goals for myself. If I don't, my efforts are irregular and less effective. And of course, Szifra does better pursuing a general eating approach rather than a goal. Both of us hide our favorite snacks—not from each other but from ourselves.

I hired a local bike coach and worked with her for a year. The next fall I switched coaches and increased my riding time to six to eight hours a week. Szifra commented on my increased power. I continued with that coach for a second year, increased my per-week ride time to eight to ten hours, and again made a perceptible leap in my ability to climb and maintain speed on flat sections. Szifra kept encouraging me. Slowly our average ride speeds on the tandem moved upwards.

After Szifra saw how my first year of indoor winter riding helped me, she decided to ride her single, hybrid bike on an indoor trainer once or twice a week during the next winter. And she did some lightly structured High Intensity Intervals. But like her early gym work, they were done when she felt like it and only for as long as she felt like. Her avoidance of specific training goals and sessions still kept her away from a tightly organized plan. On the other hand, she was persistent about attending group classes at her gym and generally stayed in good shape.

We each tried to nudge the other to expand the scope of their training. She encouraged me to try yoga. Yoga doesn't seem like fun when you're less flexible than a wooden chair and get hurt every time you do it. And solitary training on the bike doesn't seem like fun if you're a person who hungers for social contact. Our efforts failed to recruit each other. Apparently, there was no synchronizing our approaches to conditioning. Differences like whether to set goals or how far to push oneself into discomfort were significant roadblocks to coordination, even off the bike.

Szifra told me that early in their marriage He had told her he was a runner. I assumed that she meant he ran for exercise. But no, he meant he ran from tough feelings and emotional challenges. Szifra explained her approach: When she felt a tangle was imminent, she liked to "walk on down the beach" and avoid it. She had certainly picked a person of another breed when she chose me. I find that discomfort, well managed, is exhilarating. It's a gateway to improvement, whether the discomfort is physical, emotional, or cognitive.

I was an anxious kid who wanted to stay safe but made conscious choices to push into discomfort, to explore the boundaries of my self-control rather than recoil in fear. I survived, thrived, and came to see discomfort as a signal that beyond the warnings lay growth, satisfaction, and even fun. As I researched riding techniques and physical conditioning, I learned that brains are extremely sensitive to the potential danger of overdoing exercise. They tend to send an early warning long before there is any real physical danger. They send pain signals that our legs are going to seize up and that we need to stop. If we don't stop, they cause suffering in order to try to talk us out of continuing. It became exhilarating to work on developing my mental game, to better manage my brain's anxiety about pushing into discomfort.

Szifra prefers not to ride as close to the edge. She *is* willing to dip into discomfort—sweat is fine, heavy breathing is fine. She is more likely to push herself now, but she used to listen to her head when it screamed that she was overdoing it. She's less anxious than I am but is more respectful of the anxiety she does feel, particularly when she's concerned about injuries. She sees few reasons to poke her nose into areas that seem sure to cause her anxiety. This was another difference we had to negotiate on and off the tandem.

During the second or third year of our relationship, we were still spending more than twenty minutes in negotiations around communication tangles. In fact, we'd both become so convinced we were in the relationship for the long run that I could get away with kidding her about her twenty-minute rule. Her response was, "You have an uncommon and bizarre tendency to remember everything I say. You don't let things go."

I retorted, "I assume your statements hold unless you specifically withdraw them."

She countered, "You're weird! No one but you would pay that close attention."

And in there was a perennial question: Was it normal or unreasonable how we each handled our emotional road rash, our responses to the other person drafting instead of pulling, and our need to chase down the other's competitive breakaway (i.e., leaving the main group to try to win on your own)? We didn't feel our relationship was at risk, but we wanted an outside point of view on how we might grow less reactive.

We decided to find a relationship coach—a therapist. I characterized the possibilities as a fun chance to grow. Szifra looked at me with disbelief and said, "If you think therapy is fun, you are strange. Nobody who's normal thinks like that." Her derisive opinion struck me as humorous for a talk therapist.

Our effort to find a suitable therapist was an undertaking not unlike a hard training ride. Even though Szifra was less motivated to get counseling, I was less comfortable making cold calls. She did the major work of finding therapists for us to interview. Each time she identified a candidate, we rode into the meeting with profound affection for each other, but still significantly out of sync about how high a hill we were tackling.

The interview process was fun and frustrating. We followed up on referrals, tried out a few therapists, and found we tended to blow past our prospective collaborators on even small hills. We both agreed that we weren't willing to simply coast and let their assumptions dictate the route we'd take. We wanted therapy to be more like riding a triple, not like a tandem following a single. We knew we had a lot to learn, but we also knew we had a lot to add. The right therapist would recognize our individual weaknesses and encourage us to use our strengths. No cookie-cutter training programs please. We wanted a coach who would customize our workouts.

It was quickly obvious when a prospective therapist assumed I was a stereotypical male—a viewpoint that is neither true about me nor many other men. They assumed that since Szifra had made the phone calls, I was reluctant to come to the sessions. They didn't adjust to the fact that I viewed therapy as a hard but fun experience, that I expected to grow personally and as a couple. They didn't grasp that I was the primary one promoting therapy or that during my life I'd been in more therapy than Szifra. Nor did they grasp that, although Szifra-the-Therapist appreciated the process, Szifra-the-Wife was surprisingly less willing to spend her time processing emotional and relationship details than I was.

I also wasn't willing to sit through an hour listening to an introductory lecture from a half-baked listener about blame and responsibility. I would interrupt and say, "I think you'll find we absolutely understand that concept, even if we find it hard to implement." If they pushed back defensively, I would try with less subtlety, in an attempt to move them past their standard opening gambit. Szifra would jump in to clarify our understanding and acceptance of the basics. She would also explain that I wasn't who the therapist assumed I was. The first sessions rarely ended with the therapist sounding like they heard us.

One therapist fired us on the spot, "I don't think I can work with the two of you. I'm not sure you're ready to work." We laughed our way home—both aware that he may have known what he was doing, but if so, he hadn't helped us get synced with him.

Eventually we were referred to an experienced guy who didn't posture as an expert. He shared his impressions rather than pontificating. Over time he rode the rougher sections of our road with us, and occasionally fell and bruised his ego. On those occasions Szifra claimed I bumped him hard enough to knock him off. He said he'd leaned too far into his opinion. His willingness to risk road rash, and not get competitive, modeled how we might reflect rather than react when we stumbled.

Month after month we used our sessions to do cognitive and emotional High Intensity Intervals. We developed endurance—the capacity to tolerate stress and keep pushing. And we developed strength—the ability to tolerate additional discomfort as we climbed the steeper issues. The emotional conditioning also improved our abilities to solve problems on the bike and set an example of how we needed to respect each other's physical training techniques.

Chapter 25: Hills and Miles

Our new tandem was what we had hoped it would be. We could ride longer, harder rides with more climbing. We signed up for our first Eastern Tandem Rally (ETR) in Vermont that year—there are rallies in different regions of the country, each bringing together hundreds of tandem teams. We knew we needed to train for the Vermont mountains and for back-to-back days on the bike. It was during one of those training rides that Szifra tried riding with a heart strap. Once she realized she was riding more casually than she'd thought, she began to experiment and discovered she was able to handle more intensity for longer periods than she'd realized she could. She told me she'd been way too cautious about wearing herself out. I still have to fight that tendency.

The next few rides blew apart any hesitancy she still had to try longer rides with steeper climbs. We rode 35 miles with our local tandem group, where we tackled the most climbing we ever had in that distance, a little over 2,000 feet. Later, on a ride near our vacation home, we decided to try a quarter-mile long local hill that was incredibly steep compared to previous hills we'd climbed. We started at the four-way stop, and the "Grade" readings on our bike computers immediately began clicking up from 5% to 6 and then 7%. As we passed the spot where the trees give way to a sloped pasture and where the stone wall had been rebuilt, the grade increased to over 8%. Concurrently our speed dropped to 4.5 mph. But the grade wasn't resting on its laurels. Within another hundred feet our readings passed 10%, and our speed settled at 3.5 mph. Neither of us was talking.

At the midpoint on the hill I began to lose my focus, turning from a just-turn-the-pedal head set, to a gasp-to-gasp desperation. The distance left to climb grabbed my hope and throttled it. I began to fall into a death spiral of worry about my leg strength and wondered, if we faltered, would I be able to get my foot out of the pedal clip and planted on the inclined road surface. Would I be able to gasp to Szifra that I was done and needed her help to keep us upright when we stopped? With effort, I kicked the thoughts out of my head and focused on how I had climbed lots of tough hills, "Don't let this one kick your butt! Keep pedaling!"

And we kept climbing at a tolerable pace. We passed the point about three-quarters of the way up where an old farmhouse had once stood overlooking our hill and the pasture and forests that dropped back to the lake. All that remained was the foundation, a square of large granite blocks, half buried in the grass. Slowly, at that point, we both felt we had a good chance of making it to the crest. Then the hill slapped us in the face with an 11% grade. With each twenty feet it continued to climb, 12, 12.5, and then 13%. But the end was in sight. Breathlessly I gasped to Szifra, "We're making this!" And we did roll out at the top with enough strength left to keep going for a block before we stopped, stood, and sagged over the bike. I rested my arms on the handlebars and dropped my face onto them. Szifra spoke first through her restoring deep breaths, "We did it! We're awesome! Nice work Livingston!"—Szifra's endearment for me is to call me by my last name.

"Nice work Birke!"—Szifra is tickled that her last name is one letter off "bike".

We remounted and had a great ride down the winding road on the other side and then continued a dozen miles later onto a mile-long section of ride that threw extensive 9 and 10% inclines at us. Our bike could climb. Szifra realized she could climb. I was getting stronger. Our conviction that we could handle most challenges soared.

We were ready to tackle almost any road or hill. Although we still look very respectfully at inclines of more than 13% and avoid 20% grades both up and down. A 20% downhill grade makes me feel like I might slip over the handlebars, like I won't get any traction if I put my foot down. Szifra just looks at them from the car and says, "No way!"

We aren't ready for grand tours—multiday races with stages of one to two hundred miles per day. But if the total distance is sixty-two miles or

185

less, we're game for more than we ever originally imagined. And on some forty-mile rides, we can even get into that fifteen-mile-per-hour range that eluded me on my first century ride.

We went to the Vermont rally full of self-assurance. But when we looked at the planned rides, we hesitated. On one day, all the options were long rides. When combined with the mileage, the climbs seemed too demanding for us. We decided to choose a route that was shorter and less hilly.

All that day's routes started together and joined again near the midpoint for lunch at a tourist farm. Shortly after the start we hit a road-construction detour. A rally organizer stood at the side of the road and waved everyone to the left. We followed the pack. That was the last we saw of the moderate route we'd planned. We suspected we were off our route a few miles in but had no idea how to find it. After almost an hour of following distant bikes over gently rolling hills, the road we were on came to a T intersection. A tandem ahead of us had turned to the right. We stopped. Going to the right immediately put us at the foot of a big hill. We now figured out where we were. We'd been waved onto one of the routes we'd thought was too challenging for us.

As we stood there, two other tandems rolled up beside us. The middle-aged captain on one of the bikes exclaimed with dismay, "I think this is the route with the big hills."

Some things are too obvious to comment on. But not commenting was too unfriendly. I settled for "Yup. Looks like it."

We paused to fuel up. I ate another fig bar while Szifra chewed on whatever snack she'd decided to try that day. We both took a long pull on one of our two water bottles—both to hydrate our bodies and to lighten the weight we'd have to carry up the hill. The other two tandems pushed off and I asked Szifra, "Ready?"

She replied, "Just a second." And after a few seconds, "Getting on." Then, "Ready."

I said, "Go" as I pushed against my footed pedal, paused to clip the other one in we were off toward the hill. One by one the other bikes slowed, wobbled, and stopped to recover. We put our heads down and kept methodically turning the pedals. We weren't fast, but we kept moving. The time we'd invested in training to climb began to pay dividends. What looked overwhelming in its aggregate wasn't as steep as the hill near our house. It was long, but doable one pedal stroke at a time. We not only made that hill, we also rode another and the one after that.

Lunch at the tourist farm was a buffet of salads, fruit, and grilled meat. Among the hamburgers and hot dogs I found a covered serving dish full of veggie burgers. All was good. Satiated, we remounted and rode a few miles to a village green where a volunteer team was handing out ice-cream sandwiches from a cooler. They melted deliciously in our mouths.

After a bit of further socializing to allow all the food to settle, we set out for the last section of the ride. A few miles in, we hit a pitch that was almost as steep as our hill at home but shorter. I shifted into our low gear. We leaned into our pedals. Szifra didn't miss a beat; we were both willing to push into discomfort. Perhaps best of all, we realized we weren't the day's lantern rouge—the last place rider of the Tour de France.

Time in the saddle was also a limiting factor for Szifra. On rides longer than three hours she would cringe. Saddles and butts are only tolerable acquaintances. Saddles and other "lady-part" contact points are even less friendly. Padded shorts and chamois cream help, but don't make the saddle into a cushioned chair, and cushy saddles can make the issues worse.

Szifra spent a couple of years looking for a solution to the irritation and pain her saddle caused. She tried different saddles, slathered chamois cream on every thirty minutes, and interviewed gynecologists, PTs and NPs. She questioned other woman riders. No solution appeared.

There were ice packs, weeks off the bike, and we missed the next year's ETR in Gettysburg, PA. We read articles and Molly Hurford's book, *Saddle Sore,* on the subject. Slowly we began to face the possibility we might have to give up tandem riding. And then she found a pair of shorts that helped, and at the suggestion of a woman GYN NP cyclist, she added Vaseline to her prep process. I tweaked her saddle position again and something, or all of it combined, finally gave her consistent relief. (Szifra isn't alone in dealing with the issue. Literature suggests that more than 75% of pro women bike racers are significantly affected, including a frighteningly large percentage who eventually need surgery for the results of abrasion.)

Before she found a solution, rides that called for long hours in the saddle were a cause for major concern. Early on we'd taken the tandem for a Half Century on a remarkably flat course, and she'd done fine. So, pure miles were less intimidating than slow miles, or miles with lots of climbing. Szifra began assessing long rides by time and elevation.

Once she'd figured out a regime that worked successfully, she was game to increase the length of our rides, and to once again take on significant elevation gains. We signed up to do a Metric Century—one hundred kilometers or sixty-two miles. She noted the elevation we'd have to climb, and we created a pre-event training of about the same length, but with a few hundred feet of additional climbing.

Potentially challenging rides that end up manageable are boring to report. Our training was effective, and the Metric was a grand success. We rode hard with complete confidence that we could finish. Without focusing on speed, we ended up riding our fastest ever for a ride of more than three hours. We took a bit over three and a half hours, clocked 16.5 mph, and attacked the last half hour as if we were just getting started. We thought that wasn't too shabby for a couple in their mid-to-late sixties.

There was one more barrier to eliminate before we could stop worrying and ride any events or trips we wanted. We needed to ride more than two hours a day for multiple days. In Vermont, we'd alternated long rides with short ones. Two years later the Eastern Tandem Rally was in Geneva, New York. It was the place to check off long, multiday rides. And indeed, in four days we rode our butts off without actually riding our butts off.

The next year we checked off two other challenges we'd previously resisted, longer steep climbs and really long climbs. We checked off the former when we rode with our tandem group to the top of a ski mountain. A few years previously I'd had to get off my single and walk a section of the steep slog. The really long climb we notched when we followed a ride listed on an online site called Ride with GPS. It had been posted by an unknown cyclist, and we could start it a mile from our lake house. Midway, at an intersection with a major highway, we paused, waiting for a break in the Saturday traffic, then zipped across through a brief gap and continued around a sweeping curve on the tree-lined sideroad. We passed a few modern houses tucked into large plots of mown grass and a 1900's farmhouse with a barn in serious disrepair. At the end of the curve, a steady hill rose up in front of us. We didn't know it yet, but we'd unintentionally gotten onto the longest hill we'd tackled so far, a three-mile, 5% plus climb. The Vermont hills hadn't been the event, but the training ground.

The pavement lifted unexpectedly through a delightful forest of dappled sunlight and cool shadows. Mature birches leaned out of the shadows of large pines. A red squirrel screamed at our audacity in invading the afternoon's stillness. Around the first corner the road lifted even more. Over the next crest it lifted again for as far as we could see. And as we topped the next and the next crest and rounded each corner, the rises kept coming and coming. After a mile we began to giggle incredulously, between gasps for breath. "Where did this come from?" "Will this ever end?" "Can you believe we're doing this?" And finally, Szifra invoked pro-biker Jens Voight's command, "Shut up legs!"

As farmhouses and stonewalls crept by at barely walking speed, we glowed with how far into tiredness we had pushed. The lift eased a bit as we approached a bend to the left, whose resolution was hidden by a grove of young birch trees. We slid around the corner and the road threw a steep little rise at us. I spurted out, "Stop or go?"

Szifra just gasped "Go!" and on we went.

When the top finally came, the grade flattened until the slight upgrade fooled our eyes into thinking the road was flat—bike jargon calls this a false flat. We still didn't believe we were liberated until the road began to gently slope down after a few hundred more yards. And even then, as we rolled across the flatter sections, we warily waited for one more surprise. But we'd made it and were about to earn the treat that most hills offer, the ride down.

At the four-way stop that stood alone at the corner of four pastures, our route turned to the right and dropped abruptly, straight back down. Somewhere in the tree-covered valley, the road ended back at the busy highway we'd previously crossed. We pushed off and glided on tubular air. The breeze of the descent blew through our sweat soaked jerseys and chilled us. When we got to the bottom, we discovered one more surprise. We were on the road beside our favorite ice-cream stand, where the kiddie dishes are so big that by the time you finish, you're spooning for the dregs of melted flavors, and the cones need to be attacked with focus or you end up with a cream-covered hand.

We waited off to the side of the line for our order, quietly babbling celebratory appreciations about our accomplishment. When my dish and Szifra's cone came, we returned to the bike, which was carefully leaned against the side of the clapboard building. There in the parking lot, as our arms and hands tried to eat faster than melt speed, our brains began to freeze, and our tongues turned numb and ineffective. We let the ice cream and silence take over and leaned into each other's shoulders. My love for this woman beats ice cream on a hot day anytime.

The bike, our chauffeur to togetherness, has reached through our desire for independence and coordinated our lives. We'd come miles from Szifra's no-hills rule, miles from our single lives, and miles from His shadow. We were an unbreakable team.

We were getting comfortable riding hills, but the mountains began to call my name. Two years ago we decided to extend our cycling season by riding in Tucson for two weeks during the winter. We packaged our tandem in a long, cardboard box, shipped it by FedEx to Arizona, reassembled it, and rode for two weeks while New England hibernated under a cascade of snowstorms. Tucson is one of the most bike friendly cities in the US—wide bike lanes everywhere, a hundred miles of dedicated bike paths, and flat rides along dry river banks. One of the major draws for me was the pro-training rated climb of 9,157-foot Mt. Lemmon.

That first winter we went at the climb of Mt. Lemmon as an exploration of how realistic it was to think we could climb a real mountain. Pedal stroke by pedal stroke, we climbed eight miles of the twenty-two-mile, 5-8%-grade, two-lane road. We rode until we got tired and then stopped at an overlook to enjoy the views of Tucson on the desert floor below, set between mountain ranges to the East, North and South. Looking down at the valley we'd climbed out of, the saguaro cacti looked like birthday candles stuck on every surface of the hills and flats. The green-armed giants stood wherever there was a bit of space along highways and streets, in open stretches between subdivisions of single-story homes, tucked between houses and up mountainsides toward us, until they were repelled by the potential of freezing nights and snow.

We stood in a cool breeze drinking water and eating fuel bars while Tucson baked in 85 degrees. When we were satiated with cacti and views, we turned and coasted back down the swooping hairpin turns. Single cyclists who had pedaled passed us on the way up were overtaken and passed on the way down. It's intoxicating to be able to drop into conversations that you've ridden eight miles up a mountain, and I found lots of places to drop that fact. But around Tucson, it only brought encouragements that we needed to "ride to Windy Point overlook. That's where most cyclists turn around. That's the end of the steepest part." Windy Point is fourteen miles, six miles beyond where we'd stopped.

We enjoyed Tucson so much we decided to return for four weeks the following winter. I set my sights on tackling the fourteen miles up to Windy Point. Fourteen miles goes on for hours at our climbing pace of four to eight miles-per-hour. But the first eight miles had proved we could climb for more than an hour.

The first week back in Arizona was rainy and cold. But by the third week we were getting back into riding shape and one morning we set out to take a crack at Windy Point. The climb never relents. The panoramas never quit. And my partner never faltered. We spun at eighty revolutions. We spun at seventy. We occasionally ground along at sixty, but we kept spinning. We stopped a few times at beautiful turnoffs, caught our breath and ate energy bars and gels without fear that a deep breath might inhale a crumb of fig cake or a rivulet of honey. We took long swigs out of our water bottles, celebrating each time that our load was lightening. We climbed past campgrounds, past rock outcrops, past dead squirrels and broken glass. When we passed two cyclists stopped beside the road, we asked if they needed anything and slogged on when the answer was "Thanks! No." And then they returned the favor when we stopped and they passed us.

At just over 7,000 feet, as the road wound back toward the Tucson-side of the mountain, a sign announced Windy Point was coming up on the left. We were relieved but not desperate. The overlook faced the valley to our South. Across from the pullout a small pile of snow leaked a stream of melt water into the crushed gravel shoulder. 5,000 feet below, Tucson and thousands of saguaro cacti shimmered in the heat currents that rose off the desert floor. We stood over the bike and drank our fill, knowing that we'd need very little water for the trip back down. A retired gentleman from a small RV agreed to take our picture with the little pile of snow in the far background. Just before we left, a young woman from a car with a Wisconsin license plate took Szifra's phone and framed us against the valley and the surrounding mountains.

As I've said, the downhills push our anxiety buttons. Neither of us gets any thrill from pushing our luck, from depending on three-quarter inch wide rubber tires to resist the centrifugal force generated by three hundred pounds of people and bike. Neither of us is willing to risk major injury or road rash for a quick descent. Age, with its slower recovery and less resilient fitness, has pushed safety into the foreground.

The trip down was even more tense and slow than we imagined. The disk brakes on our bike hadn't been centered since reassembly after shipping. They screamed, smoked and chattered. Only creeping along at less than ten miles per hour quieted their and our anxiety. The refreshing breeze, generated by our motion, cut through my wet jersey, and quickly threatened hypothermia. Even at our glacial pace, and with a windbreaker covering my jersey, I had to regularly stop in the protective shelter of rock outcroppings to rewarm my quivering core. Szifra worried. I shook. My teeth chattered. Szifra tried to rub heat into my back and arms.

Anxiety, cold, aching hands from holding constant brake pressure and a relentless scream from the bike swallowed the joy of our accomplishment. Our delight didn't return for over an hour, until we'd rewarmed in the comfort of Tucson's bosom.

Chapter 26: Death Is a Part of Life

Death is a regular topic in our house. Some conversations He motivates, some are kindled by lost friends, parents, or pets. One of the questions I struggle with, and that I randomly throw into quiet places, is why we don't have a more natural way to deal with death—to accept that it is coming into our lives again and again.

Part of my responsibility as a dog behaviorist was to help owners validate their profound sense of loss when their dog died. It's common that well-meaning, non-dog-loving friends say careless things like, "It's a dog. You can get another one." Some research suggests that the loss of a pet arouses more grief than the loss of a spouse. I don't know about more, but I have certainly seen equal amounts. Dogs aren't judgmental, are always ready to forgive, engage life with a beguiling innocence, and like us unconditionally. That's a few more credits than any spouse I've met.

Death is often unpredictable, and surprises are disruptive. But death is also inevitable. Why doesn't that inevitability temper the surprise and grief more? Why is death so hard to manage? The concurrent question that I grapple with: Do multiple deaths over the years prepare us better for future deaths, including our own, or do all the deaths make us raw with trauma and less able to cope, so we go numb?

My mother has lived well into her hundredth year. To make life easier, she said she thought it was time to move into what I labeled a "concierge living" arrangement—her retirement community calls it assisted living. And now, four years later, as the tasks of daily living became overwhelming, she has moved into the health unit of her complex. Visit after visit and call after call, she reports on her friends and other residents who have died. She expects these deaths and is sad for them and their families, but she's not overwhelmed with sadness. Her experience suggests that for her, death is becoming a normal part of life.

I often think about a Buddhist story I read as a twenty-year-old. A guru's young son died. The guru remained cheerful and his devotees asked why. He responded, "I was happy before he came. Why shouldn't I be happy now?" Szifra lived a long time before He came into her life, why shouldn't she enjoy remembering their good times without sadness? That's a tough hurdle to clear. But what purpose does grief serve? Lots of questions. No easy answers.

When it was clear Szifra and I were getting beyond merely serious and into life-partner territory, she announced in no uncertain terms, "You are not to die before I do!"

My family is pretty long-lived. My prairie-living, paternal, great-grandfather lived to ninety-three. My prairie-born, paternal grandmother and grandfather both died at ninety-three. My father lived to ninety-three. Ninety-three seemed like a safe bet as my mother had reached ninety-six and outlived her birth family's average of eighty-something. A great-uncle on her side lived to a hundred and two.

With that background, I was comfortable promising, "I won't die before you." In retrospect I suppose my promise took away a responsibility that was rightly hers. The death of important others and the attendant grief is each of our liability to manage. It's the toll we pay for the joy of loving someone.

When I'm riding either the tandem, or my single, I do find myself thinking about my promise to her. My risk tolerance has never been very high, but since the promise I've reduced it a bit more. But sometimes the level of risk isn't clear until it hits you—or almost hits you.

One summer Szifra's thirty-year-old younger son, my niece's husband, and I went backpacking in California. We took the mountaineers' route up Mt. Whitney in the Sierras. The five-day hike was demanding in the low oxygen at 14,000 plus feet.

The penultimate morning, as the sun rose, we slogged up a melting-snow field to the hundred-foot-high, rocky chute that leads to the summit. The chute is a daunting sight of large rocks and scree. With some trepidation we continued, carefully scrambling up, over, and around huge boulders. We slowly worked our way up, being sure with each step that we didn't knock any rubble down on anyone entering the chute below us. Small stones traveling at the speed of gravity can injure, even through the plastic climbing helmets we donned for this section. And beyond loosening stones, each step carried a slight risk of slipping into a free fall. When I'd researched this climb before we'd come, I'd read about the death of a climber a few years back in this very chute. He'd slid on snow and ice, which was now mostly melted in the summer heat, lost control, and tumbled head over heels down the chute, slamming into boulders. The momentum catapulted his body right over the cliff at the chute's terminus. The risk to us was small, but tension dominated our heads and actions.

At the summit, we climbed over a rocky lip to join dozens of backpackers who had ascended during the morning by the easier mule trail. For an hour we walked around the flat summit, enjoying the spectacular views of the valleys and mountains of Central California. When we were ready to descend, we returned to the chute. Looking down, the steep route we'd taken up wasn't visible beneath the rocky lip. The first step would be into emptiness. I took a deep breath, shifted my load of panic, and said I'd go over first.

My rock-wall-climbing stepson anchored himself on an embedded boulder and I tied our climbing rope around my chest. He belayed me as I squirmed backward, over the edge into the apparent void. Although they were initially out of sight, there were plenty of foot and hand holds. The rope functioned as more of a security blanket than a necessity. The three of us worked our way deliberately down and around the boulders. Above us another party entered the chute just where we had. Finally, we got to the last shelf, a hundred feet or more below the initial lip. My stepson found a position above us and off to the side to once again act as a safety belay for the last eight-foot drop. As we prepped the rope, a loud voice rang out from above, "Rock!" Immediately it was followed by a second, louder, more insistent scream, "Big rock!"

I looked up. Directly above me a boulder as big as a small car was bounding down the almost vertical rock field. It hit something, bounced clear of the rocky jumble, and dropped right toward my nephew and me. I body-slammed myself and him down and against a three-foot-high ledge a single step up from our position. I hunkered down into that broken-rock corner, tucked my chin tight against my chest, and leaned into the mountain's bosom. In the second or two that elapsed, there was plenty of time to think about my stepson, sudden death, and my promise to Szifra. Somewhere in those seconds, the world went deadly silent—the multi-ton rock had hit so close that the blast temporarily deafened me faster than the sound could register. In silence, I watched behind me as the mammoth rock bounced high and flew off the end of the chute, off the edge of the mountain thirty feet away, off the edge of my world, following the path of that ill-fated climber.

Sound returned slowly. The rattle of smaller debris rained around me. I yelled to my stepson who had been perched thirty feet away, out of sight. "Are you all right?" He didn't respond and my promise to Szifra to not die flooded me. I knew she would have instantly revoked her wish for my survival if it assured his. Failure washed over me. And then his voice rang out, "I'm ok!" He froze when the rock hit right where we were, so close to us that it crushed and melted our nylon rope three feet from where we hunkered. I had felt the monster give a glancing brush to the soft fabric of my backpack, which stuck a few inches above the ledge.

We exited the chute aware of how close death had been. On our way back down the snow field everyone we passed was talking about the accident in the chute. Word had catapulted down ahead of us. "Did you hear about the rock slide? A huge rock was kicked loose by some climbers and it almost hit some people in the chute."

"Yes, we heard. We were the ones under it." Would the news be broadcast nationwide? Would Szifra hear about it before she heard from us?

Was not dying enough or did my promise include not almost dying? Not almost getting her son killed?

That rock comes back at me in all sorts of situations. In the wilderness, the timing of its fall is thought of as happening in geologic time. Mountains fall down over eons, but parts have to fall regularly or the mountain would just sit there. Geologic time is made up of thousands of beautiful, event-free days, interspersed with a few that have "Big Rocks!" We were unlucky enough to be there that day rather than during the thousand years it had rested safely in its assigned place. We were lucky enough to be there the day its neighbor stayed put rather than also fell, but perhaps on our head. The rock came from above and was as big as a car. Cars come from ahead or the side, and are as big as that rock, but they don't wait thousands of years between close calls.

One day I asked Szifra the question that still occasionally accompanied thoughts of Him or arose when Szifra was irritated with me. "If He came back to life, who would you choose?" I think that death is permanent, but I guess I fear that her exclusive love for him is too, that perhaps love's intensity is determined by the sequence of its occurrence. I know that my experiences of love have deepened with each occurrence, that I love Szifra more after twenty years than I loved my other wives on the day I married them. Maybe my insecurity about her love for me is a product of the intensity of my love for her.

If the realization that death stands beside life, waiting for its turn, intensifies the experience of love, then I'm glad death isn't yet comfortable. Perhaps that's one more gift He left for me. But did Szifra also get that gift? When I ask, she says she did.

Chapter 27: Screaming Yellow

I take a quick glance back in my helmet mirror. A white pickup or SUV, the little images tend to look the same, has pulled onto the street about a block behind us. I check the street ahead. About three hundred feet up, a black pickup is parked at the point where the street slopes down. The pickup is at the right curb with its left-side mirror sticking out into our lane. I look hard but can't see anyone in the driver's seat. I come out a bit and leave some space to avoid a sudden door opening in my face—"dooring" is a major risk of riding on city streets; people open them without looking back for bikes.

We've had a great ride. We left the house at 8:00, over two and a half hours ago. The morning has been warm, very pleasant for a late-September. We rode two hours yesterday and now, over two today. Other than tandem events, we don't usually ride consecutive days. We pushed hard both days— not backing down on hills, pedaling assertively even on flat sections. Not much let up the entire ride, until now. What a way to spend a Fall Sunday morning. A block back we made the left turn onto this street and eased up. It's time to gently spin our legs and begin the cool-down process as we close in on home.

Since we're not pushing anymore, we have spare breath to talk. From behind my back, Szifra proudly speaks up, "That was great! I kept pushing long after my legs were telling me to stop. That's two days in a row I've pushed hard. I feel great!"

I had the same experience. Two days of hard riding. Lots of hills. I'm impressed at how much harder I can push and for how long, compared to a few years ago. After a ride like this, I feel confident I can give even more on future rides. Once you've pushed into the realm of "Shut up legs" there's less temptation to hold back, to save anything. I'm getting better at knowing how much I have in the tank. Szifra is also exploring her limits at the same time, which makes it even better.

"Me too! That was fun," I say into our intercom system. Szifra rests her hand on my back. I never get tired of the serenity and love that gesture sends and elicits.

I lean imperceptibly, and we're out around the black pickup and onto the downslope. This street is a wide, empty suburban boulevard at this time on a Sunday. Another quick mirror check. The white vehicle is still back quite a ways, not closing on us. Maybe it's waiting to turn somewhere soon. The road dives under the freeway and I note the slight chill as we pass through the shade it casts. I move us just a tad back toward the wide, paved shoulder. The road remains empty, except for that white SUV. Or is it a pickup? Still quite a way back.

We're gliding at 25 mph. No need to pedal, just glide and enjoy. I keep my legs turning over at a languid pace, not pushing, just keeping them limber, and helping to flush out the residue of all the work. Everything feels right. My lightweight, screaming-yellow jersey was a good choice for today's temperature. It's wet from sweat and the breeze generated by our downhill plunge feels cool and nice. I touch the brakes to keep us under 25 mph.

Screaming yellow isn't a sophisticated fashion statement like black, or as interesting as a multicolored jersey, but it's visible. In the car and on the bike, Szifra and I both tend to comment on the obliviousness of riders in subdued colors. They seem to have no idea that black, dark reds, and even mild yellows and greens can blend into the background. At event rides, in a sea of jerseys, the screaming yellow, neon green and orange ones jump out like bright lights floating in a non-descript sea of muted colors.

Visibility on the bike has always been a priority for me. It's part of that promise to Szifra that I'll do everything I can to be certain I don't die before her. Not dying is another way to differentiate myself from Him. A few years ago, when I first started century rides, I noticed I was one of only a few bikers who wore neon yellow and had both my front and rear blinking lights on during daylight hours.

My bike-riding friends make derisive comments about my helmet mirror, "What are you going to do by seeing a car back? A mirror doesn't make you safer." About my jerseys, "You look like a neon sign." And about my lights, "You have to remember to charge them. What good do they do during the daylight?" I offer my rationale into the wave of negativism, "I keep the lights on in my car. Statistics show it increases safety. Has to help on the bike."

One day a driver slowed as he drove by us and said, "Boy, you guys are visible!" And a truck driver honked at me at a rural intersection and shouted, "Those lights are great! I could see you a half-mile away." Our tandem group also appreciates, sort of, my bright orange socks. On big event rides we get lots of comments about our matching stunning-orange helmets and my orange socks—we're willing to risk dweebness for safety. And at events, I can always tell where Szifra is because her neon-orange helmet is an I'm-here signal.

This morning I feel wrapped in a protective cocoon of us. We're working in sync, we're a presence in the quiet world, we're sixty-some-year-olds who have just done two and a half hours of moderate to high-intensity exercise. We're inoculating ourselves against brain and heart failure. What a way to start a morning.

Ahead on the right, a compact, light-grey car on a small side street pulls up to the intersection. Visibility also means placing yourself on the road where you'll be most obvious. A quick mirror check, the white SUV is still way back, still not closing. I have plenty of room to maneuver. I slip toward the center of our lane, out where we'll be most visible to the car, out where they'll be looking for oncoming traffic. Still, I ride the brakes just a bit harder. I want to bleed off some of our speed and more importantly to shorten my reaction time, just in case the car doesn't stop.

When I used to train dogs, I'd tell owners that cars were predators and the owner had to teach their dog to avoid them. A dog isn't safe unless it automatically stops at curbs and never crosses without permission. I carried that attitude onto my bikes. Cars are predators and I want to protect my stoker and me. And I want to be certain I can fulfill my promise to her.

I watch the car. It stops and stays completely stopped. We're a gazelle and the predator apparently isn't hungry today. It isn't crouched and stalking us.

There's a certain confidence we feel with our blinking-white, front light. When we first got it, we tested it by walking up the block, looked back at the bike we'd left resting against a tree and saw how bright the light was. It jumped out from all other activity on the street. We also tested our back light. When we're on a busy street, I know cars approaching us from the rear can see the bright, red-blinking light a long way away. A few months ago, Szifra and I went a step further, we put an additional blinking, red light on her helmet. We figured a second one, up higher, might be seen through a following car's windshield. And of course, even if they miss the lights, it's impossible to miss the screaming-yellow jerseys or the neon orange helmets—or our orange bike. We continually congratulate ourselves on this when we notice the visibility of other riders' kit and lights, which like ours are eye-catching. Szifra always wants to stop and tell riders with black jerseys and weak taillights that they're almost invisible.

Relationships are also vulnerable to predators. When we first got together we talked about the danger of being sexually attracted to someone outside the relationship. Even there we don't ignore possibilities. Each of us could catch sight of clear examples of dangerous liaisons in our rearview mirrors. Each had unbidden lust tear apart a past relationship. We both knew it was important to flash a visible warning, to alert our partner, to actively work at repairing whatever relationship weakness may have contributed to the threat of stray longing. We never considered waving a screaming-yellow flag, or wearing a white-blinky light, but we'd agreed a verbal equivalent was important. That said, neither of us has had to evoke the warning agreement. We've apparently each found a partner who generates enough of a fire in us to keep us focused inward. No stray sparks here. Age also has a way of easing temptations, age and overall satisfaction.

**

A beautiful September Sunday morning, an almost empty street, the satisfaction of a ride well done, the glow of her hand still on my back. I glance at my speed, still 25. I look up and something is dramatically wrong. It takes a fraction of a second to process it. The stopped car is pulling out right in front of us.

There are some things that, if you haven't practiced them in your head a hundred times, you won't do them when there isn't time to think. A hundred intersections, a hundred thoughts about what our bailout positions are, a hundred times telling myself to never take it head on or to allow a direct T-bone from the side.

I remember Szifra yelling something over top of my shouted "Hey!" I remember pulling as hard as I dared to the right. Rather those hundred iterations pulled the bike to the right before I could think about it. Hit it side to side or dodge the bullet and get behind it. Don't get in front of it. Do not let it hit you! I remember thinking of Szifra. I don't remember what I thought, just that she was in my thoughts before the nothingness.

Szifra got the worst of it. We sideswiped the car. The police report said the driver's mirror, door and rear door were damaged. We didn't hit it head on. My left hand apparently got caught between the bike and car, my finger needed seven stitches. Szifra had no cuts, just some rugged bruises on her legs, an elbow and shoulder that screamed they were hurt, and intense worry that spiked to the trauma level as I lay unconscious on the road. Being blanketed in nothingness for four minutes isn't such a big deal for the person who has checked out temporarily. Waiting four minutes for your partner to come back from nothingness is a terrible ordeal.

One minute He was there, and the next his brain was damaged beyond repair by a bullet. One minute I was there, and the next my brain was shut down and the damage I'd sustained was unknowable. Szifra said she expected me to come back. But she had no idea how severe the effects would be, or how long or how complete, or incomplete the recovery might be. She told me she knelt in the road and laid her hand on me. She reassured my prostrate form, "It'll be all right." She told me, "Someone called an ambulance. It's on the way." She checked to see if she was making contact, "Nod your head if you can hear me."

Days later, we laughed about her request for me to nod my head—the last thing an injured person should do is move their head. Reacting correctly in an emergency is a learned skill which takes hundreds of iterations of practice.

A witness to the accident, Szifra thinks it might have been the driver of the white SUV behind us, stood beside her and timed my unconsciousness as they waited for the ambulance. "He's been out for four minutes," he informed the EMTs. Waking up from an unconscious state is a process. Talking and hearing return before sharp cognition or memory do. I'm told I stirred, I opened my eyes, I talked to the EMTs, "I have a normally slow heartbeat. My quads hurt. How's my wife?" My talk only relieved Szifra's worst fears. As I was being prepped to be loaded into the ambulance, she asked a question about our dog who we'd left at home that morning. I blankly responded, "I have no idea what you're talking about."

While Szifra waited for me and the ambulance, a police officer arrived and told her a couple of times, "You couldn't be more visible!" Yet the driver kept desperately wailing, "I didn't see you! I didn't see you!" And a pedestrian incorrectly reported, "They came off the sidewalk at the intersection." The man in the white SUV who had followed us down the street was clear and definitive, "They were riding in the middle of the street and he pulled out right in front of them."

After I'd been taken from the scene, the police continued to question Szifra until a witness spoke up, "You know she was in the accident too?" Like a comedy routine, everyone looked over at our bike, now laying near the curb, and realized it was a two-person bike. Suddenly the second pair of EMTs were focused on Szifra, "Ma'am, would you mind lying down so we can check you out?"

Szifra said, "No problem." Out of an abundance of caution, they gave her an ambulance ride too.

In some way the ambulance rides, my one-day-observation stay in the hospital, the massive bruises we both had on our quads, Szifra's painful elbow and wrenched shoulder, my stitched finger and bruised rib, were all quickly secondary to a more profound sense of loss. The bike's fork—which pivots the front tire—had been driven back into the carbon frame when we hit. The carbon tubes fractured into black splinters. Both frame and fork were a total loss. There was also ancillary damage to derailleurs, wheels, shifters, etc. But the most acute loss I felt over the next few weeks was the loss of our joint activity.

We had no idea when or if we'd be able to ride again. How we'd get our tandem replaced. Whether we'd have the nerve to ride again. Just when we were feeling the fittest we'd felt in years, there was a big hole in our together-time schedule, an enforced time off. Research shows that if an older athlete is out of the game for too long, they may never get back to the fitness level they were at before the interruption in training. We had no idea if any aspect of the accident would bring a permanent loss for either of us.

Without the tandem focal point—the place we reconnect so easily and well—we stumbled. Connection became a problem. Every time we got physically close, something hurt. Hugs pushed on ribs and shot pain through Szifra's shoulder. Even an affectionate lean from our Airedale made me jump as his short, hard tail banged on my bruised legs. My finger hurt and my lip was split. Szifra retreated to her corner and I to mine. Both of us felt what was happening and started to issue relationship alerts. No one else was threatening us. Distance was the threat. We both wanted to diminish the risk of painful touch, to hunker down and closely control our individual worlds. The relationship was slipping apart. We were out of sync.

We used the tandem metaphor in some of our conversations. Our relationship fork and frame were damaged. We couldn't go and couldn't steer. We felt silly being so tied up with a bike. But it was the touch point we'd developed, the place in our busy lives where we focused exclusively on each other.

It hadn't always been that way. We had started working together a few years back, so work and relationship conversations found their way onto

205

our early rides. One day we made a pact to leave work and any family problems off the bike. It took a few reminders, but eventually the bike became the place we worked to be in the moment of our life together.

Szifra admitted she felt scared, and angry at the driver who had ruined our good times. We had conversations where she voiced her reluctance and said she wasn't sure it made sense to ride again. I felt like we were being pulled apart by fear. It was hard to identify what held us together. I was distressed and panicked. We loved each other. We couldn't imagine being with anyone else. But there was that screaming-yellow flag warning us we might have to reinvent ourselves.

After a week I was cleared to ride my single bike on the indoor trainer, where there was no chance of a fall and repeat concussion. Pain still shocked and burned my legs whenever I stood up from a chair, but amazingly I could pedal pain-free. Three weeks later I was cleared to take my first ride outside. Our tandem was ruined so I was still on my single. I wasn't sure how I'd manage the physical and emotional remount, but the ride went fine. I returned home after an hour and reported to Szifra that it worked out pretty well but "I flinched at intersections."

In the car, we both also found ourselves jumping when anything slightly unpredictable happened on our right. On the freeway as we passed a car, it drifted a bit toward our lane. Szifra recoiled. Cars waiting in driveways felt threatening. Intersections seemed full of menace. Even bikes or pedestrians approaching from the right caused us to flinch.

Despite the hypersensitivity, I was ready to ride. But we couldn't ride together; the tandem was ruined. I'm not sure who it dawned on first, but one of us remembered that we did have an option. Hanging overhead, from a bracket, in our garage was our original, perfectly serviceable Grand Junction tandem. If we chose, we could ride. For the first time in weeks, I felt hope.

Szifra was still hesitant. I tried to work through the possible compromises, "We can stop as often as we need to. We can take it very easy. But I think we need to try it." Her fear drove her to look for the safest solutions. She suggested we only ride on empty dirt roads, until we discussed the risks of riding on dirt and the paucity of such roads in our riding area. We also discussed never riding through an intersection with a car at a cross street but imagined how profoundly it would disrupt a ride.

I said we could watch every car like they were out to get us. But of course, that was what I had been doing up to the moment of the accident. Szifra asked, "What about staying off busy streets?"

I pointed out that we were on one of the quietest streets at a quiet time, and still we got hit. The feeling of hopeless vulnerability was crowding back in. I needed us to try to ride!

I put it out as clearly as I could, "We need to try." Szifra reluctantly agreed we did. She was bruised, but since pedaling hadn't hurt me, she didn't think it would hurt her. The thought of riding brought a mix of delight and trepidation for me. She felt mainly fear and said, "If you weren't here, I'd probably never ride again." Something more profound was happening for her than me. Was this about stoker vulnerability?

Both of our neon-orange helmets had been cracked in the accident. Hers front, mine rear. When we went to replace them, orange was no longer available. We chose screaming-yellow ones and hoped they were at least as visible as our old shocking-orange ones. We talked a lot but had little idea what we could do to prevent a future accident, and the change of helmet color felt like doing something. But there was no longer comfort in visibility, only doubt.

I lowered the old tandem down from its retirement roost. Tires that had been left to deflate for a year were filled. Seats were readjusted, both sets of power pedals switched over from the ruined "good bike," the seat pack restocked, bike computers remounted. But Szifra wasn't ready. She said that she'd have to bury the fear too deep in order to get on. She needed more time to heal. I went for another ride on my single.

A few days later Szifra said she felt better. She was ready to try a ride. I asked, "Are you pushing yourself too hard? We can wait."

She gave me a hug, "I think I'm ready to try." I dressed, filled our water bottles, pumped the tires, and stalled. Szifra finally came out and stood by the bike.

I put on my helmet and pushed the tandem out of the garage. We mounted and pushed off. The flow was reestablished.

We made it through the twenty-mile ride with a minimum of fuss or fear. Although every car from the right caused us both to flinch. And we crept through every intersection, looking everywhere for lions hiding in the bushes.

Chapter 28: Involuntary Flinches

Our first tandem ride wasn't one-and-done, and our first accident wasn't either. It was one and not done, even after the skin healed and the bike was replaced. Like fairy-tale romances, fairy-tale recovery isn't usual.

The driver's insurance company was stunned a replacement bike could cost over $13,000 dollars. They started asking us for paperwork and both Szifra and I said, "Too much. Let them deal with a lawyer." And we sat back for the long miserable process of having our lives disrupted form by form and doubt by doubt.

It quickly became clear that passivity wasn't going to get us a tandem by the time we were scheduled to go back to Tucson for our second winter riding vacation. We're spoiled. We didn't want to ride our old bike if we could get a replacement in time. I called da Vinci and ordered a frame and fork that they said could be built and delivered before we left for Arizona. I told them I wanted to reuse anything from the wrecked bike that was still in good shape, "Please start building the frame as soon as your schedule allows." Almost simultaneously the insurance company called and said they wanted the bike evaluated by the manufacturer. Was I willing to ship it to Colorado at their expense? One of their few convenient requests.

The professional inspection concluded that we needed a new frame and fork, wheels and shifters, derailleurs, and other parts. I gave permission again to build a new bike and we sat back to check off each week as we waited to hear it was ready. After a number of months, the insurance agreed to pay for the new bike. Step one!

Getting it in our hands was step two. Da Vinci shipped it three months later. It was delivered to a Tucson FedEx the day we arrived. Opening the box was like opening a birthday present. We felt relieved the orange bike inside looked like our old one, and because it looked so much like our old one it was a bit of a letdown. There were drops of ambivalence mixed with a flood of pleasure and relief.

Shipping a bike is really about shipping bike parts, some of which—like the handlebars or brake calipers—are entangled with the basic frame by wires, cables, or hydraulic tubes. As I pulled the pile of semi-attached parts out of the shipping box, being careful that the front wheel, which was zip-tied to the frame, didn't bite into the cardboard box and make it useless for shipping the bike home later, it was a bit like untangling a mobile. Only, once they were released from their zip-tie restraints, each part of the bike was hanging by a fragile wire or hydraulic thread that threatened to harm itself before I got everything attached and stabilized. Setting the bike down outside the box, with only the rear wheel in place, risked getting grease on the floor and damage to chainring teeth. To add to my concern, I worried that I'd damage the new paint job before it ever saw a road.

It had been months since we'd gotten back on our old, steel horse after being thrown. But we hadn't ridden outside in months—New England had been buried in blanket after blanket of snow. As I pieced our new bike together in Tucson, neither of us thought about the fear we'd had to manage on our last few rides. But when we took the bike to the bike path for a test ride, there it was again.

The wide, paved path is isolated from most cars except at a few intersections, but it's a collage of bikes, walkers, dogs and roller skaters. Users merge from numerous entrance paths and converge at narrow bridges. Friends wanting to ride or walk together come at you two-by-two, or in some cases three-by-three. There are dips under streets where you're forced to blindly roll into corners, which may harbor a slow or wrong-sided person.

We emerged from one of the dips to a bike entering from our right side, and we both flinched. Szifra spoke up, "That scared me. I'd like to slow down."

We were in warmup mode. "It really wasn't very close and I'm only going ten mph, but I'll take it back a notch."

For the entire time we were in Tucson, Szifra flinched at any sudden actions on her right. Again and again, she reported, "That made me flinch. I just jumped. My heart just shot up." When we returned home our lawyer asked her whether there were any residual effects from the accident. That question made Szifra realize that she needed to treat the accident like the traumatic experience it was and get some good counseling help.

She went back to a therapist she'd worked with, one who used EMDR—Eye Movement Desensitization and Reprocessing—a technique that has been helpful for many trauma survivors in reducing unwanted reactions. The brief description is that the method uses a rhythmic eye movement created by following a finger, sound, or other signal from side to side. At the same time, the trauma is reported and reexperienced in some detail. Strange, but effective in some cases.

Szifra described the accident to her therapist several times, and then suddenly she was overwhelmed by the memory of her experience of coming home and seeing Him lying dead, under the trees in their oval driveway. She'd truly gotten the worst of our accident. She'd consciously held it together to be sure I got the help I needed, but unconsciously she relived his death. I'd promised not to die first, but I'd made her live through the next closest thing.

The day after that session was the warmest day of the spring so far. We had ridden the tandem only once since we'd gotten back from Tucson, and we'd put a riding time in our schedules for that day. As we began to prepare, Szifra froze. The therapy had brought too much to the surface for her to easily turn it off. She couldn't get back on the bike.

Trauma is complex, and Szifra deals with layers of it. Because most of her family's grandparents' and parents' generations were murdered by Nazis, the trauma was handed down to her. Her father repeatedly heaped abuse on everyone, including her at times. When she was eight, a man who managed a bowling alley molested her, and she hid the upset to protect her little sister. Her second husband put a gun to his head and ended his life. And in her sixty-seventh year, her third husband lay on the road, his fate unknown for four minutes.

These shocks compound and mix. Without warning, little things can overpower her rational stability and set off potent memories of one or more of them, memories that stimulate many of the emotions of the original incident. Therapy caused some minor things to overwhelm her carefully built wall of resilience, caused her round bottom boat to tip too far for her comfort, resuscitated Him back into our lives.

Over the next two months, therapy helped subdue the feelings. The flinches remained but were reduced and softened. Szifra got back on the bike, and within a couple of weeks we were taking long rides again. Slowly the trauma receded back to a ridable level, and we rode with the tandem group for the first spring ride.

Chapter 29: Where We're Headed?

There are games designed to declare a winner and a loser. Once the winner subdues all opponents, these finite games come to an end. The winner feels the temporary joy of dominance. Other games are infinite, designed to be played for the fun of playing, no conquest, no winner. Some rides are planned to take you out to a predetermined spot to conquer a certain hill. Some are just time spent wandering and pedaling.

I was raised by a father who eschewed competition for a variety of reasons. Some of those whys were locked in his closet of childhood traumas and disappointments. The reason he gave for encouraging play without winners or losers was that we should include everyone who wanted to play without regard to their skill or experience. Volleyball became a game to see if each side could set up the ball at least three times before passing it across the net for the other team to pass around. The purpose of this type of infinite game is to always keep the play going––unending, perpetual, non-stop. The best relationships are like that; they work to keep the play going.

In an infinite relationship game, you need to respect your playmate, to avoid even temporarily striving to craft an individual win or ascribe blame. You need to find ways to help all players use their strengths and celebrate the team's and each other's accomplishments. The best tandem teams enjoy playing the unending relationship game.

If a captain and stoker don't ride with the goal of keeping themselves and each other engaged in the ride, they're on their way to a finite game. Watch tandem captains who are competitive, and you often see them riding like they were on a single. If they're comfortable pulling through an intersection, they go. If they want to suffer to keep up with the group, they pedal until their legs ache and perhaps blame their stoker for coming up short. "She doesn't like hills. Her pedal stroke is inefficient." Or the ever-popular, "She doesn't train." Other captains might quietly chastise the complainer with a wink, especially if stokers are within earshot. The complainer is reminded that, "Stokers make no mistakes." But negative comments can be contagious, and a murmured example can start a quiet circle of critical solidarity.

Stokers can foster their own circles of grievances. And because the critiques are about their captain's competitiveness or insensitivity, they sound more justified. But comments from either captain or stoker are often attempts to win sympathy points from other riders. The dangerous, finite game is afoot.

Each couple must figure out what game they want to play. And, if they agree they want to play an infinite game, they need to decide where they're going—how far, how fast, how much climbing, and how many stops. I once read about a mountain climber who doesn't consider the climb finished until he's safely back down. Bike rides are like that, they aren't complete until we're safely back home.

If Szifra and I start together, ride together, and come to the finish together and healthy, we think our ride was a success. "Enjoy ourselves" is the obvious goal but begs the question, "What do each of us enjoy, and what do we enjoy doing together?"

Much of what Szifra enjoys are the social aspects of group riding. She started with a goal of being with the group at the finish so she could fully participate in the social time. Her secondary goals were to arrive not so physically tired that she couldn't enjoy herself, to not spend so long on the saddle that she was sore, and to not exacerbate any chronic joint or muscle issues she might have. It quickly became apparent that this was one of those situations where "You can have some, but not all of your preferences."

Initially I didn't have the leg power to carry us along with the faster, younger riders, or even the middle-of-the-pack teams. But I wanted to try to ride with the group more than I cared about how I felt at the end. Secondly, I wanted to ride the "big kid's" ride. If I couldn't ride one of the longer routes in a reasonable time frame, I felt like a junior member of the group. Szifra and I begin to negotiate ride-goals as soon as we hear about an upcoming ride.

Once we had a few hard rides in our team's palmarès—a term for bike racers' notable accomplishments—it gave us insight and the courage to attempt more ambitious goals. It also became easier to negotiate the conflicting desires between and within each of us. Sometimes we decide to give it our best and aggressively ride a shorter course. We aim to arrive back when the group does or to meet them at a junction that is within our capabilities of accompanying them to the end. Other times we start before the rest of the group to give ourselves a head start. At the point on the route where they catch us, we push to stay with them. We'll most likely still finish after them, but we aren't too far behind. One ride, we wanted to congregate with everyone at the top of a ski mountain and were willing to tolerate the fact that the effort we would have to invest in the first half would slow the second half. We knew we'd probably be late for the afterparty.

Negotiations weren't and aren't always easy. We have to trust each other to speak up about our needs and desires, but this means trusting that each of us knows what we need or are capable of. Sometimes I have a hard time getting off my single-bike mindset. Other times I'm not sure what we're capable of on a given day and route, how much fatigue is in our legs, and how the teams we're riding with might motivate us to push into our discomfort zone. When we ride without a group, it's easier.

We laugh about our individual savant-level abilities. Almost always, I can judge the time it takes to ride a route. I will usually get us home within a few minutes of our desired time. Some of this is just having more riding experience in the local area. I tend to know how long different rides take and can intuitively add or subtract snippets. Szifra has a similar ability to look at a container and know whether certain contents will fit into it. She packs the seat bags; I choose the routes.

Even though Szifra doesn't follow a prescribed training routine, we often decide that the ride is a training ride. She understands how important High Intensity Intervals are to health and longevity and encourages us to incorporate them. This means a ride will be a certain block of time, an agreed upon intensity effort, and fit into my specific—if flexible—pattern of frequency.

A fun ride goes down a pleasant rural road, along a quiet river, or passes a great place to stop for lunch. Routes are evaluated on a combination of length and elevation. Either they have to meet our training requirements, or they have to support the experience we're looking for.

Szifra has an allegiance to the tandem. Given the choice, she will always ride it instead of her single. She has women friends she rides with occasionally. She's ridden her single bike on a six-day trip with a friend. She even rides the bike path or neighborhood streets by herself occasionally. But any offer of a tandem ride is her highest priority.

We kit up and pump the bike tires. She fills the water bottles and packs her nutrition. We put on our helmets and turn on our lights. I walk the bike to the street. She closes the garage door. "So where are we going?" I ask. She answers, "I don't care!" But of course, she does care, as I do. We care for the team and the other person. But as long as we're riding together, we are where we want to be.

Chapter 30: He Still Hangs Around

We have the privilege of affording new bikes—singles and tandems—when compelling features or upgrades are introduced. We've converted from nine-speed to ten and now eleven-speed rear gear clusters. Shifters that were once mechanical are now electronic. Older rim brakes gave way to discs and now hydraulic discs. On my single, I've switched tube tires for more flat-resistant tubeless ones. I now ride on compliant seat posts that flex with bumps. Aluminum handlebars have been replaced by carbon ones to dampen vibration. Our present bikes are much more comfortable in the third and fourth hours of a long ride and yet have no compromises that slow us down.

Over the years, our relationship has made similar advances. We're much more effective at putting on the brakes when we're heading into a rough patch, at shifting into a gear that will be most effective at keeping our momentum flowing, at making U-turns without dismounting, at communicating what we need the other person to know, and at steering around gaping holes left over from life experiences.

We're pulled back time after time to invest more energy in training for the next twenty-five or thirty years of this ride. And we both see that our hard work has paid off. We aren't afraid to climb tough hills. And when we're flying along a flat, straight section, we delight at the wind on our faces and the well-oiled operation of our relationship where ups and downs are translated into forward motion.

It's going on twenty-two years since our first coffee date and twenty years since we got married. I've been with Szifra longer than He knew her, but he still hangs with us occasionally. He showed up for a while when Szifra was working to sort out the bodies of her motionless husbands. There's another of my jokes that may be too much, but it isn't too soon.

I opened my toolbox the other day and one of the wrenches He bought years ago was the one I chose to use. I have a collectible brass magnifying glass of his that sits on my desk. I like it, it goes well with my grandfather's brass compass, and it is a soft connection to the man whose life became so painful that he stepped aside and left room for me.

When Szifra talks about Him with her boys she calls him dad. At first I cringed. He was a stepfather and so was I. No one called me dad, or even stepdad. In fact, my stepsons didn't like me introducing them as my stepsons. I had to call them Szifra's sons. And when they introduce me, I'm most often "my mom's (or Szifra's) husband."

It took many positive experiences and a few harrowing ones as my relationships with them grew and changed. One Father's Day I got a card from my younger stepson. He had come to understand something about the pain I felt at never having children. His card obliquely acknowledged my importance in playing a small piece of that role for him as a young adult. It's a treasured gift. And at a gathering recently, he referred to Szifra and me as "his parents."

I've become more understanding of what a gift He gave my stepsons. He loved them and was a steady hand on the handlebars during a major transition in their lives. That's a gift I never underestimate the value of.

He lives on in many ways in our lives. His daughter visits us regularly. References to "Dad" float through conversations. Szifra and I have visited his family and his grave in Utah. A part of Szifra's retirement savings is due to the sacrifice He made working in a corporate environment that didn't always appreciate him. Szifra's and my early story is richer and more uncommon, and our connection may be stronger because of what he added to our early relationship.

He's still here, but now he's the outsider. It took a while to move him into his new circumstance, but we're comfortable that he's settled into that spot. He's still allowed into our conversations and even the bedroom, when we're talking. After all, he's part of our family, and always will be.

This spring, just before the accident, we upgraded our Joint Venture tandem to Shimano electronic shifting and hydraulic brakes—an admission that my thumbs don't like the effort the previous Campagnolo mechanical shifters required. Relationships are like that. They require continual tweaks to meet our needs as we gain experience and lose some of our physical drives.

Part of the reason He hangs around less and less is that he can't learn and upgrade himself the way the rest of us do. The early threat I felt when he was a glowing memory has softened into a gentle sadness that he is more like our first tandem—an important remnant of a previous time and place, but the memory also makes me glad I don't have to pedal that hard anymore.

Acknowledgments

Thank you, Kara Cheek, for introducing us and hanging in there as we drove each other crazy figuring out how to settle into a couple/team on and off the bike.

Thank you, Joe and Kathy Marino, for your inclusive and caring introduction to tandem group riding and for demonstrating a level of athleticism that evades us and many other riders.

Early readers shape a book in profound ways and then slip into the background. These readers need to be appreciated for their feedback that made this a more interesting and cohesive story. Many of their thoughts put our expectations back where they rightly deserved to be and helped corral Jay's tendency for wandering adjectives and overpopulated sentences.

Professional editor Jane Harrigan read a compilation of chapters and made suggestions for a book that pulled itself together around a more organized style and flow. With additions and subtractions, those ideas formed the content that professional editor Rochelle Sharpe helped shape into a manuscript very similar to the one you're reading.

Sarah Reiff-Hekking has always volunteered to read Jay's writing and offer her valuable feedback to clarify and clean up his language. Our friends David Kahn and his wife Kathie Roche-Goggins invested their precious reading time to see if our tandem riding experience and re-creation of a couple had any touch points that matched theirs.

Susan Fentin, a longtime tandem stoker, went through the manuscript with the same precision she brought to her law career and found many criminal uses of language, yet showed tremendous leniency for Jay's looser style.

Judy Cohen read with a solid view of the precursor to these experiences and gave it a passing grade and a wry smile. Her support was generous and kind.

Roz Birke, sister and sister-in-law, slogged through the written conversations that she would probably be loath to participate in but was willing to suffer through to offer her voracious-reader's thoughts.

Likewise Jay's late cousin, Andy Sharpe, focused his thousands of hours of experience with books and gave us his wise counsel, "It's good, but it will never be a best seller." What can we say?

Jay's once-professional-bookseller brother, Kent Livingston, went way beyond requirements to find a workaround that allowed him to rest his weary eyes and have the manuscript read to him electronically. And still he added editing corrections and big-picture advice. And similarly, David Wood, Jay's friend since high school and one of Jay's original inspirations to write, strained to read the book when he so easily could have declined. We appreciate both their efforts to offer us support and advice.

Evelyn Gosnell, a lifelong bicyclist and tandem rider was willing to read a manuscript of barely known fellow tandem riders and offer thoughts and support about all the coordination it takes for a couple to live and ride together.

Lesley Guyton and Seph Bloedoorn, a formidable tandem team, friends, and observational whizzes, looked for worn-out cliches and detours they'd never ridden and found a few we'd missed.

Louise Baribeau focused her critical line editing eye on the manuscript and found what many others had missed.

Belinda Juran generously offered her ideas about word options that better captured the gist of the story.

Marilyn Mbombo Dike lent her design mind to the final version of the front cover, helping us with tie-breaking decisions.

Todd Shusterman of da Vinci Designs invested an inordinate amount of energy to assure himself and us that the mechanics described here would actually do what Jay said they do. Thanks Todd, for the quality control.

Caren Bianco, co-founder of Adventures in Tandem, read with an eye for the experience of coordinating a bike driven by two individuals and gave us a pass on our checkout ride.

Molly Hurford, writer, editor, bicycle racer and activist for young women, looked at the words about tandems and couples and recognized the love we have for both bikes and each other.

Andy Applegate is an exceptional cycling coach and part of a competitive tandem team with his wife. His willingness to spend the time to look over this story was an unexpected gift to us.

Lisa Hochstein, an artist and designer we've always appreciated, offered valuable early input toward an interesting cover. Without her critique the photo would have been a muddled snapshot of indistinct province.

Kevin Harkins, professional photographer, agreed with Lisa's critique and produced a wonderful series of alternative photos.

Thank you all,
Jay
Szifra

Who is Jay?

Jay has learned to live his life more fully through many iterations of careers, relationships, and interests. Szifra and the tandem are two manifestations of that practice.

Jay has a master's in counseling psychology, which was more useful than an English degree, but less helpful than all the lessons he learned on a bike, in the woods, in discussions, from sailing, and from his loyal dogs. It's possible to get a sense of how he spread himself too thin by hearing that he was a master mechanic, a prize-winning wooden boat restorer, the head of a hospital's emergency response team, a certified EMT, an acclaimed dog behaviorist and an executive coach to nationally recognized sports, business, and performance professionals. Along with ten or more lesser jobs.

Jay is an expert in the human factors of leadership and management. He's particularly interested in how to motivate practice and change. His previous book is *Simple Steps to Change Your Business, Your Life*. His soon to be published books include *How to Improve Your Racing Performance in Small Sailboats,* and *Simple Steps to Stop Procrastinating and Start Riding: Improve Your Motivation, Persistence, Endurance, Mental Game, and Performance on Your Bike.*

Jay's life is more exciting and pleasurable because it now includes his granddaughters Rachel, Samantha, Paige and Adeline and his great nieces Sierra and Charlie.

Who is Szifra?

Szifra Birke is a personal and professional connector, whether bringing people together to aid new Americans or to volunteer at a new nonprofit. But she has never been satisfied with knowing people casually. Her career choices include Psychotherapist and Executive Leadership Coach. She is the author of *Together We Heal* about group therapy.

An avid exerciser, Szifra spent 35 years off bikes before a tandem bike seduced her back on. Once she was pedaling, the habit stuck. Besides her love of an active lifestyle, she came to the new relationship with two adolescent sons, a stepdaughter, and a love of marketing and public relations.

Offered the captaincy of the tandem, she demurred with a "Not on my life!" Her freedom from watching "every little thing in the road" allows her to enthusiastically acknowledge all drivers, walkers and porch sitters. She also strives to keep the conversation interesting and rolling along.

Influenced by her parents' Holocaust experience and inspired by their tenacity, Szifra has been personally and professionally involved with Holocaust survivors and their families since 1973 while a graduate student at Purdue. For the past twenty years, she has mentored and assisted immigrants and refugees from Southeast Asia and Africa.

Szifra co-produced a documentary about her outrageous dad, her beloved mom, and their quirky store. It can be viewed at: BrowsingThroughBirkes.com.

Her life is far richer because it includes her four granddaughters Rachel, Samantha, Paige and Adeline, and her six grandnieces and grandnephews Sierra, Charlie, Theo, Kaiah, Max and Taizen.

Made in the USA
Middletown, DE
04 December 2022

16648163R00129